R. Hook, G. D. Hook

Through Dust and Foam

Travels, sight-seeing, and adventure by land and sea in the Far West and Far East

R. Hook, G. D. Hook

Through Dust and Foam
Travels, sight-seeing, and adventure by land and sea in the Far West and Far East

ISBN/EAN: 9783337179632

Printed in Europe, USA, Canada, Australia, Japan

Cover: Foto ©Andreas Hilbeck / pixelio.de

More available books at **www.hansebooks.com**

THROUGH
DUST AND FOAM:

OR

Travels, Sight-seeing, and Adventure

BY

LAND AND SEA

IN THE

FAR WEST AND FAR EAST.

By R. & G. P. Hook.

Illustrated by
OVER 200 ORIGINAL ENGRAVINGS.

PUBLISHED BY SUBSCRIPTION ONLY.

HARTFORD, CONN.,
COLUMBIAN BOOK COMPANY
BLISS & CO., NEWARK, N. J.; F. DEWING & CO., SAN FRANCISCO.
W. E. BLISS, TOLEDO, OHIO; ANCHOR PUBLISHING CO., ST. LOUIS, MO.
1876.

PREFATORY.

This Book is one of the unforeseen and unpremeditated consequences of a series of travels by land and sea toward the setting sun, initiated by a rambling excursion to the plains and mountains of Colorado, and continued by alternate journeyings and sojournings until the starting point was again reached and a trip around the world had been accomplished. In preparing it, we have attempted to describe some of the interesting objects which we saw, and to record the novel incidents and personal adventures which came within our observation or experience.

The routes by which we traveled took us over the waters of the Pacific, Indian, and Atlantic Oceans; the China, Arabian, and Red Seas; the Gulf of Siam; the Bay of Bengal; the Straits of Malacca; and the channels of the Japanese and East Indian Islands. Japan, China, Farther India, Malaya, Ceylon, Arabia, Egypt, Sicily, Italy, and other countries were visited; and in most of them ample time was taken for sight-seeing and observation.

It may be proper to add that our travels were undertaken solely for pleasure, and in that point of view were a success—a greater one than we can expect our book will be. Still, we have been agreeably entertained and fought many of our battles over again while reading the proof-sheets; and we have become interested in the pictures—deeply so in those wherein are delineated

THE AUTHORS.

List of Illustrations
Engraved by
FAY & COX
105 NASSAU ST. N.Y.

		PAGE
1. The Land of the Pyramids,	*Frontispiece*	—
2. College Nights,		18
3. Bachelors of Art,		19
4. "Buffalo!"		20
5. Toting Him Out,		22
6. The Bachelor's Welcome,		24
7. The Colorado Sphynx,		25
8. A Narrow Escape,		27
9. A Bloody Reception,		30
10. Sunday Recreations,		31
11. Fully Convinced,		32
12. Monument Rocks,		33
13. Inviting a Treat,		36
14. Indian Squaws on the Hunt,		39
15. Adventure with Wild Cattle of the Plains,		40
16. A "Foul" Dinner,		42
17. A Night in the Woods,		46
18. Summit of Gray's Peak—Colorado,		49
19. A Mutual Scare,		51
20. Novel Descent from the Mountain,		57
21. Slam and his Buyer,		64
22. Ecstatic Passengers,		67
23. Mountain Flora,		68
24. The Serpent of the Mountains,		69
25. Salt Lake Apostles,		71
26. A Row on the Lake,		74
27. The Gem of the Mountains,		75
28. Ready for the Plunge,		79

ILLUSTRATIONS.

29.	CALEB'S RACE-COURSE,	80
30.	CROSSING THE FERRY,	82
31.	BOUND FOR THE VALLEY,	84
32.	CALEB TAKING THE VEIL,	85
33.	WOMANS' RIGHTS ADVANCING,	86
34.	ABOVE THE FALLS,	87
35.	WATCHING THE CAMP-FIRE,	88
36.	CALEB'S PERILOUS DESCENT,	89
37.	"QUITE SHOWERY,"	91
38.	THE RESCUE,	93
39.	AROUND THE LOG-FIRE,	96
40.	YOSEMITE VALLEY,	100
41.	THE BROTHERS,	103
42.	COUNTING IN THE GOLD,	104
43.	THE STOOL-PIGEON,	107
44.	"HERE I AM AGAIN!"	108
45.	BACHELORS' HALL,	112
46.	BOUND FOR JAPAN,	115
47.	"ONLY A RIPPLE, SIR!"	119
48.	CASTING BREAD UPON THE WATERS,	120
49.	A STEERAGE PASSENGER'S FIRST DIVE,	124
50.	A TRYING TIME,	126
51.	A QUEUE-RIOUS SEPARATION,	127
52.	GOING ASHORE AT YOKOHAMA,	129
53.	A FORE-RUNNER OF CIVILIZATION,	133
54.	THE GREAT ORIENTAL EXPRESS,	134
55.	INDIA-RUBBER BOYS,	137
56.	NEW JAPAN,	139
57.	NATIVE SWEETMEATS,	142
58.	FOREIGN SAUCE,	143
59.	A SMALL WATER-PARTY,	144
60.	APPROACH TO THE JAPANESE METROPOLIS,	146
61.	DINNER AT YEDDO,	148
62.	A BOOTLESS VISIT,	149
63.	BEFORE THE HIGH AND MIGHTY,	151
64.	A JAPANESE TEMPLE,	153
65.	THE LATEST INNOVATION,	155
66.	THE WIDOW'S MITE,	156
67.	TOUCH AND BE HEALED,	158
68.	"GETTING USED TO IT,"	161
69.	WILDAIR'S WARRIORS,	162
70.	WILDAIR AS A GEOGRAPHER,	163
71.	SOCIAL EQUALITY ILLUSTRATED,	164
72.	OLD JAPAN,	165
73.	THE PIRATES' DOOM,	167
74.	STREET SCENE IN HONG KONG,	171

75. Starting up the Leader,	173
76. A Down Grade,	175
77. Abating a Nuisance,	177
78. Street Gamblers,	179
79. The Opium Smoker and his Wife,	180
80. Amusing the Natives,	182
81. A Barbarous Barber,	184
82. A Study of Hats,	186
83. Chinese Mistress and Maid,	187
84. Sidewalk Artisans—Hong Kong,	188
85. A Policeman and his Victim,	189
86. Our first Rat-soup,	193
87. Opium Smuggling—Canton River,	195
88. Ploughing like his Father,	198
89. Agricultural Scene—China,	199
90. The Guardian Pagoda,	201
91. "Rock me to Sleep Mother,"	202
92. An Attack in the Rear,	204
93. The Gentle Rower,	205
94. Improvements on the Race,	207
95. A first-class Rat-seller,	208
96. The Gutter Snipe—Canton,	209
97. A Covered Street of Canton,	211
98. Poking Fun at Him,	214
99. "They Seemed to like it,"	215
100. "The Grim Iron Barrier Prevented our Egress,"	217
101. The mysterious Box,	219
102. Priest with Alms-box.	220
103. A long-nosed Ancestor,	221
104. A Pig-tail Excitement,	223
105. A dignified Chinaman,	224
106. Specimens of Architecture—Canton,	225
107. Before the Throne,	227
108. A Chinese Mandarin,	228
109. More Ornamental than Useful,	232
110. Third-class Passengers at Dinner,	235
111. Our State-room Visitors,	236
112. "The Captain frequently Hovered near Them,"	237
113. The Banks of the Saigon—Farther India,	238
114. Native Boats,	239
115. Assaulted by Amazons,	242
116. An Adventure in the Dark,	244
117. "Your Foot very small,"	246
118. A Siamese Prince,	249
119. An Anam Aristocrat,	251

120. Deck Amusements—Gulf of Siam,	. . . . .	253
121. Dot Wins the Night,	. . . . .	254
122. A Meteoric Shower,	. . . . .	256
123. Diving from the Ship's Deck,	. . . .	257
124. On the Road to Singapore,	. . . .	259
125. "He Is Hungry,"	. . . . .	261
126. "Go it you Cripple,"	. . . . .	262
127. Boat life in Malay,	. . . . .	266
128. A Burial in the Bay of Bengal,	. . .	268
129. The sick Frenchman and his Chinese Wife,	. .	269
130. A Princess of Malay,	. . . .	270
131. Our Ceylon Pilot and his Boat,	. . .	271
132. An Insulted "Guide,"	. . . . .	274
133. One of our Passengers,	. . . .	275
134. Ceylon Jugglers—Mysterious Balls,	. . .	277
135. "Many of Them Improved Surprisingly,"	. .	279
136. Ceylon a Fraud,	. . . . .	281
137. Initiating a Candidate,	. . . .	282
138. Running for Life,	. . . . .	283
139. An Indian Mosque—Taj Mahal,	. . .	288
140. A Brahmin Devotee,	. . . . .	290
141. A Fight in the Jungle,	. . . .	293
142. Fun on Deck—Arabian Sea,	. . . .	297
143. Heads and Tails—A Scene at Aden,	. .	299
144. Eggs-traordinary,	. . . . .	301
145. A Meeting in the Desert,	. . . .	306
146. Fruits of Competition—A Scene on the Desert,	.	307
147. A Stiff-necked Egyptian,	. . . .	309
148. Lost in Cairo,	. . . . .	310
149. Hard on the Donkeys,	. . . .	311
150. Entrance to the Great Pyramid,	. . .	317
151. Plan of the Interior,	. . . .	318
152. The Grand Gallery,	. . . . .	319
153. A Hard Goose to Pick,	. . . .	325
154. Morning Recreations,	. . . .	326
155. Bed-time Exercises,	. . . . .	326
156. A Touching Scene,	. . . . .	327
157. Return of the Hunter,	. . . .	328
158. A Mighty Archer,	. . . . .	329
159. Subterranean Hall of the Bulls,	. . .	331
160. Doe and Fawn,	. . . . .	333
161. Transporting a "God,"	. . . .	334
162. Yankee Pyramid-builders,	. . . .	335
163. Ruins on the Nile,	. . . . .	338
164. Egyptian High Art,	. . . . .	339

165. Mummy-case,	. . . .	341
166. Street Scene in Alexandria,	. . . . . .	343
167. Cleopatra's Bath,	. . . .	344
168. Cleopatra's Needles,	. . . .	345
169. Pompey's Pillar,	. . . .	346
170. Wildair Expresses an Opinion,	. . . . .	348
171. A Strike on the High Seas,	. . . . . .	349
172. The Shores of Italy,	. . . .	352
173. A Colorado Ghost,	. . . .	357
174. "Take Him out,"	. . . .	360
175. An afflicted Neopolitan,	. . . . . .	363
176. Bacchanalian Dance,	. . . .	364
177. Mutual Recognition,	. . . .	367
178. Three Young Ladies of Naples,	. . . .	368
179. Tunnel at Naples,	. . . .	370
180. Enticing a Victim,	. . . .	371
181. Result of Paying off the Boys,	. . . .	374
182. Dissatisfied Damsels,	. . . .	377
183. Herculaneum—The Theatre,	. . . . .	380
184. 'Our Horses Were fiery, and We Gave Them the Rein,"		382
185. "Our Assailants soon Lost their Legs,"	. . .	383
186. "I Let My House out a little,"	. . . .	385
187. The Great Catastrophe,	. . . . . .	388
188. Excavated Street of Tombs—Pompeii,	. . .	389
189. A Warning to Burglars,	. . . . . .	392
190. The Tragic Theatre,	. . . .	393
191. A Sudden Stop,	. . . .	395
192. Arches of Ancient Rome,	. . . . . .	396
193. A Drive through Rome,	. . . . . .	399
194. The Procession of Trajan,	. . . . . .	403
195. Ruins of Caracalla's Baths,	. . . . .	408
196. "We Shuddered as we went along,"	. .	411
197. "They Kiss the Toe of St. Peter's Statue,"	.	414
198. The Sacred Steps,	. . . .	415
199. The Old Man's Pet,	. . . .	429
200. "A Wild-looking Man with a Cudgel in his Hand,"	. .	430
201. Our funny Fellow-passenger,	. . . . .	433
202. Imperialism at a Discount,	. . . . .	436
203. Park and Fountain at Versailles,	. . .	438
204. London Beggary,	. . . .	441
205. Among the Roughs,	. . . .	443
206. Going to hear Spurgeon,	. . . . . .	445
207. A tipsy Emigrant Going Below,	. . . .	451
208. A Dance on Deck,	. . . .	453
209. A President and a President-maker,	. . .	456

And Other Smaller Engravings.

CONTENTS.

CHAPTER I.
THE START WESTWARD.

College Days Being Ended, Caleb and Wildair Start out on Their Travels—Westward Ho!—Scenes on the Plains—"Buffalo!"—The Rendezvous at Denver—"Yonder Goes Caleb"—Caleb and His Ponies............... 17

CHAPTER II.
WANDERINGS IN COLORADO.

Among the Herders of the Plain—A Magic Valley—Pleasant Park—The Bachelor's Welcome—"Tewat," the Old Man of the Mountain—Bear-Rock—Purgatory River—A Squirrel Hunt—Treeing the Game—Wildair Perplexed—The old House by the Roadside—The Hopkinses—A Bloody Reception—A Sunday Bear-hunt—Among the Prairie Dogs—The Gardens of the Gods—Monument Creek—Double Falls...................... 23

CHAPTER III.
LIFE ON THE FRONTIER.

Lively Experiences of a Circuit Preacher—Along the Arkansas River—The Romance of Hardship—Las Animas City—Fort Lyons—The Sunset Gun—A mixed Congregation—Stove-pipe Hats at a Discount—Indian Wives of White Men—War between the Utes and the Plain Indians—Visit to an Indian Camp—The Squaws Institute a Search—Dreary Solitude—Encounter with Texan Cattle—A Lady's Experiences in Colorado—Kind young Bachelors—A "Foul" Dinner—Proposals of Marriage—A reformed Bachelor—Bound for the Mountains—Petrified Stumps—A Night in the Woods—Fire-works—In the South Park—Mining Camps.............. 35

CHAPTER IV.
ASCENT OF GRAY'S PEAK—IN A HORN.

Up the dark Gorge—The Quartz Mills by Night—A Midnight Halt—A Bivouac among the Willows—Approach of Daylight—Sunrise—In the dense Forests—A mutual Scare—Ascent of the Peak—Mysterious Tracks—Suspicions of Grizzlies—Wildair's Pepper-box—On the Summit—The Continental Divide—Novel Descent—At the Foot—Cities in the Wilderness—Slam and his Slanderers—The Town "Busted"—Wildair's Ride—Slam and his Buyer—Final Catastrophe...................... 49

CHAPTER V.
WESTWARD BY RAIL.

A Wanderer—Palace Cars—At Cheyenne—Mountain Flowers—The highest Altitude—The Laramine Plains—The North Platte—The Continental Divide—Green River—The City of the Saints—A Sunday in the Tabernacle—Salt Lake Apostles—Excursion to Lake Tahoe—Donner Lake—The Sierra Nevada—Sacramento Valley.................................. 66

CHAPTER VI.
A FLIRTATION AMONG THE BIG TREES.

The San Joaquin Valley—Mariposa—A pleasing Arrangement—Wildair Falls in Love—Incidents of the Ride—Ready for the Plunge—Down Grade—Caleb's Race-course—The Ancient Couple—A startling Disclosure—Crest-fallen... 76

CHAPTER VII.
SIGHT-SEEING IN YOSEMITE.

Bound for the Valley—Caleb's Night Ride—At Bridal Veil—Moonrise—A Climb Upwards—Above the Falls—"I Won't Go Home Till Morning"—Caleb's Camp-fire—Night Adventures—Perilous Descent........... 83

CHAPTER VIII.
A CLIMB OUT OF THE VALLEY.

"Quite Slippery"—Vernal Falls—Interviewing a "Guide"—His Warning Voice—Resolve to Visit Glacier Rock—Up the Gorge—A Perilous Situation—Holding on for Life—The Rescue—"Where is Caleb?"—Found at Last—Return of the Wanderers—Around the Log-fire............... 90

CHAPTER IX.
EXPERIENCES IN SAN FRANCISCO.

Looking for Caleb's Denver Friend—A Fruitless Search—A thrilling Narrative—Miners and Their Burdens—The obliging Stranger—"Let's Have a Drink"—The Stool-pigeon—"Plodding Joe's" Discovery—Inquest and Verdict—"Ben Butler" at Home..................................... 99

CHAPTER X.
FIRE AND BRIMSTONE.

Visit to the Geysers—The Witches' Chaldron—The Laboratory of Nature—Bachelors' Hall—Santa Rosa Valley—Petaluma—The Coast Ranges..... 111

CHAPTER XI.
POETRY OF THE OCEAN.

Arrival of a Japan Steamer—Good-Bye to San Francisco—Bound for the Orient—Conversations with the Pilot—Rough on Wildair—We Are not "Sea-sic-hic"—Scenes at Sea—Meeting a Steamer—"All's Well"—The "America".. 114

CONTENTS.

CHAPTER XII.
A VOYAGE ON THE PACIFIC.

A Seaman's Yarn—Chinese Passengers in a Storm—Offerings to the "Gods"—An Eccentric Calendar—A Trying Time—From Gay to Grave—Adrift at Sea—Land of the Rising Sun—Anchor in Yeddo Bay—Japan at Last. 123

CHAPTER XIII.
SIGHT-SEEING IN JAPAN.

Going Ashore at Yokohama—Pleasant Scenes—Musical Japanese—Are They Men or Women?—An economical Dodge—A Tea Party in the Suburbs—Paper Butterflies—India-rubber Boys—The Sensible Mikado—A Strange Upstart.. 130

CHAPTER XIV.
A COUNTRY RIDE TO YEDDO.

Four wicked Ponies—Our tattooed Runner—Japanese Farmers—Tea Houses—Pretty Waiter Girls—Native Refreshments—American Ingratitude—A Young Ladies' Bathing Party—Approach to Yeddo—In the Great City—Dinner at Yeddo—Wildair's Encounter with Burglars................ 140

CHAPTER XV.
THROUGH THE TEMPLES.

The Forest Parks of Yeddo—Imposing Tombs—Massive Gates, and shaven Priests—Pompous Ornamentations—Up the shining Stairs—An august Object—Solemn Ceremony—The Deserted Palace—Two-sworded Retainers—The chief Temple—The Widow's Mite—The Altar and the Priests—Ghastly Pictures—The "God of the Smokers"—The Goddess of Mercy—"Touch and Be Healed"—St. Francis Xavier the first Missionary to Japan—The early Christians—Massacre of Priests—Japanese Exiles. 150

CHAPTER XVI.
SOCIAL PROGRESS IN JAPAN.

An American Bride in Yeddo—"Getting Used to It"—Japanese Seclusion—Commodore Perry's Visit and the Result—Western Ways in the Ascendant—Foreign Teachers—A model School System—Liberty of the Press—Downfall of the Aristocracy—The Birth-right of Twenty Centuries Abdicated—Condescension of the Mikado—A new Holiday.............. 160

CHAPTER XVII.
FROM JAPAN TO CHINA.

A Voyage along the Coast—White-sailed Fishing Junks—Terraced Mountains—Fortifications—An enchanting Scene—Volcanoes—Rendezvous of Pirates—Fate of the Deceived Pirates—Chinese Fishermen—The Typhoon—Approach to Hong Kong—The Signal Gun—At Anchor—Sampans and their Inmates—Broken China—Importuned by Sprightly-looking Girls—Rowed Ashore by the fair Sex—How they Paddled!—A Scramble at the Landing—The Girls Beaten back and the Chairmen Triumphant....... 166

CHAPTER XVIII.
ADVENTURES IN HONG KONG.

Some Things We Liked—Chairs and Charioteers—An Excursion—Results of Starting up the Leader—English Convicts—Government Gardens—Chinese Washermen—A down Grade—A nice Trick—An Astonished Celestial—Our Chairman's Revenge—An uncharitable Landlord............... 170

CHAPTER XIX.
MORE ADVENTURES IN HONG KONG.

Caleb's Rashness—Gamblers—The Curse of the Country—Among the Opium Smokers—The faithful Wife—Smoking-houses—Imitative Natives—Bridget's Story—Cutting a Swarth—A Perfect Scare-crow......... 178

CHAPTER XX.
THE LAST OF HONG KONG.

Chinese Fashions—About the Women—Street Scenes—Policemen—Funerals—Processions—Weddings—Dinner at a Restaurant—A Suspicious Dish—The Mystery Solved—Caleb Excited—"A mean, dirty Swindle"....... 185

CHAPTER XXI.
UP THE CANTON RIVER.

Opium Smuggling—A Detective—Dilapidated Forts—Reminisences of War—Agricultural Scenes—Guardian Pagodas—Approach to Canton—Junks and Sampans—No Buoys for Girl-babies—At Anchor—Beleaguered Passengers—Female Hotel-runners—Wildair Surrenders—An Attack in the Rear—Rescued by Our bright-eyed Captor............ 194

CHAPTER XXII.
CANTON.

Seven Chinese Girls—Semi-celestials—Connoisseurs of Chinese Beauty—The Foreign Suburbs—Native Ladies—A Festival—A Floating City by Night—Rides about Canton—Native Industries—Inhuman Punishments—Caged Men—On the Great Wall—Tartar Soldiers—Belated—Canton at Night—Locked Within the Gates—Final Escape............ 206

CHAPTER XXIII.
AMONG THE CHINESE GODS.

The Mysterious Box—The Chinese Religion—Priests—Ancestral Worship—Superstitious Customs—Buddhism—Sacred Swine—The God of Longevity—Temple of the Dragon—A Helpless God......................... 213

CHAPTER XXIV.
THE EMPIRE OF THE CELESTIALS.

General Features—Canals—Inland Commerce—The Emperor and his Wives—The Mandarins—Soldiers—Tartars—The Coolie Trade............ 225

CHAPTER XXV.
OVER THE CHINA SEA TO FARTHER INDIA.

Life on a French Steamer—Third-class Passengers—The pretty German Girl—State-room Visitors—Handsome French Ladies—Scandal on Shipboard—Up the Saigon River.. 233

CHAPTER XXVI.
FUN AND ADVENTURE AT SAIGON.

A dismal Prospect—Disembarkation of Soldiers—Going Ashore—Droll Encounter in the Suburbs—Dot a Prisoner—Escape from Amazons—Saigon by Night—An Adventure in the Dark—Hasty Retreat—"Pulling on ze leetle Shoe"—A Note for Mademoiselle—Siamese Customs—The Brahmins—Temples of Siam... 240

CHAPTER XXVII.
VOYAGE TO THE LAND OF THE MALAYS.

Morning on Deck—Airy Costumes—Amusements—Playing "Frog" and "Log"—Caleb's Promenade—Dot's Troubles—The Malay Peninsula—A Swimming Tiger—Singapore Harbor—Malayan Divers............... 252

CHAPTER XXVIII.
EXCURSIONS IN SINGAPORE.

A Drive to the City—Scenes on the Road—Among the Malays—At the Mercy of Jehu—A hungry Horse—A Malayan Arena—Jehu Prepares for a Storm—His Garments Overboard—Mysterious Dogs—An abominable Swindle—Among the Monkeys—Boat-life in Malay................. 258

CHAPTER XXIX.
CEYLON'S ISLE.

In the Bay of Bengal—Nicobar Islands—A Burial at Sea—The Frenchman's Oriental Wife—A genuine Princess—"Spicy Breezes"—The City of Point De Galle—The Pilot and his Boat—A dazzling Display—At Anchor—An Excursion on Shore—A brazen-faced Intruder—Tricks of the Trade—An Insulted Runner—Guide or no Guide?—Buying Parrots......... 267

CHAPTER XXX.
RAMBLES IN AND AROUND CEYLON.

The Forts—Sidewalk Jugglers—A Traveling Menagerie—Cinnamon Gardens and Cocoanut Groves—Remarkable Cripples—Adam's Peak—Impudent Rascals—Ceylon a Fraud.. 276

CHAPTER XXXI.
EASTERN CIVILIZATION—THE BRAHMINS.

Effects of Western Ideas—In the Temples—The Mysteries of Priesthood—A Religion of Caste... 284

CONTENTS.

CHAPTER XXXII.
OVER THE ARABIAN AND RED SEAS.

The Journey Resumed—Veteran Bear-hunters—A Storm at Sea—Fun on Deck—The Doctor's Pranks—Araby the Blest—A Town in a Crater—Sight-seeing in Aden—Wonderful Eggs—A gulled Gull—Mecca—Mt. Sinai—Suez.. 292

CHAPTER XXXIII.
GETTING ACQUAINTED WITH EGYPT.

Lazy Arabs—Moses' Well—An Evening at Suez—Rolling over the Desert—Caravans—Egypt's new River—Scenes on the Desert—Cairo—A Stiff-necked Race—An Oriental Paradise—A Beauty Unveiled—Hard on the Donkeys.. 302

CHAPTER XXXIV.
A VISIT TO THE PYRAMIDS.

The Guide and Donkeys—The Arabs of the Pyramids—"Beware of Your Pockets"—On the Summit of Cheops—A tempting Proposal—"Old Traditional"—Down in a Dungeon—Pharaoh's Telescope—The Grand Gallery—Who Carried off the King and Queen?—Ruins of Memphis..... 312

CHAPTER XXXV.
SIGHT-SEEING UNDER GROUND.

A Visit to the Catacombs—Immense Excavations—Old Ben Hassan—Weak young Ladies—A mighty Archer—A Memento and its Fate—An Egyptian Swindle.. 324

CHAPTER XXXVI.
THE LANGUAGE OF THE MONUMENTS.

The Obelisks—An Ancient City—The Papyrus Manuscripts—Early Picture-writing—Ingenious Lexicographers—Egyptian High Art............. 334

CHAPTER XXXVII.
THE VESTIBULE OF THE OLD WORLD.

Alexandria—Street Scenes—Donkeys and Camels—Mementos of Cleopatra—Pompey's Palace and Pillar—Manufactured Relics—Imperial Tombs—Unpleasant Experiences—Besieged by extortionate Arabs—Demoralized Baggage—Detained by Force—A Strike on the High Seas—Wildair Quells a Mutiny—Escape from Enemies—A parting Curse.................. 342

CHAPTER XXXVIII.
FROM EGYPT TO SICILY AND ITALY.

Farewell to Africa—A peaceful Sea—First View of Italy—Up the Straits of Messina—On the Island of Sicily—The Evening Bells of Messina—Mount Ætna—Stromboli, the Light-house of the Mediterranean—Aboard an Italian Steamer—Along the Italian Shores—Picturesque Mountains—Elevated Houses—Bay of Naples—A sleepy Landlord—A Colorado Ghost. 351

CONTENTS. xv

CHAPTER XXXIX.
NAPLES.

Impoliteness to a "Guide"—Sunday in Naples—The Church of San Martino—Visit to the Great Cathedral—Story of Saint Januarius—Public Exhibition of Miracles—Beautiful Statuary and Paintings—Sights on the Street—Wax-work Miracles—Visit to the Bourbon Museum—Objects of Interest—An Ecclesiastical Procession—A Stroll through the City—Three young Ladies.. 359

CHAPTER XL.
WONDERS OF THE COAST WEST OF NAPLES.

The Villa Reale—The Grotto of Porilipo—Tomb of Virgil—The Dog's Grotto—Cruel Tourists—Pozzuoli or Ancient Puteoli—Steps where St. Paul Landed—Ruins of the Amphitheatre—The Temple of Serapis—Boat-fights of Gladiators—A big Scramble—Cicero's Villa—Lake Lucrine—The Ruins of Baiæ—A Temple of Venus—Dancing Girls................... 369

CHAPTER XLI.
HERCULANEUM AND VESUVIUS.

Descent to the Buried City—Hidden for Eighteen Centuries—Wondrous Relics of by-gone Ages—Bound for Mt. Vesuvius—Reminiscences of the Volcano—Abused by the Guide—A Villainous Assault—At the Foot of the Cone—Climbing Upwards—Red-hot Lava—At the Crater—A hasty Retreat—Ride down the Mountain—A beautiful Sight—Another Swindle. 379

CHAPTER XLII.
THE BURIED CITY OF POMPEII.

A dry Storm—Approach to Pompeii—A wayside Inn and Its Lodgers—Diomede's Mansion—Serene Sleepers—The Tomb of a Prize-fighter—The Welcoming Inscription "Salva"—Calls at the old Homesteads—Nobody at Home—Inside the Houses—The Forum and a Dungeon—Grimy Diggers—A petrified Burglar Caught in the Act—The deserted Stranger—The brave Roman Soldiers Who Scorned to Flee...................... 387

CHAPTER XLIII.
FROM NAPLES TO ROME.

Surprising Charges—Railroad Experiences—A Blue-eyed Wonder—A Country Station—An old Story—Peasant Life—Italian Sunset—First View of Rome—Model Hackmen—Astounded Foreigners—Sight-seeing......... 394

CHAPTER XLIV.
AMID THE RUINS OF ROME.

Descent to the Forum—Reminiscences of Cæsar—Scenes of Departed Glory—Rome's last Conquest Pictured in Stone—The Coliseum and its Scenes—The Arch of Titus—Towering Ruins—Nero's Palace—The ancient Etruscans and Their Tombs...................................... 401

CHAPTER XLV.
THE SPIRIT OF THE ETERNAL CITY.

St. Clement's Subterranean Church—St. Paul's Prison—The Underground City by Torchlight—Ghastly Scenes—Retreats of early Christians and later Robbers—St. Peter's Cathedral—Scenes within—The Priests and People—The Scala Sancta—The Pope's Palace—Ancient Manuscripts. 410

CHAPTER XLVI.
FLORENCE AND VENICE.

Beautiful Florence—A Morning Excursion—Slighted by the Guard—Boboli Garden—An ancient Church—The Palazzo Vecchio—In the Museum—A remarkable Bridge—Smoky Tunnels—Approach to Venice—The City of the Sea—Looking for a Carriage—A Ride in a Gondola—Crossing the Grand Canal—The Piazza and St. Mark's—The Rise and Decline of Venice—Souvenirs of dreadful Days................................ 418

CHAPTER XLVII.
OVER THE ALPS.

Milan—Lake Como—An Evening by the Lake—Colico—A lovely Valley—Peasant Life—Amid the Foot-hills—Scenes by the Way—At the Foot of the Alps—Lively Times at a Swiss Village—Among the Vineyards—Singing Girls—"Sour Grapes"—A Start up the Gorge—Torrents and Waterfalls—Among the Clouds—A Snow-storm in the Mountains—On the Summit—The Descent—Zurich—An Excursion into Germany....... 427

CHAPTER XLVIII.
PARIS AND LONDON.

Continental Passports—Relics of Barbarism—Down-trodden Paris—The Tuileries—Relics of Imperialism at Auction—An American Lady's Bargains—Versailles, Its Parks, Fountains, and Palaces—Louis XIV and Madam de Marntenon—Sleigh-riding in Summer—Country Scenes—Unbeaten Beets—Holland Canoes—Paddling Peasants—London—Underground Railroad—St. Paul's—Westminster Abbey—The "Poets' Corner"—The British Museum—Assyrian Account of the Deluge—The Crystal Palace by Day and Night—The Great Fire—Going to Hear Spurgeon—London Beggars—The Lord Mayor's Show—Among the Roughs—Rescued by Policemen.. 435

CHAPTER XLIX.
ACROSS THE ATLANTIC.

A Separation—Wildair Starts Homeward and Takes Passage in a Liverpool Steamer bound for N. Y.—Irish Emigrants Taken on Board at Queenstown—Drunk, or very Jolly—A Look into the Steerage—Going Below—A tipsy Bridegroom—Tin-ware Falling—Asking for More—The Lower Depths—Evening Entertainments—Ominous Weather—A fearful Gale—Anxious Nights—The Storm Abates—Land Ho!—Home again from Foreign Shores. 451

SUMMIT OF GRAY'S PEAK, COLORADO.

CHAPTER I.

OFF FOR THE MOUNTAINS.

WE flung our hats, our "sheep skins" we flaunted in air; our college days were ended! Many a time we had sat over our Latin and Greek as the rattling cars went galloping westward over the prairies, and thought, ere our lesson was finished, that train would be out among the scampering buffalo of the plains. We longed to be there, too; but those Greek and Latin roots bound us within the college walls. These were glorious studies, and even to this day I recollect them with emotions of joy. I look back and see ourselves sitting side by side with those dear old books on the table just in front, nodding, ever nodding. Now we were stuck on a Greek root, and after long and weary toil Caleb succeeded in unwinding its entangling fibres, then looked round exultantly, but only to find me asleep. Poor fellow, it was a little discouraging, but his only alternative was to nudge me in the side, and heavily my eyes drew open.

Again we became perplexed over some hard termination or other, and of course I passed into the land of Nod. That was not the worst of it. Upon awaking, instead of finding that he had adjusted the difficulty, it was only to perceive that I had been aroused by his snoring. It was my time then to become discouraged, and after a few jerks under the short ribs with my elbow he was brought to his senses—*not* to learn that I had solved the difficulty, but that it was after midnight and we must go to bed without our lessons.

But musty Greek roots were no longer to coil their tangled meshes about our minds; buffalo, climbing mountains, storms at sea, visions of Oriental climes, adventures, scares,

COLLEGE NIGHTS.

activity, life, "hip, hip, hurrah!"—such things as these were shooting through every artery of our being.

Later in the fall Caleb, being rather of a religious turn of mind, went out upon the frontiers of Colorado to preach till spring, while I remained at home reading history and novels. We completed our plans through correspondence during the winter—and such plans as were occasionally suggested! They comprised everything this side the moon.

The snowy folds of winter having rolled away, green spring was beginning to smile upon the earth; so toward the first of April, 1873, I was off. The first evening, as I sat looking out into the darkness, my eyes filled with tears, for I had a long, hazardous journey before me, and had left friends behind to whom I had given a long, and it might be a last good-bye. In the western part of the state I stopped a few days among friends whom I had not seen since I started for college, all of whom greeted me kindly, and were anxious to have me tarry; but I must on.

So I jumped into the fastest train and was soon rolling down between breakers into the Missouri valley at Council

Bluffs. As far as the eye could reach up and down this beautiful valley it was perfectly level, with high bluffs, from five to ten miles apart, on either side of the Missouri river. Yes, here was the Missouri river, so black that the dirt seemed to bubble up to be carried away on its surface. Yet this muddy stream was a mighty one, extending from where the gulf's billows ever roll and roar, to where the earth's tossed billows rear their snow-capped heads above the clouds like breakers on the upper deep. Tracing his downward course from his home in the mountains to his larger home in the ocean, he creeps along gathering strength, until angrily he throws a coil against one side of the bluffs of the valley, and another against the opposite, his shifting tides in turn striking every point of the bluffs, undermining and crumbling them down into the broad extensive valley as smooth as a table.

BACHELORS OF ART.

In early times when the Indian roamed over the Mississippi valley, an exploring party under Lewis and Clarke ascended the Missouri in skiffs, and crossed the mountains over into Oregon. While passing near Sioux City, Floyd, one of their number, died. His comrades buried him on the highest bluff they saw, and erected a large cedar post to his memory, thinking they had given him a secure, though a solitary, resting place. Many a time the Indian's tomahawk chipped that cedar post, but nothing disturbed the sleeper's rest till one of the shifting coils of the stream attacked this prominent bluff, undermining where the quiet sleeper lay. His remains appearing in the side of the bluff next the river, a man was let down by ropes to secure them, and now they are resting farther back upon the same bluff, to sleep on till again disturbed by this unsatiated stream, or awakened by the trump of God.

But westward! the plains! the mountains! the Indians! the new, the wild, the unexplored! To me these were thoughts of a magic charm, impelling me onward with an electric thrill. Rolling over the fertile prairies of the Platte one hundred and fifty miles, then shooting like an arrow three hundred miles more across a placid sea of green where the only land-marks were the wrecked carcasses of buffalo, we entered a half barren track where the sand ap-

"BUFFALO"!

peared between the bunches of buffalo grass from eight to ten inches apart—where great numbers of prairie dogs scampered to their holes to give the closing scene of hind legs and tail twinkling in air—where droves of antelope skimmed the prairie away from the approaching train until, beyond danger, they turned upon their heels to stare a moment, and then unconcernedly continue their grazing—where buffalo were frequently seen in the distance, but always proved to be a knoll, or other object, upon approaching. Now a gentleman exclaimed "buffalo! buffalo!" All rushed to the opposite windows, and lo! a Thomas swine was making a sturdy quick-step along the track, grunting as he went.

Rolling on through a country growing rougher, and still more so toward the mountains, passing bluffs, and at times apparent islands with perpendicular rocky sides, rising high above the level country around, and on till in the distance rose up the snow-capped mountains dazzling in the sunlight upon the canvas of white clouds beyond, growing closer and closer as the cars wound around the foot hills through snow fences and sheds, the train halted at Cheyenne, 516 miles from Omaha.

Denver was 110 miles south, and I changed cars to soon be shooting along from fifteen to twenty miles from the foot of the mountains, yet apparently much closer. Long's Peak, forty or fifty miles to the right, appeared only a few miles away, while Pike's Peak, eighty miles beyond Denver, seemed but twenty or twenty-five miles distant.

The country along the track was somewhat barren and broken; we occasionally passed a valley productive by irrigation, and the whole was a fine grazing country. Greeley was in a rich valley about half way between Cheyenne and Denver. Its many ditches told of irrigation, and everything looked new and flourishing. On toward Denver the country was smooth and productive, and thousands of cattle roamed over the green prairies.

As the train moved up to the depot I looked out for Caleb, but no Caleb was there. Next day, when in the post office I accidentally raised my eyes and looked out into the street; at once I exclaimed to myself, "Yonder goes Caleb!" The personage in the street rode along a few yards, alighted, and tied his ponies. While doing this I stepped up with a smile, put out my hand, "How are you, old fellow." Caleb was taken completely by surprise, and of course grinned all over.

"How fleshy you are, Caleb; Colorado preaching must agree with you."

"Who wouldn't be fleshy! That lazy pony would afford exercise for a professional spurrer."

"Come now, don't slander that pony; you know those dear old sisters have been pampering you on Methodist chickens."

"I am but too sorry those dear old sisters, as you call them, left their chickens in the States. But, by the way, Wildair, I brought that pony along for you. Now you, the

TOTING HIM OUT.

smaller, jump on him the larger, and I, the larger, will jump on this one, the smaller, and we will be off for the livery."

"I suppose your policy in riding that small one is that upon his becoming mired, you can catch the pommel of the saddle, carry him out to dry land, and jog along without having the trouble of getting off and on."

"Mistaken; this small one never sticks, and he can beat the world at kicking. Were I to ride that one he would mire sure, and my only alternative would be to get a long lever, raise one of his ends, jump on my pony, wrap his tail round the pommel of the saddle, and tote him out!"

CHAPTER II.

WANDERINGS IN COLORADO.

LIKE the wild herder without home save his pair of blankets, frying pan, cup and coffee-pot, and without tent save the sky above him, we mounted our saddles for a ride through the plains and mountains of Colorado; at night, lying down beside a dry pine log fire, while our ponies grazed their fill and then came to nod and sleep in the camp light. However, if some cabin about sunset seemed designedly thrown in our way, we unceremoniously unsaddled and stopped with the bachelors for the night—that is, if they were not all away from home; in that case we modestly built our fire outside, though herders frequently assumed the duties of the house in the absence of the inmates—perhaps having supper ready when they returned.

Our first few days' ride, however, was not out on the broad plains where the herder tends his cattle in sight of vast droves of buffalo; neither was it in the narrow mountain gorges where the miner in the foaming stream washes out the shining metals—but between these two extremes, where the mountains and the plains met in embrace, and laughing streams coursed their way along numerous valleys. Here the herders in many cases had wives, comfortable homes, and small farms yielding wonderful crops. They did not ask for the rains of heaven, but looked to the snow-capped mountains, whose melting waters they turned from their natural channels into artificial ditches, winding around the hill sides or along the borders of the valleys.

About half way from Denver to Pike's Peak we struck a spur of the mountains, shooting out into the plain and dividing the waters of the Platte from those of the Arkansas. We had heard of a lovely spot of earth situated somewhere in this locality, a few miles from the road. So ere the departing sun drew through the mountain gaps her golden ribbons, we turned up a green valley which, though miles in length, was as straight as the last threads of light that streamed down this magic way. It was so regular, so lovely, I imagined an angel had inverted a rainbow and with it plowed his course far into the mountains.

Along the bottom ran a careless Indian trail through the carpet of green, while far up the curving sides were groves

THE BACHELORS' WELCOME.

of evergreen with inviting retreats almost inducing us to leave the path. By and by forms of monuments appeared among the evergreen on our left, as though rocks, like trees, could grow from the green unbroken turf.

At the end of the valley we halted. Below us lay Pleasant Park, surrounded by lofty rocks, stony fortifications, within whose walls were towering ruins as of a mighty city shaken down by the hand of God. Some of the standing walls were red like brick, others white like marble. Long we watched the fitful lights and shadows of the moon play their wondrous charms among those eternal remains. In that green and level valley from which they arose stood groves of lofty pines, like tender household plants in the door-yards of a deserted city.

Down in the park, in a secluded spot, we found a cabin of three bachelors who bade us welcome as old friends. On the walls were great horns upon which were racked their guns, while about the room lay Daniel Boone's complement of dogs. One of the men, wearing buckskin pants with five hundred dangling strings, cooked us a good supper; then we lay ourselves down on furs and buffalo robes among the dogs to sleep.

Next morning they pointed out, two miles distant, the side view of a monstrous Indian face. The Red man of these regions called him "Tewat," as the stern visage looked like their chieftain of that name. Men may have carved the Sphynx of Egypt, but no human ladder ever reached up this perpendicular rock, a thousand feet high, to cut this face. It must have been a grand thought to this Tewat, that

TEWAT.

the Great Chieftain had stamped his image upon the eternal rock as a witness of his commission to rule.

But a stranger phenomenon was the picture of a bear on the face of a rock. The longer I looked at it the more I was puzzled. So perfectly in shape, size, and color, did it resemble the brown cinnamon bear of these regions, that a number of rifle balls had been fired into it, apparently through mistake. These scars, which were about an inch in depth, gave us a better opportunity of inspection; but, like every subject that is unfathomable, all light only revealed new mysteries. Had it not been for these perforations, showing that the color extended at least an inch in depth, I would have concluded that an artist of some race inhabiting this country prior to the Indian, had painted this picture upon the stone, immortalizing his skill, though his name and race had vanished. But I know of no paint that will saturate a stone, and yet not leave the outlines perceptibly blurred.

This pictured rock, I believe, has never been described by any traveler, though it is well known to the Indians, Mexicans, hunters, and the settlers. It is situated in a canyon of Purgatory River, twenty-five miles above Fort Lyons. The people all wonder how it was formed, and the idea has somehow spread among them that a bear standing near had been photographed by a flash of lightning.

After riding round through Pleasant Park among the monuments until tired of seeing and admiring, we keeled over on the green grass in the shadow of a lone rock as steep as any wall, towering up into the sky perhaps two hundred feet.

The rocks of this park are the same layers as stand on their edges so grandly thirty miles to the south in the Garden of the Gods, in which the traveler may wander up narrow grassy streets between smooth perpendicular walls that seem to tower into the sky: the same also as form such imposing entrance to Masie's Hole, known in early days as Devil's Hole. The entrance was then guarded by a band of horse-thieves, while the interior formed a corral large enough for ten thousand horses, with abundant pasture. It is now occupied by farmers and herders who have put a gate across the entrance, keeping their cattle within from mixing with outside herds. This place of wondrous beauty is about fifty miles south of the Garden of the Gods, and many miles of the country between are colored red as blood with the dust of these crumbled monuments. When those lofty granite mountains to the west of this region popped their heads through the ground, they must have thrown the whole crust of the earth along here on its edge. Only the hardest layers of rock yet remain.

As our ponies were grazing, the luggage on the small one worked to one side, touching him in the flank, when, as quick as the flash of a gun, he went into a fit of kicking. Wildair was considerably frightened, but I took it coolly, for I had seen that pony kick before. What did I now care for his kicking? My foot was not in the stirrup! Finally he freed himself of everything save the saddle which slid down on his tail; then he streaked it toward a deep ravine, turned a somersault, and alighted at the bottom of it.

We had just got ready to start again, when Wildair espied a squirrel. Off he goes, I after him and he after the squirrel,

A NARROW ESCAPE.

leaving the ponies to take care of themselves. The squirrel runs up a tree, but that is just what Wildair wants; I never saw such a fellow; he never gets tired of shooting. The second shot brings the squirrel, over which Wildair seems as delighted as if he had shot a buffalo with a cannon seven miles off. As we stow him away, Wildair continues to boast over his shooting and the fine aim he took, to which I assented:

"Oh, certainly, certainly, I never heard of such tall shooting! Only think of bringing a squirrel from the top of a tree with a revolver no longer than your finger!"

A few rods more Wildair is off again, and I after him. This time he sights fine, but the squirrel doesn't come. I take aim with my large revolver, that gets on a high, discharging all the barrels at once, but the squirrel doesn't come. Wildair also loads up his seven barrels again and again, he standing on one side of the tree and I on the other, shooting, but the squirrel doesn't come. He now climbs the tree and shoots, while I, to keep the squirrel in his sight, stand off on the opposite side, throwing clubs and stones, which seem more likely to hit Wildair than the squirrel; but the squirrel doesn't come.

Then Wildair creeps up to another limb, though anxiously solicited not to proceed higher. At last the squirrel is on the tip-top limb spreading its tail as if about to fly away, and he right beneath it reaching up his arm.

"A little closer, Wildair; reach a trifle closer, and you know the powder will save us the trouble of singing."

Bang! Bang! and down comes the creature; but the moment it strikes the ground away he bounces in the direction of a large rock, up which he scampers, while Wildair scrambles down with triumph to get his squirrel; but the squirrel is gone. I dangle my feet in the air, laughing, while he rolls and tumbles me over and over in search. In vain I assure him that I have done nothing with his game; he is inwardly convinced that the fall would have killed any squirrel, though he maintains to this day there was no room for such a catastrophe in this case.

As we rode on we passed a house by the roadside which I

watched with the deepest interest, and when on the hill I turned and took a last, long look: I seemed to be parting with an old friend. Wildair desired to know what interest so deep could be connected with such a common-looking house; so I soon found myself relating the story.

"It was here as a lonely wanderer I ate my first supper in Colorado. I then was a stranger, as you know, to every human being in the territory.

"I was on my way to Southern Colorado or any place else. When I left Denver in the morning I inquired the way to Colorado City, and was told there were two or three roads, but that the one by West Plum Creek was the nearest, though roughest, as it kept close to the mountains. Then I asked who lived along West Plum Creek about a day's ride distant, and was referred to a Mr. Hopkins. I inquired if they ever had preaching near by, and was informed that they did in a school-house of the neighborhood about five miles beyond, and that the preacher often stopped with this family. I rode on enjoying the mountains and the new world around me. I did not have a bite for dinner, but lay down at noon on the grass under some pine, to drink in the enchantment of the strange, beautiful scenery of the mountains, which, range beyond range, rolled away into snowy peaks amongst whose infinite vastness I longed to wander.

"When my pony neighed, and then went down to the stream to drink, I concluded he had eaten grass enough, and again rode on.

"He was the oddest pony I ever saw—cinnamon colored, white sided, white striped, white footed, ball faced, glass eyed, and fat; but I wouldn't have cared for all that only he pretended to be able to know when it was time to stop for the night.

"Just at dark I inquired the distance to Hopkins', and was informed that it was eight miles. Then commenced a scene of whipping and spurring, which, before it was through with, almost hardened my heart against all ponies. I spurred until compassion arose, but as soon as I commenced pitying he stopped to pity himself. There was no moon, but the playing lightnings lit up the summit of the mountains, whose dark bases appeared like black clouds right before my face, but which I seemed never to approach.

"But it wouldn't do to lay out in the face of a storm; and finally the pony concluded to jog slowly on.

By and by, with joy I saw a light near the road, for, strange as it may seem, they had a window in their house. Hopkins

A BLOODY RECEPTION.

was not a bachelor. At the door I dismounted and knocked. A motherly-looking woman opened it.

"'Is this where Mr. Hopkins lives?' I inquired.

"'Yes, sir.'

"'Do you receive preachers into your house? I am on my way to Southern Colorado, and would be glad to stop over night with you.'

"'O! certainly; come in; leave your pony; some one will take care of him.'

"In half an hour more in came half a dozen large, stern-looking frontiersmen; but the sternest, most dauntless looking one was Mr. Hopkins. I seemed like a tender child before their hardy natures, and felt almost as much like running as speaking. Their hands and arms were bloody from skinning a bear which they had killed that evening.

"Next morning just after breakfast, a large grizzly bear came down from the jagged mountains, ran across the broad grassy plot before the door, and disappeared on the left among some low, shrubby oak. Out started all the men with their guns, calling to the dogs as they ran. Some went around the rocks and

SUNDAY RECREATION.

woods to scare him out, while Mr. Hopkins took up a position near the road to shoot the bear as he returned. My nature was to go too, but you see it was the Sabbath. Soon, however, they returned without any bear, Grizzly having scampered back safely across the road.

"Somehow, that house seems strangely dear to me, because the scenes were so new, the people so kind, and I so lonely."

Finally, as we proceeded on our way Wildair became interested in shooting at the little prairie dogs, which, on our approaching their village, skedaddled, each to his mound, where he stood barking faster and faster as we approached. When we came so near one that he could bark no faster, he popped into his hole, and we heard a last rapid whe-we-we and saw the final twinkle of his tail.

But Wildair would persevere in showing how straight he shot, and how his balls struck right on the opposite side of where they sat. So, after having told him a hundred times, even if he did shoot one with his little revolver he could not

FULLY CONVINCED.

get him, I tried making fun of his shooting. So when he said—

"Did you see that? the ball struck exactly on the opposite side of where he stood;" I replied, looking in the opposite direction—

"Oh, certainly, certainly, you put a hole through one every time; how can I doubt that, since seeing your performance on that last squirrel?"

But that remark only whet his appetite; so I rode on, telling him I was so fully convinced I thought it useless to tarry longer. When last I looked around I espied him four miles away, still pulling trigger at those barking puppies of the desert.

When Wildair overtook me I was sitting upon a jagged rock of the wall of the Garden of the Gods, watching the zigzag lightnings play about the summit of Pike's Peak just beyond. That great battery, having become charged with electricity, telegraphed to the clouds, which came flying—gath-

TEMPLES OF TIME. 33

ering as they flew—until the elements met in wild fury and fierce array around the awful summit, while unseen wires became red as flame and fiery javelins pierced the mountain.

It seemed fit that down from those awful heights the furious gods should come to spend their calmer moods in this garden, from whose surface, so level and green, towered variously colored rocks of startling grandeur yet fantastic forms of beauty.

But we wandered outside the garden, far away along Monument Creek, where the white columns of their ruined temples arose amid the evergreens and over the valleys, as strange, if not as fanciful, as any that ever adorned the heathen temples of ancient Greece and Rome. Though the ceiling had fallen, yet frequently a broad flat stone remained strangely poised upon the top of a column. The music that used to echo here was the wild ocean's roar, as declared by the pillars of cemented gravel.

MONUMENT ROCKS.

We next wandered up amid the mountains, to the Soda Springs, whose gaseous waters formed a flowing soda fountain that would both raise bread and elevate one's

3

feelings. After drinking large draughts it seemed that springs were under our heels, and we were soon up about the "Double Falls," loosing large stones to dash and plunge into the unseen depths below, while all the chasms around echoed back every boom and crash, or prolonged and modified them to suit their hollow voices. We tried our lungs; we had only to open our mouths and the chasms opened theirs to the mountains, and the mountains spake back to the chasms. We grew wild with delight—we hallooed—we whooped—we modified our voices in a thousand strains while waving our hands, gloating upon the vastness around between rocks and mountains, who, as if full with utterance, spake back to our ravished senses such tones as we had never heard—tones larger than Pike's Peak and deeper than five hundred wells. Creation seemed our speaking trumpet, while we were raised in feeling above the mountains.

At evening we wandered back to Colorado City, with its crumbling buildings speaking of its high but fallen hopes.

CHAPTER III.

FRONTIER LIFE.

I HAD some lively experiences before the arrival of Wildair. My circuit extended over the scattered settlements from the Green Horn Mountains to Fort Lyons, a distance of one hundred and fifty miles along the Arkansas River.

Here I found all the romance of hardships I desired. My appointments were mostly in log cabins without floors or windows, the people from Texas even complaining that the cold required them to daub up the cracks. Upon entering them I could not see a particle, but said: "How do you do?" They managed to find my hand and we had a sociable time. Were it too cold to throw open the door, they lit a faint candle or punched the fire so I could see to read the hymn; then we were all right for the rest of the services, though I looked in vain for tears to be shed—it was too dark.

Las Animas City, within a mile of Fort Lyons, I found the excrescence of creation; the scum of railroad towns floated down there and lodged round a military post. I first entered this village one Saturday evening just as the echo of the sunset-gun was dying out over the plains. The people were on a high. Before me passed a young girl with a cigar in her mouth, cracking her fists, and reeling toward a saloon where men were gambling. Up to them she marched, interrupting their game, and gave them distinctly to understand that she was around, and must have a treat, or some of them would enjoy the luxury of bloody noses.

Next morning as I tried to hold services in an unoccupied

room, the clatter of hammers against horses' shoes in the adjoining shop was the chorus of each song.

During the day one hardy frontiersman sought the opportunity of an interview with me. As he began to talk, tears filled his eyes, which had not wept for years. He told me from an overflowing heart and in pathetic language, of the new life and hope that once dawned upon his mind; of the higher bliss, the more rapturous joy he then experienced and felt to be not of earth, but streaming down from Heaven. Then he deplored the condition into which he had drifted—not so much through his own fault as through the downward tendencies of all around him. Upon the currents of unmixed evil he was here thrown, and borne farther and farther away from the

INVITING A TREAT.

things he used to love. With bitterness he told me it must remain so; he could not stem the tides. Upon leaving he firmly grasped my hand, and with emphasis said:

"For God's sake, be firm."

In Boggsville, near by, my first congregation were Indians, Mexicans, Europeans, and a mixture of these that I have not arithmetic to express. However, the gentleman in whose house I held the services had a splendid mansion, while around him were the cabins of his tenants, forming a village. As every one gazed at my tall hat until it went out of sight, I threw it away, and my host gave me one from his store with a low crown and a broad drooping rim. I also found it quite convenient to resort to his smith shop when my pony needed shoeing; and his harness shop proved very handy when I wanted to swap my old sinch for a new one. He had an immense herd of cattle, and several square miles of land. The latter, I understood, he received as a premium from the government for raising a number of children equally related to the Indians and the whites, as a civilizing policy. His wife sometimes left his fine mansion and ran away to the wigwam of her childhood, but as often he brought her back. But still she would be an Indian, strapping her papoose on her back, and hiding about the house like a wolf. The daughter of Colonel Bent—her neighbor—though a half-breed, was refined, could play on the piano, entertain guests, and had a warm, noble heart, yet her sister was as tameless as a fox, preferring to spend most of her time with her mother's relatives.

She belonged to the Plain Indians who are the eternal enemies of the Mountain Indians. Formerly both were friendly to the Whites, passing up and down the Arkansas to meet on the war-path. The last time the Plain Indians passed up this way they came with their rifles, breathing vengeance against the Utes of the Mountains. But no sooner had they arrived at Colorado City, than they treacherously wheeled about and returned, scalping the helpless settlers who had permitted them to pass and made no preparation for such betrayal of trust. I was shown the tree near which two little boys, brothers, were killed while driving home the cows. Almost every neighborhood had its fortified house where the people collected in time of danger. The Utes were still friendly to the Whites, passing up and down the Arkansas River, as of old, to replenish their store of buffalo meat. I might tell of Indian scares innumerable, of families fleeing from tribes of friendly Utes mistaken for Plain Indians, and wives and children sorely frightened during the absence of the heads of families.

One day a neighbor woman rushed into the house where I stopped. I knew at once the cause of her fright, and immediately hastened to her home, to find a number of peaceable Utes at the door. The warriors, with their flashy colors, continued to pass for an hour in gangs of three and four, riding up to the house to beg, or trade for arms. Their very looks were frightful. Then for a couple of hours passed scattered squads of squaws, driving ponies loaded with tents and bundles of poles, one end dragging on the ground.

As the mantle of darkness spread around, the war-whoop of these savages rendered the night air hideous; so I wandered thither, far, far down the river to them. In a cove-shaped nook of timber their wigwams were pitched, and lit up by a common camp fire around which a party of braves were still dancing. It was a beautiful scene, so nature like; there were their groups of nodding ponies. Upon entering the camp an Indian poked out his head from a wigwam with the salutation "How, how; come in," and in I crept. Around a little fire whose smoke ascended through the top, curled the lazy inmates, apparently a part of two families, forming a circle, the head of one being in contact with the feet of another, while the back of each individual touched the tent. Upon a couple of hot stones were slapjacks baking. When ready to turn, they were leaned against some pegs before the fire to give the other side a scorching, then thrown to the stupid savages to devour.

When they desired to retire for the night, they had simply to draw the curtain over their eyes and the thing was effected. Or when the squaws wished to prepare breakfast, the only requirement was to rub their eyes, raise themselves upon their elbows, and go to baking—without the vexation of dressing, washing, combing the hair, or even moving a peg.

Upon their begging for matches and tobacco, I indicated I wasn't a smoker, when these suspicious savages (a couple of squaws, by the way) concluded that seeing was believing, and at once instituted a search. So I climbed out of that—not that I had much money to lose, for in those days I lived upon charity myself. The "head" of the hovel crept out after me, whispering slyly in my ears "whiskey, whiskey." As I had none to give, he took me aside and secretly inquired, the best he could, as to the whereabouts of the Plain Indians, whom they dreaded to meet in open country, but with whom they would have rejoiced to battle among the rocks of their own native hills.

But Wildair and I visited them at their homes in the mountains. We did not wonder that they were peaceable, for they had nothing more to lose; their game was all gone, never to return, and when the charities of the Whites fail, all these tribes must go to work or starve. After having traveled two days in a region so wild that the Indians must feel gloomy, our provisions failed us. In the afternoon, at the head of a fertile little valley, we passed the ranche of some bachelors, but they had nothing for us, though we were cut with hunger and almost begged for a little of their greasy side meat and a few sad biscuits.

ON THE HUNT.

Next morning I heard a wild pheasant flapping its wings; 'twas the loneliest sound I ever heard. I wandered up amid the rocks, and climbed above frowning precipices, but could not tell from whence the sound proceeded; it seemed to come from every stone around. I climbed to the summit, full of lonely, dreamy thoughts.

> I lay upon a wild and rugged rock,
>   O'erpowered by chasms deep,
> And gazed into the desolations round
>   Where Nature lay asleep.

> The bleaching bones of vanished buffalo
> Foretold the Red Man's fate;
> No more amid those rocks he pens his game,
> For else, too desolate.

But in these parts remained a few mountain sheep, and an occasional wild Texan ox escaped from some herd. The people have found that Texan cattle must be kept on the plains. So wild are their natures that, should a drove see a man alone and on foot upon the broad prairies, his life would be in danger. One day as I rode across the plains far from the river, I noticed Texan cattle unherded coming on the run toward me. My horse was white, and attracted their attention far

WILD CATTLE OF THE PLAINS.

and near. By swinging my coat, and plunging my horse at them, I managed to keep them at bay, and finally put the drove to route. It would have required a swift horse to keep ahead of their stampede.

We stopped over night with a solitary but well-to-do bachelor. He cooked our supper and breakfast, swept the house, and more, accommodated us with the luxury of a tolerably comfortable bed.

But, take it all in all, bachelors are the roughest set of housekeepers that ever undertook such duties. Their dirt floors, their greasy pokers, their jams, their door-posts, seemingly rubbing posts for hogs—are enough to frighten any lady or even the Old Scratch himself. My sister visited me in Colorado, and being romantic, I bought her a pony, on which she accompanied me once around the circuit, which was a distance of nearly four hundred miles. One day, my pony having given out, we rode up to a herder's cabin, round which we saw several ponies grazing, to banter them for a trade.

The young bachelors were very kind, and invited us to have some dinner with them. With joy we alighted and entered, for I was always hungry in Colorado. But Roxanna was taken by surprise, although I had tried to picture to her the mode of life these weary men lead. Our meal consisted of beaver tail and beans, served in a black pot set on a low box before us, into which we dived one at a time, filling our tin plates, and eating with forks that had long since lost their handles. One of the young fellows politely used his fingers. The beds, blankets, and saddles, were twisted up in an inglorious pile on the floor.

At another place where Roxanna and I took dinner, we were all eating away with great satisfaction and relating incidents of our lives; as one fine-looking man whom they called "Major," was telling some of his hardships in Libby Prison—how it shattered his health, how he came to the territory to recuperate, and of the wonderful vigor he was beginning to feel—an incident transpired that cut short his remarks.

An old hen, happy with the thought of having become the mother of an egg, came flying from some back apartment for the open door, and with a loud cackle and wonderful flounder, lit plump in the great plate of fat meat, throwing the pieces and gravy all over the table and into our faces! Then, with another fearful bound, she flapped her greasy wings over our heads, and was off. But the Major caught the worst dose, as the chicken's feet slipped out from under

A "FOUL" DINNER.

her with great violence, a time or two, in the direction of his face. That invading form! I still sometimes see it in my dreams. The Major did not finish his story.

Though a young lady could hardly be in Colorado a week without receiving a number of proposals, yet Roxanna received too greasy an introduction; all their propositions slipped off. Were I a lady, before I would marry one of these bachelors, I would require him to burn down his greasy shanty and build a clean one, throw all his clothes to the flames, scour himself with a brick, syringe the drooling end from his mouth, and even then I would not have him, for nothing can reach his mind, to purify the fountain of his thoughts that have been corrupted by the scenes of his surroundings. Yet there are exceptions to this rule, when the sudden presence of a pure and lovely angel at his home brings back, like a flash, the remembrances of former times, for many of them had been reared in the lap of luxury and ease, and once knew the charms of refinement.

One day, cold, dripping and wet, Wildair and I rode from early morn through the mountains, amid clouds of fog and descending snow-flakes. In the afternoon we came upon a cabin, where we stood the rest of the day like hungry, dripping rats, on the rickety hearth in an unearthly looking house, while back of us were four men of intellect, but fallen refinement, who, eager for excitement and thrilling events, had come to this wonderful West. There they sat, round a table that they would once have shuddered to touch, gambling over money they had received through the grand lottery of the West—gold mining—while filthy words and vile oaths rolled from their mouths.

By and by, in came another man who looked as if he belonged to civilization; he tarried but a short time, seeming to have something to do, something to occupy his mind this rainy day. Making inquiries, we learned that he owned a saw mill, and lived in a house not three rods distant, which was hidden from view by the clouds.

When supper time came, to our delight he invited us to his house. As we entered, our eyes first caught glimpses of clean paper trimmings upon the shelves, and the white stand table covering, upon which were a few little trinkets tastefully arranged, and we seemed to have seen an angel—yes, another step and there she stood, as neat as a white pigeon and pretty as a dove. Three weeks before this man had been living as these other bachelors were; but he had the good sense and fortune to go down toward Denver and get him a jewel of a wife. How his heart leaped with joy as he sat down around a table with a snow-white spread, on which was inviting food served in beautiful dishes. I had seen so much of dirt that I came near rejoicing aloud, but I quenched my feelings. When at night we lay down in a soft clean bed, her angelic presence seemed to hover round, and I then and there said in my heart some hard things against bachelors.

I thought this reformed bachelor—reformed like a magic, his feet taken from the pit and miry clay and set upon flowery beds of comfort and beauty, and his weary head laid upon a snowy pillow—enjoyed more comfort in a single hour than one of those other lonely, filthy greasers would enjoy in a lifetime of vexation, disappointment, and sorrow. A man robbed of the society of woman is the filthiest looking brute I ever saw. The deer, the rabbit, the wild birds of these regions, seem born of the sky in contrast.

At this time Wildair and I were on our way from Colorado City westward into the mountains, bound to stand face to face with the grandest of those distant eternal pillars of the sky, that had beckoned me thither ten thousand times when riding on my weary rounds on the plains. They had called me with a passion, day after day for months, and now, with Wildair equally wild in his first enthusiasm, I was at last to approach those mighty forms, and try to throw my arms around their infinite vastness.

Next morning the clouds were lifted high, and drifting down the mighty gorge toward the plains like great chunks of broken ice on the upper deep. The bright sunshine played between the pieces down into the ethereal river, while above, on either shore of the stream, stood the eternal peaks clad in their mantles of purity and bright in the clear sky of heaven. Soon the sun came out, the snow fled up the mountains, and stretching carpets of green spread themselves beneath our feet.

Toward evening we found ourselves upon an elevated ridge, and before us in the west opened a scene of vast extent. The rolling mountains, dark with evergreen, rose higher and still more rugged in the far-off distance; but far beyond these, set in the golden sky, were snowy ranges of peaks so remote they seemed to be the eternal spires that lined the bound of creation. The clouds rolled away, opening distance beyond distance, then dropped their golden spires down to meet the silvery spires of earth, as if to form portals through which to pass to heaven. To angels they must have appeared as the gates to this dark earth, through which only scattered rays of light were shining; to us they appeared as openings leading into the Beyond, illuminated by the smiles of Heaven.

Near the roadside we visited the "Petrified Stumps," about twenty in number, scattered along a grassy valley. Out of the hollow of one over a dozen steps in circumference, had grown a large tree whose trunk had fallen and now lay mouldering in the grass, while the original stump seemed to laugh at its decay.

In these high altitudes, the atmosphere is so thin that there is no covering to break off the splendor of the sun, or none to keep what heat he gives, so that the moment he sinks from view the warmth flies upward, leaving the world and poor campers like us to shake with a fit of ague until his return. But still there were charms in sitting before the bright blaze of the camp fire flashing out under the boughs of the deep green foliage of pine—fun in roasting our venison on the end of a long pole, and relish in eating it. Four pounds disposed of gave a wonderful amount of pleasure to a couple of huge animated lumps that keeled over on the grass to contemplate mischief for the evening.

On the side of the ravine where we lay was a forest so dense that no eye could discern that beneath the lofty foliage towered a grand mountain. Up the grassy valley here and there stood solitary evergreens, their silver-coated foliage glittering in the moonlight. Up, up they rose, tapering into perfect cones that seemed to pierce the sky. On the opposite side of the valley many had been killed and badly burned by the fires, yet their leafless trunks stood as long, straight, and tapering as the arrows used by the mighty angels during the fierce battle of heaven.

"Look here, Wildair, I can't see a particle of sense in sleeping over here by one fire that's likely to go out before morning, when we can enjoy a dozen over there, and have a sure thing of it. You can stand any amount of cold; it don't faze you, but I can't sleep so sound. If I didn't creep out in the night and run through the brush, packing limbs to throw on the fire, you would be a frozen icicle one of these mornings and wouldn't know it. Look here, I lost my watch chain last night, and almost scratched my sleepy eyes out."

"Well, agreed; let's pack our saddles over there and build

A NIGHT IN THE WOODS.

fires on every side of us, for I can venture to say that one of my sides alternately cooks and freezes every night."

"Here, here, Wildair, is the very place. See, the logs lie round in a circle!"

After starting fires far and near to moderate the whole atmosphere, we sat down to watch the blazes flash, wane, shoot into the air, and play their various pranks, until, tired and sleepy, we placed three torches in the encircling logs, then lay down in the centre to rest. We had just fallen deep into the arms of Sleep when we began to dream of infernal regions, of the torment of their flames—I'd never had such dreams before—

"O! rouster, Wildair, blazes! good heavens! get out of here—"

"Ho! Oh—oh—what's this?"

"Fire! fire! come—"

"O! where, how, back, Caleb!—"

When we found ourselves we were standing off about fifteen rods, scratching our heads—a little scorched they were.

"Do you know what I was thinking about, Wildair?"

"Certainly; about that fire."

"No, not that—how near we came needing no more roast venison."

"Well, I'd been worse than an icicle in a moment, had you not awakened me."

"The Indians, I imagine, must have barked those logs for pommel soup."

"Why, what of that?"

"A good deal; it causes all the pitch to settle in the peeled portion, and the people in Southern Colorado split this into candles!"

"The end of yon elevated log—a snorting candle that!"

It was not long before the wind arose, sweeping the flames from tree to tree up into the denser and denser dead pine trees, until it seemed like a mountain of burning fire sending its blaze toward heaven. It didn't go out that night, neither did we sleep much.

Somewhere far out among those endless mountains, one day before us opened South Park, a mighty basin deeply sunk in the snow-capped mountains that girt it about like eternal barriers of ice piercing the clouds. Far, far beneath us lay that gem of spring, carpeted by grass. Raising our glasses to our eyes they revealed thousands of cattle grazing down in that level lawn, drove beyond drove, until they appeared like myriads of ants—then vanished from view beyond the centre.

We now started for the summit of Gray's Peak, in sight, a short distance to the north; but there was a snowy range to be crossed, over which mining prospectors were beginning to pass on snow shoes. So we had either to pack our ponies over the range, or traverse a round-about way. We did the latter. Along a gorge winding in every conceivable direction, we followed until I thought we were nearly back to Colorado City—at least we came to where we could see the stream bursting out upon the plains. Then we started up another gorge between other folds of the mountains, toward the peak we were bound to climb.

The squads of miners whom we passed driving their pack mules into the mountains looked curiously at us, but on we wound our way up South Clear Creek, along one of the grandest gorges that ever cut its course through granite.

The early miners who went out with pick, shovel, and sandpan, have here left great signs of their work. The stream had ground portions of the mountains into gravel, through which the miners have dug for the gold that had been crushed out of the stone and settled on the bed rock. Mile after mile the smooth round stones and gravel had been washed over and piled up in great fields and innumerable mounds.

But as if this stream were too slow, impatient man had directed his ingenuity and powers to crushing the precious metals out of the mountains. On one hand, donkeys were packing ore down the steep side of the mountain along a winding path to a neighboring crushing mill; on the other hand, a rail-road cart came rolling out of the granite wall, bearing to a stamping mill its precious load. We rode into one of these tunnels, with the dripping rock above our heads and the chilly air around us, until we came to a machine on wheels, drilling the sparkling granite with augers whirling at lightning speed preparatory to blasting. They were still driving the tunnel into the mountain, expecting by and by to strike a far richer vein. The machine was run by compressed air, which was conveyed hither through pipes from the air pump at the entrance. This pump received its power from the dashing stream.

CHAPTER IV.

ASCENT OF GRAY'S PEAK—IN A HORN.

GRAY'S Peak had been in our minds ever since we left South Park. Seemingly we had come around creation to get here, and now the miners told us that we could not ascend, that the snow yet covered all the mountains. They had a hard time beating this into our understanding, for it looked like summer at Georgetown. But that was not the point—we were bound to set our feet on the summit of Gray's Peak, or fail trying: so they told us that just before day-break would be the best time to ascend, as the crust would then bear us up without snow-shoes; besides, we could then obtain a grand view of sunrise upon the mountains. No doubt they thought this would be a stunner. But not so; we were delighted with the idea. How romantic; nothing could be wilder!

So, as evening was throwing her dark mantle over those mountains, we started up the principal gorge, with the dashing stream far beneath us like a streak of silver light seen by glimpses through openings in spruce and pine. The dark rocks reached up half a mile or a mile on either side of the chasm, over which a pitchy cloud soon moved, but only to bring out the stars which shone from the entrance to shafts, tunnels, or doors of miners' cabins, whose houses seemed in the sky up the sides of those eternal rocks. We thought that now their damp, dreary day's work was done, and that they were preparing their little meals, soon to lie down and dream of finding gold as abundant as stones, and then of hastening home to far distant friends awaiting their coming.

Occasionally we passed a large quartz mill with lights in the windows. Thump, thump went the fall of the iron-heeled stampers, night and day. We heard the heavy jarring sound until lost in the roar of the stream. The sound was as though the gods were still forging those mountains.

About midnight we were tired. The snow began to lay around in great patches; but we found a dry place among some willows, and built a fire. The cold wind came whistling through like mournful music, as we crouched low, and curled around the fire, while the ponies forced their way into the brush, and stood with their heads over us. When we fell asleep the fire managed to die out, as we had nothing larger than willows to feed it. In a couple of hours, the sky being clear, we hastily ate a bite with our chattering teeth, and long before the stars drawing the rosy-wheeled chariot of morning appeared, we were on our way exultant with the thought of standing on that lofty outlook of heaven and beholding from its summit the Flaming Rider with reins of fire burst through the mantle of night, casting a myriad of golden wreaths upon a world of marble brows—first upon the one touched by our feet, then upon one far remote, then upon another, and another, until descending lace of transparency had fallen over each pure white breast. Then, sitting down on this pillar of the sky, we would watch the playing lights and shadows of the peaks across the mighty chasms between.

Soon the forest became so dense that it was almost impossible to ride farther. But I had scarcely dismounted, when before me was an animal apparently as large as a tiger. I suppose my lively imagination exaggerated the size, for the innocent creature turned and ran off through the starlight before I had shown my courage by remounting. Well, it is something to see a large panther in the woods, and know how it feels to be scared, after all.

Hitching our ponies, we started on foot, giving us a splendid opportunity of warming ourselves. In crossing the stream we got a view of the peak before us—more, we got our boots full of water, but that only made us care nothing for the snow.

Just before the sun arose we had come out from under the forest, and were commencing the ascension of the peak, which was without trees.

"Look toward the summit, Caleb, what does that mean?"

"Those are tracks, sure."

"Of what? Not men, for they told us at Georgetown none had yet ascended."

"From the way they have plowed down the side, I should judge they must have been grizzlies."

Instinctively we halted; but it was only a moment; we had endured too much to turn back now; besides, Wildair

A MUTUAL SCARE.

banished fear by flourishing his "pepper box." It wouldn't salt a prairie-dog—but he verily seemed to think it would season a grizzly. To redeem its character seemed to be his idea, while I lamented I had left my "bushwhacker" behind.

After more than an hour's climbing, the snow had gradually become so steep that a misstep, or losing of the balance, would have sent us rolling wildly, with ever-increasing velocity, toward the bottom. How carefully we beat the toes of our boots into the almost impenetrable wall of snow. It was now almost perpendicular—we dared not even look back. A rod more would bring us over the difficulties. It was passed, and we felt relieved. But look; we gaze with astonishment upon a mighty basin.

"Oh, Wildair, what a scene; I never saw anything like it before!"

"It looks like the billows of the storm-tossed ocean."

"Or like the frozen crater of a volcano."

"Caleb, do you remember those great bear tracks? Here is where they end!"

"I see where they started, too." (Using the glass.)

"From that perpendicular rock almost at the very summit."

"Wildair, I understand the mysterious bear tracks now."

"So do I;" and both at once tried to explain, the one to the other, how small pieces of stone had crumbled off of the great rock when the side had been warmed by the sun, to go rolling upon the softened snow, collecting with every roll, augmenting at each bound, until finally every leap became as the plunge of a ship, finally bursting, and heaving at the bottom as breakers against the shore. We had fun scrambling over these billows, and fun ascending where the snowballs had plowed.

Then it entered our mind, what sport for a party of boys and girls to snowball on the side of this mountain of a warm afternoon, when the showering balls would fall to chase each other like rolling moons. But if one of the parties should stumble, somebody's darling would soon be but a sweet coriander seed in the centre of a tremendous rolling snow-ball. Only the sun could suck her out.

By and by we arrived at the rocks from whence the snowballs started. As we passed up among them we came upon some white pigeons which lost their wits and fluttered about dumb-puzzled; we also saw the tracks of Rocky Mountain sheep.

From these heights we started large stones from their balance, which went crashing down, loosing a multitude of others in their course, all racing over the yet frozen snow at marvelously increasing speed.

A few more hard scrambles, each trying to be the first to enjoy the scene, brought us to the summit which had so long evaded our approach. The view which opened around us is beyond the power of imagination to picture. We stood in awe; but in a few moments we noticed that far and near were peaks higher than the one upon which we stood. Our happiness was gone. We knew we had missed Gray's Peak, which was considered the highest of any in these regions. There were two that seemed to equally claim that distinction. One was south of us across the principal gorge from which we had ascended; the other was just to the north across a branch of the same gorge. The thought of climbing from the bottom of the principal gorge again was too horrible to indulge a moment; so we decided that the peak on the north was the higher—the highest of all.

Now, there were two ways of reaching this peak. The direct way, was straight across the branch gorge; the long way was by the ridge leading around the head of this gorge several miles away, then back along the ridge on the opposite side. We would have taken the ridge, had it not been capped by a number of minor peaks, over whose summits we would have to pass before arriving at the desired point. We decided to cross the gorge.

The snow on the north side was like feathers, having never been thawed and frozen. So down the steep side we bounded, leaving deep peg holes in the snow, fifteen feet apart. Descending that mountain was a sport next to flying. Most of the time we were in the air, and when our feet touched the snow it was as though the soft wing of a bird was beneath them, lifting us into the air. When near the bottom we came upon the true tracks of a bear, and from their size we judged they had been made by a grizzly. Pines, with the arms bent down by the snows of long and dreary winters, skirted either side of the gorge.

Now began the long and tedious ascent. When somewhat above the top of the first peak we had ascended, we imagined that a few more struggles would bring us to the desired summit; but unexpectedly there opened before us another descent, though less than the one we had just crossed. Wildair still preferred to take the direct way, while I chose to follow around the head of this gorge. As each was decided in his own opinion, we separated. He soon became like a speck below me, while I could just make him out, waving his hat as a sign of triumph. He seemed to have completed half his journey, while I had hardly made any progress—indeed, was slowly climbing farther away.

Finally I reached the ridge at the head of the new gorge. I was now on the summit of the Continental Divide. It was so steep before me that a stumble would have sent me dashing hundreds of feet below. I took up a handful of snow, and placed it a yard away from where I had picked it up, and that determined its course into the Pacific instead of down the Mississippi into the Atlantic. So a single decision determined our course toward the Pacific, and around the world. I walked on along this sharp "Back-Bone" of the continent, looking down into Middle Park—indeed, careful lest I should tumble into it. I could have followed this ridge round all the gorges to the other high "peak" that had claimed our attention. Indeed, I believe I could have followed it far away to South Park—or, in the opposite direction to North Park. I would like to see a railroad built along this "Back-Bone of the World." Would it not be a grand ride through this Switzerland of America past the Parks fifty and one hundred miles long? All the railroads in the world could not, in the least, compare with it for an excursion route.

I now looked down at Wildair, who seemed to be making poor speed, having to rest every few minutes. Finally we both called up all our energies as we neared the meeting point. I fell first, and Wildair tumbled across me, almost burying me in the snow.

"I b-e-at you," was the pertinent suggestion of Wildair as soon as he could gain his breath.

"You di-did—"; the n't was cut off by a mouthful of snow.

"We'll consider that when we are re-sted."

After nine hours of the most incessant toil, we finally reached the summit. Neither pen nor pencil can reproduce the scene which confronted us on every side. One could only feel in silence, rather than exclaim—What an elevation, what yawning chasms, what vastness around! One snow-white range or peak beyond another until the eye was led away one hundred and fifty miles, through an atmosphere so pure that even at night a mountain at that distance can be distinctly seen.

Middle Park, comprising an area much greater than that of Rhode Island, lay beneath our feet and seemed like a deep-sunk gem of green with snowy fingers grasping it from circumference to center. Beyond were the unexplored mountains. South Park, across two ranges, with its green-tinted basin rimmed with evergreen, nestled in the everlasting hills, and seemed to perform no part except to add beauty to the snow-clad mountains around.

Then we cast our eyes toward the plains, but their endless carpet of green opening far beyond Denver, seemed to be but the foot-stool to these spotless sanctuaries of the skies.

The high upland prairies of North Park led the eye to the border of the territory, but beyond, the peaks of the Continental Divide reached into the unseen.

The Continental Divide mustered its hosts from the horizon in the northwest to the horizon in the south, presenting a line of about three hundred miles of peaks, separated by depressions like hanging festoons. About one-half of the distance was taken up in a grand sweep around three sides of Middle Park, branch ranges shooting off from the angles to complete the enclosure of the Parks—each branch range perhaps forming a divide between two great rivers on the same side of the Continental Divide. It is as difficult for this or any range to run a long distance in one direction without branching, changing its base of operation, or breaking suddenly up, as it is for a school-boy to cover his ball without having branch seams.

These branching streams or veins among the mountains are constantly wearing them away, and bearing portions of them, age after age, into the ocean, or over the valleys.

When the sun was well along in the western sky we went jumping down the mountain side, but were not long in finding that our springs were considerably worn. In truth we felt like old wagons, and concluded to try turning ourselves into sleighs; so, sitting down upon the soft snow, we slipped and ploughed our way downward, regardless of our pantaloons, until, finding ourselves going too fast, we used our heels and hands as brakes. The sport was fine, and we struck up a race, letting our sleds out at a pretty rapid rate. I was heavier than Wildair; and was gaining, I thought, a slight advantage of him in the ride, when suddenly we approached a point in the side of the mountain, where the grade became rapidly steeper. We slapped on the brakes with a vim, but instead of slackening the speed the snow clogged in front of our hands and feet, the quantity increasing as we shot downward. To my sorrow, my sleigh was now driven decidedly faster than that of Wildair, and was becoming so large that I feared it would begin to roll. When I reached the bottom I was driven clear through it. Looking up from the tumbling snow which almost buried me, I saw Wildair sitting upon his snowball, which was twenty feet high. He afterwards said, that from the way I looked up I must have thought an avalanche was coming upon me. When composed I hallooed:

"Ho! Wildair, I beat you badly that time."

"Yes, I confess you did; you look like a gorilla frozen fast in an iceberg!"

"Come, come, now—just be neighborly for once and step down and help me out of this."

"Stars! you have the advantage of me now; how the blazes do you imagine I am to get down there?"

"You'll be down before you're aware of it, I am thinking."

Finally he did jump from his ball to mine and dug me out.

On looking around we found that we had descended the peak just below where the gorge forked. Our ponies had broken loose and were browsing near where we left them at daybreak. We felt like browsing, too, for we had eaten nothing since long before that time, as we expected to return to Georgetown, for dinner. Our boots were like wet rags, yet our other clothing had no reason to be ashamed of them.

DESCENDING THE MOUNTAIN.

It was nearly dark when we reached Georgetown.

Soon afterwards we crossed a low mountain range to the head waters of North Clear Creek. Here we found a ditch winding along near the summit of the ridge, conducting water to some of the dry mountain gorges to be used in washing out the shining metals. Around us, and for many miles in front, the mountain sides were thickly covered with stumps of trees which had been cut for running quartz mills and propping the walls of the mines. The mountain sides had, during past ages, crumbled down into slopes, but almost every square rod had a freshly dug pit. Out of part of these the miners were taking a soft ore containing small particles of free gold that were easily separated.

Here and near by we found three cities—Nevada, Central, and Black Hawk—as closely united as the three Fates of old. We imagined ourselves Indians coming out of the wilds of the West, now for the first time looking upon a city, so strange and unexpected did these high walls and rich and stylish streets appear. I am not sure but the Indian on his pony would have felt more at home than we did on ours, looking as we did. Mincing ladies, in silks and ruffles, walked the streets, or looked out of windows hung with lace.

Concluding to sell our ponies, we rode around to the different livery stables. It was fun to see the curiosity of the collecting crowds at these places. No one offered to buy our ponies excepting a drunken man, and his comrades wouldn't let him pay us the money.

We knew that ponies were selling very low at Denver at that time; so I, as well as Caleb, thought we had better try to sell before we got there. When a mile or two out of Central City, upon the old road to Denver, we stopped at an old stage station to try our luck. A couple of gentlemen seemed inclined to purchase. Caleb asked fifty dollars for Indian, while I thought Slam was larger and finer looking; somehow, just then, too, it crept into my head that he was getting better of his stiffness; so I put him at sixty dollars.

After looking at Slam a few moments, they paid their entire attention to Caleb's Indian. All I said seemed, to my indignation, to fall unnoticed upon their ears. One of them offered Caleb a shot gun and a few dollars in cash for Indian. Of course Caleb didn't want the shot gun. The other offered him forty-five dollars. That was not Caleb's price, and so we started on.

When a few yards away "Shot Gun" called to us to return. We rode back. He brought out his wife's gold watch, offering that as an even trade for Indian. In a moment his wife came out on the portico and said that she "did not want to part with the watch," that she "wouldn't have such a pony," and that she "would never go to church with her husband if he got such a thing."

Still her husband wanted to trade. Caleb did not want the watch, and thought she needed to go to church.

As we were about to depart, his "angel of sweetness" said that she would let the watch go. The husband remarked, as he had before, that "it was not running just at that time, it needed cleaning, but that it was a No. 1 time-keeper." A little spoiled girl holding her father's hand, just then remarked:

"The watch won't run."

"It is not running just now."

"It never would run."

Both father and mother looked sheepish, grinned at each other, and we rode off.

In half an hour we stopped beside a spring to let our ponies graze awhile. Looking down the road, we saw a couple of horsemen with guns on their shoulders. They were riding toward us.

"Caleb! yonder come those very men."

"Wonder what that means."

In a moment they spoke to us and said that they had followed a pathway down into the woods, hunting squirrels, and were returning by this road. They started on. Shortly, back trotted the one who had made the cash offer, gave Caleb his price, and led away his Indian. They had slighted Slam almost from the very first. I was not feeling very well over that, and as Indian was led away I remarked to the man:

"You will be hunting squirrels towards Denver. When you meet us I suppose you will buy my pony."

His answer was, "Your pony isn't worth the little end of nothing whittled down to a point."

Many a time I have tried to think of my reply, but never could, and Caleb never could.

From this place to Golden City, Caleb and I took turns riding and walking. We met several parties with teams, and asked them:

"Are you wanting Slam? O! excuse me I mean a pony."

Slam was in every respect gentle, except when any one wanted to look at his teeth. I was very glad of that, but I can solemnly swear I never taught him that trick. Only one man was ever able to look into his mouth, and he remarked, after his scrutiny was over—

"I can't tell within sixteen years of his age."

From time to time, as the pony jerked away I thought I was all right, but at an unexpected moment I would hear that ominous demand, "Let's see him move." That was sufficient —they never bought.

As we were getting on toward Golden City, we met some miners on their way to the mountains. Our clothes were, to say the least, slightly dilapidated. We had not been bush-whacking, but the bushes had been whacking us. Right here you will remember that at the time of the gold excitement at Pike's Peak, many had written upon their wagons as they crossed the plains, "Pike's Peak or Bust." In a short time they were to be seen returning with this inscription instead, "Busted by Thunder." So these parties we were meeting seemed to think we should bear the latter inscription, and one man had the impudence to pretend to see it and to read it aloud for the benefit of his friends. I returned the compliment by making sundry gestures indicative of derision, and by informing him that the sooner he got his companions to hoop him the better.

We arrived at Golden City toward sundown, tied Slam in front of a hotel and made inquiries in regard to selling. I had now come down to fifty-five dollars, the price I gave for him. I did not like to lose on him, even were he of no account. After some inquiry, a boy told me he was wanting a pony on which to herd cattle, and thought his father would buy. He pointed me across to his father's store. I rode over that way shortly, and the father and son came out. In a few minutes a crowd gathered around. Two or three attempts were made to look into Slam's mouth. Being true to the teachings of a former master he was ashamed of his age, even jerking loose as they twisted his upper lip to hold him. He showed the white of his eyes, pricked up his ears, appeared to be full of life and fire—the most deceiving pony in all Colorado, no doubt.

The father talked of buying. He had not seen him move, our knew his age, and I thought I was all right. In a moment he wanted his boy to get on and try him. My hopes fell at once; his movement had blasted the prospect of sale several times before. As the boy started around behind to get on from the other side, the pony kicked, striking him on the leg, and sending him whirling to the ground. The frightened father picked up the crying boy. I cannot say I wanted to see the boy hurt; still, it was a great relief. However, I was astonished at Slam, in fact, didn't know he could get his heels that high. In a moment the boy was better. The father remarked:

"That's the kind of pony you are trying to sell, is it?"

"You mistake your man, sir—I never knew him to make any signs of such a thing before."

Still, the father was afraid of Slam.

Said I, "Should there be any wild fire in him, which I do not admit, the herding of cattle will soon extinguish it."

Still, I was not believed, and such remarks as these were going the round: "Bet there's fire in that pony!" "Look at the snap of his eye!"

From his looks, no doubt, at one time these remarks would have been appropriate, but from abuse and old age those days had passed many years since.

By this time the crowd had grown to be immense. Some said "Let's see him move," and desired that I should ride him up and down the street. I rather demurred, but that wouldn't do; so I mounted him. No doubt they expected to see me whirled to the ground before I should be seated in the saddle. I administered two or three spurs; he started off-on-a-slow-walk. From some cause, he was worse than usual. Two or three cried out: "Move him up!" I knew this was next to impossible without making an ass of myself, but gave Slam several terrible prods from the side opposite the crowd, concealing my efforts as much as possible. He bent his body from the spur, and moved off in a slow, wriggling, dragging, circling trot. The crowd burst into laughter, and cheers rent the air. Men waved their hats and tumbled over each other! That was too much. I turned partly upon my saddle, and attempted to speak. There was a lull after a storm.

"Gentlemen, if I knew who it was that poisoned my pony, I would"—

The storm of laughter opened anew! The town "busted;" windows and doors opened—crowds came flocking from all directions. As I passed down the street—for I didn't return—the boys followed me as though I were a circus menagerie. The thought struck me that I would get out of that as soon as possible! How I spurred! Every time I let up, the pony let up—in fact, would have stopped short had I not continued spurring. I was the target for laughter from every window, and from every crowd that collected as I jogged along. Shortly I espied Caleb in the crowd, laughing like the rest, and knew that he had seen it all. I could not blame him, but had he been in my grasp just then I would have wrung his neck.

At the hotel I alighted. Caleb stepped up to me. Said I:

"When I get this pony down to the barn, I am going to pull out my revolver, put it to his ear, deliberately pull the trigger, and see if he will go to sleep over that."

We took him down to the barn.

"Now, Caleb, I can't forgive this pony—it is utterly impossible; but as you are of a religious turn of mind, and as I have some money at stake, I will desist if you will pronounce a long, solemn blessing over him and his descendants forever."

Not saying whether Caleb pronounced the blessing or not, I soon got Slam some corn meal to eat, not for any love I bore toward him, but because I wanted him to pick up during the night, for he was to be sold or given away in the morning. As regards the meal, I did not feed him with that because he couldn't eat corn—oh, no!

Next morning Caleb took the cars for Denver, twelve or fifteen miles away, while I rode my "fine stock." I didn't try to sell him any more in Golden City; he had a reputation all over town.

On my way to Denver I met several parties, but they wouldn't buy; they had seen his gait as I rode along. I was now pretty well toward Denver. "Yonder, probably, is my last chance," I said to myself as I saw a couple of mule teams hauling flour into the mountains, a man driving the first team, and his boy the second one. I knew it wouldn't do to let them see the movement of Slam, so something began to be the matter with the girth, and I stopped to fix it. I did not want to deceive any one, but when anything is the matter with the girth, it must be fixed! As the team passed by me I was mounting.

"Are you wanting to buy a pony?"

"How much do you ask for him?"

"Fifty-five dollars."

The father got out to look at him.

"His back is sore, isn't it?"

I told him I was merely fixing the girth, at the same time showing him that the back was all right; also said that I had been riding him hard for the last three weeks through the mountains, and that he needed rest. Wasn't that the truth? Surely, if Slam didn't need rest, no pony ever did!

"I will give you fifty-two dollars for him; that is all the money I have to spare, with me."

I hesitated a moment as though not too anxious, and only a moment. He might call upon me to make him move, and of course that would be the end of the thing. Now I asked him what he would give me for the saddle. He said that he had one already. So I pulled it off, and by one stirrup threw it across my shoulder. The man got out a rope by which to lead the pony at the hind end of the wagon. I scarcely knew what to say to that, for I knew that Slam was the meanest thing on earth to lead; I had pulled at him sometimes, and the harder I pulled the harder he held back. The only possible way to get him along was to walk by his side and punch him up, or get behind and twist his tail. However, I merely told the man that he didn't lead very well, as

SLAM AND HIS BUYER.

I knew he wouldn't be any the better pleased with his riding should he attempt getting him along in that way; and more, I never like to destroy any one's felicity. I bade him good morning, and started off toward Denver on a pretty round pace, the saddle stirrup and skirts dangling and flapping in the air.

When a few hundred yards away, I glanced round, and they were just ready to start, Slam being tied behind. They started. Slam pulled back. They stopped a moment and started on. Slam braced his feet and slid along, then began rearing and throwing himself back with the greatest violence. Now I heard something crack. Out came the tail-gate, two or three sacks of flour tumbling on to the ground. The old man scrambled to the back end of the wagon, glanced at the sacks, then at me, shaking his fist violently.

"Come back, you rascal!"

I trudged on faster than ever. Slam sauntered out to one side. In a moment the old man was out to catch him. Generally he was easily caught, but now he started off on a stiff, unearthly trot. The old man halted, stood, and stared, then turned toward me, cracking his fists. I trudged on, and soon disappeared over a hill, and never learned whether the old man and his boy left Slam upon the prairie, or shot him for breaking their wagon.

Soon I was at Denver with a saddle on my shoulder, looking a little rough from having been tearing through the mountains for the last three weeks. At home, as a choice, it would have been preferable riding a goat up town to walking the streets as I looked. But what did I care? I was doing no wrong, and the faces of the people were strange to me, and I never expected to see them again. My saddle disposed of, I walked into a store, bought a new suit from head to foot, and stepped over to the hotel, where I found Caleb. Of course I told him I had sold Slam and how I sold him. He was delighted that I had disposed of him, yet somewhat sorry for the unhappy man who had been his purchaser.

I had become so used to spurring when riding Slam, that it was some time before I got over the habit. Judging from the way the sheets of my bed were torn one morning, one would think I had been having a terrible encounter with a night-mare—but it was only a ride through dreamland on that "hoss." Poor fellow, I fear he never lived to see the epizoötic!

5

CHAPTER V.

OVER THE MOUNTAINS BY RAIL.

FAR out from the habitation of man, amid the wild, wild mountains, we passed a wanderer. He had no home, no friends, nor wished for any; yet he was not lonely, he knew every mountain, every rock, far and near. His camping ground extended from Washington Territory to Texas. He was driving a couple of Mexican donkeys followed by a playful colt that sported and kicked its heels around its loaded Ma and Pa, and at night looked in at the tent door beside the dog.

Once a year he went to Denver, or "Frisco," or Galveston, or Portland, to sell his furs and buy a sack of flour, then wandered leisurely back from the haunts of men, contented and happy, with no one's whims or fancies to please, and no one's tongue or frowns to fear. But still he was sociable, and manifested an extreme delight in pouring into our eager ears the many strange stories and wild adventures of his life, as we sat one evening around his camp fire, which happened to be in sight of our own.

Out from those retreats we came and took our seats in a palace car, shooting along without a quiver, the snowy peaks of Colorado on one side, and the endless level green on the other. As the elegantly attired ladies and gentlemen glided from window to window, in ecstacy over the new world and the distant mountains, I thought of the thousand scenes hid amid those lonely retreats of which they never dreamed. With astonishment they learned the immense distance to those marble looking peaks seen through snowy gaps that opened to give us glimpses beyond. We pointed to our sunburned hands and faces as witnesses that we had wandered amid them and stood upon their lofty summits, where the sun shines without a screen and stars look down in the daytime.

At Cheyenne we were joined by other passengers. As we passed along they talked about the mountains as though we were passing among them, when in fact we were not at any time nearer than a day's ride in the saddle to anything the least worthy of that name.

The soil of these regions is of indefinite depth, having been formed by the crumbling away of limestone and rocks, upon

ECSTATIC PASSENGERS.

which vegetation has never yet fairly taken a start, but when watered and planted it has in places produced abundantly. That the increase of vegetation by means of irrigation augments the fall of rain in that quarter, has become a well known fact, which adds encouragement to the belief that those regions as well as the Plains proper—whose soil by the way is strong—will at some future day yield an abundant increase at the hand of the husbandman.

Although this section is about seven thousand feet above

68 MOUNTAIN FLOWERS.

the level of the sea, yet it is only a thousand feet above Denver and the valleys around, and is hardly as high as the parks and valleys among the mountains where it is known that an abundant yield, at least of certain kinds of produce, is the reward of cultivation. Moreover it is likely that products will be found which are adapted to this high altitude, as moun-

MOUNTAIN FLORA.

tain flowers and berries bloom almost among snow banks. We have often stood on snow and gathered them.

An hour and a half from Cheyenne brought us to Sherman, the highest point in the whole line of the Continental Railroad, though little more than eight thousand feet above the level of the sea. Thence by an easy grade we descended to Laramie Plains, a thousand feet below and green with sprouting grass. This used to be an agreeable resting place for emigrant trains of old, affording both game and fine pasture. Just beyond these Plains we crossed the North Platte, where a few companies of soldiers were drilling.

Then we rolled on, across the Continental Divide so low as to be scarcely noticeable. Here we climbed on the top of one of the cars to look around, and could see distinctly that

THE SERPENT OF THE MOUNTAINS.

the track wound like a snake around every hill and rock—for you know the Government agreed to give the Company so much per mile, besides half the land for twenty miles on either side of the track. At times we saw snow sheds in the distance, and hardly known whether we had passed through or were approaching them.

As we crossed Green River the last one third of the distance to Salt Lake began, and with it green streaks of fertile valleys, which gradually deepened into canons among which thrifty Mormons were cultivating small but beautiful farms. Soon the walls of rock became too narrow for valleys and rose boldly hundreds of feet high. Thrilled by the wildness, we again climbed upon one of the cars, as the train thundered faster and faster down Echo and Weber Canyons, past "Castle Rock," the residence of old King Time and his powerful princes, Winds and Floods, past "Devil's Slide" where from the long, deep print he has left in the sloping rock we should judge him to be twenty or thirty feet in diameter, by the "1,000 Mile Tree" from Omaha, as indicated upon a large sign suspended from a limb, on down the narrowing, deepening canyon, increasing in speed as the fall of the stream increased, shooting from side to side over the foaming abyss, plunging through tunnels in the side of the protruding wall, the cars rattling, shaking, and bounding, until we clung to the car from fear of being shaken off—and thus we were ushered at frightful rapidity from the monotony and desolation above through "Devil's Gate," full into the smiling gardens below, embraced and watered on all sides by snow-capped mountains whose forms were pictured on the bosom of the lake.

Switching off for the City of the Saints, we passed through level orchards and gardens flourishing under the most luxuriant growth, forming a scene which from contrast with the outer world seemed doubly lovely, into the rural City of Salt Lake, down whose broad and regular streets ran streams of clearest water, giving life and freshness to the vast gardens, and forests of fruit trees which almost embowered her lonely dwellings.

As I looked upon these thousands of rural homes in the bosom of plenty, I was inclined to bless Brigham as a benefactor of his race sent by a wise Providence to raise up the poor and the needy. Every visitor to Salt Lake has cursed "Old Brigham," so it does me good to remember that he has wrenched from the hand of the savage a large section of land, and caused it to smile with plenty at the touch of industry.

Early on Sabbath morning we wended our way along shady walks to the Old Tabernacle. We were shown one of the front seats reserved for visitors, where we sat watching the ignorant-looking masses as they entered. Soon, in stalked a long-nosed, hollow-cheeked, shallow-brained looking man with his family of homely-clad wives, daughters, and a few boys, perhaps a dozen altogether. Through a side door leading directly to the altar, entered now and then one of the Twelve Apostles, or a couple of the Seventy, with a very religious air, who shook hands with some of the brethren. When they had sat with their hats on long enough to mortify all pride and all etiquette, they uncovered their apostolic heads.

Following the singing and prayer, the Apostle Canon, a saint of the largest caliber, poured his volleys upon us poor Gentiles. After enumerating the dangers through which God had led them, and the blessings he had conferred upon them, which were causes for the deepest gratitude, he stated it was a great work to which they were called, requiring heroic energy and a sacrificing spirit; yet God had promised them the peace needed, and they were now, to some extent reaping it. But why the opposition they had always encountered on every hand? It would naturally seem an argument against them.

SALT LAKE APOSTLES.

But people had formed wrong opinions of them. All reformers, all good men had met with opposition: Christ himself met with opposition. The reason was that he who presented truth had to meet error, he who acted right had to combat with wrong. There were two conflicting principles at work; it commenced with Cain and Abel, and had extended down to the present. The reformers had a glimpse of light, and they met with opposition, but they had just prepared the way for the new dispensation which was then beginning to be ushered in. The church had lost its connection with God, its power of working miracles, and had been disorganized and divided; so God sent an Angel to Joseph Smith to give him a commission to restore the former modes of worship, to reorganize the church according to its former pattern, and to prepare men for the receiving of the gifts and powers they once possessed. These were bestowed upon the condition that they would acknowledge them before the world, and their faithfulness to this injunction was the cause of their persecution.

The spiritual and temporal head of Mormonism arose to close with a "few remarks," which consumed not much short of half an hour's time, and were directed toward the Gentile portion of the audience in rather a boastful, scornful manner. But he was the preacher, and we poor sinners had to bear all he hurled at us. He pictured out what an awful desert they were driven into; how barren the valley was when they arrived; how the people came to him with their discouragements, but how God had quickened the soil and made the valley fruitful like the promised land, so that every stranger praised the beauty of the city. He said their enemies thought by persecuting them and driving them upon the desert they would put a stop to their doctrines, but under the counsels of heaven it had resulted only in proving the purity of their doctrines. Now, instead of their going to the Gentiles to preach, the latter were coming to them.

During the afternoon about eight thousand people assembled in the New Tabernacle—scriptural in name, but a turtle in shape. We admired the organ, the largest we have seen in America save the one in Boston, but were surprised to learn that the unpretending citizen sitting at my elbow was its manufacturer. The discourse consisted of weak trash poured out by one of the elders, and was followed by the admistration of the sacrament, or something like it, which was passed round to all but the Gentiles.

I spent a long time reading the Mormon bible, and came to the conclusion that none but the most ignorant could be gulled by such nonsensical trash so clumsily thrown together. It was originally intended for a novel, giving in biblical style a fictitious account of the settling of this country by the lost Tribes of the Children of Israel.

Leaving Mormonism to give way before the potent influence of this assimilating age, we rolled out across the great Continental basin through regions where the alkali lay so thick upon the barren plain as at times to resemble a fall of snow; where streams lost themselves in stagnant waters around which were the fit abodes of lizards, reptiles, and low beastly Indians; past horrible lakes with horrible names, the ground here and there steaming and puffing with a sulphurous smell; on and on through this sunken Sodom and Gomorrah, till one bright morning we were ushered out into that verdant region where the tallest pines of earth lifted their heads to the sky, on the lofty Sierra Nevadas.

While waiting at Truckee for the hack that was to take us to Lake Tahoe nestled in the mountains, we sat and looked upon four out of the five races, often all represented within the space of a square rod. There was the European with his noble bearing, the Negro with his assumed dignity, the Indian with his crouching step and sly look, and the Chinaman with his subdued, submissive appearance, toiling as slowly, steadily, and unconcernedly as the ox beneath his yoke. As we passed the Chinamen upon the broad lonely desert, tending or working upon the railroad track, we had often wondered what he thought of America, whether he was not lonely so far away from home where his people by millions dwell, and earth is like a garden. As we thought of the means of riding in their country where two men become a walking locomotive to bear a third, we wondered what they thought of our locomotive whose mouth glares like the lightning, the breath of whose nostrils is like the clouds of heaven, and the approach of whose iron hoof across the desert or over the mountain is like the rolling thunder.

The coach was now ready, so we started for Lake Tahoe. Up a deep wooded ravine past a village and many a miner's cabin, all now deserted, up among large, lofty pines, spruces, and firs, where cones with bases a foot in diameter lay around beneath the giant trees, up where trees were hidden by moss, and the cushioned limbs fell upon the ground with a soft bounce, and on up to the summit rolled our coach. Then down, down, we bounded, trying ever but in vain to catch a glimpse of the lake, until as we came out from beneath the forest, the Gem of the mountains opened before us—fourteen miles in length and eight in breadth.

A little boat connecting with stage lines among the mountains steamed over the lake; but we preferred a skiff ride. We hardly knew how to launch out as the water was so clear that it seemed as if each stroke of the oar would send us against some lofty granite boulder, although the little steamer had fearlessly rode above them. As the water deepened we stopped paddling, leaving our skiff to float out upon this lower stratum of air, as we imagined it. The rocks far beneath us seemed crested with moss, with shells, with lime, while many rose up toward us, bare and grand, presenting yawning chasms into which the sun cast peculiar lights and shadows. Owing to the depth of water all were tinged more or less with a bluish green. As we touched the waters with our oars each ripple made the rocks dance, while chasing rainbows seemed ready to carry them away. We paddled out until the chasms, and then the rocks, all hid themselves in the beautiful color of the lake, while an occasional spotted trout sported unconcerned, perhaps seventy feet below us. Then we looked around over the lake; up the walls of the basin covered with impenetrable foliage; above the green to the snow-capped peaks nearly encircling this gem of the ocean and sky.

THE TRANSPARENT GEM.

After a bath in the hot spring which boiled and steamed up through the cool water near the shore, we were ready for a trout dinner at the hotel.

Having returned to Truckee we started up the apparently impassable mountains, two engines tugging and puffing ahead. Up, up, a deep gorge, we passed to and around its head—then back along the opposite side, leaving the stream and track by its side farther and farther beneath us, until finally we were riding around a point of the mountain hundreds of feet above Truckee.

Before arriving at the summit of the mighty Sierra Nevada,

we saw far below us in the forest shades the silvery waters of Donner Lake, where an emigrant party to California, in early times, was overtaken by the deep snows of winter and reduced to such straits that a part of them survived upon the flesh of those who died. We were reminded of the depth of snow which falls here, by a single snow shed twenty miles in length which covered the track along this part of the route.

At the summit an observation car was attached which gave an excellent view. Down we almost flew through a fresh cool air that quickened every nerve, whirling around lofty mountains whose sides stood out of dizzy chasms below, shooting along the sides of the precipices one or two thousand feet high, past mountains almost washed away or cut in two by hydraulic mining, always charmed by extended views of mountains with glimpses of the far off California valleys, until we had descended seven thousand feet in one hundred miles, from deep fields of snow into the scorching prairie of Sacramento Valley, where wilting vineyards were watered by hundreds of fluttering wind mills.

CHAPTER VI.
A FLIRTATION AMONG THE BIG TREES.

HEARTS were all aglow in anticipation of beholding one of the grandest scenes in nature. At 5 A. M. all were stowed away—three on a seat inside the coach, with a young gentleman and two misses on the roof. Crack went the driver's whip, the horses pranced, and we were off.

Soon we learned from conversation, that one of the gentlemen within, a fine looking man, was a judge living in Mariposa, some sixty-five miles on our way, and that the talkative lady, sitting between the judge and Caleb, had traveled a great deal; that the young gentleman and one of the young ladies above, were her son and daughter; the other young lady the intended bride of her son; and that they all were from Fifth Avenue, New York, visiting the wonders of the West.

Soon we came to a ferry; the gentlemen climbed out, it being sandy on the banks of the San Joaquin, and consequently heavy pulling. I took advantage of the opportunity to cast a sheep's-eye at the ladies above. As we were returning to the coach on the opposite bank, I caught the eye of the daughter, and I said to myself, I'll have a flirtation with that belle yet, see if I don't.

We were now passing over the broad level valley of San Joaquin, very productive generally, but this season everything was withered and parched from the drought. The judge pointed to broad fields of wheat that would not be touched by the reaper, and to the horses, cattle, and sheep by the thousands, which were being driven to the foot-hills, and into the mountains, there to browse the grass. Two or three times during the forenoon we stopped to change horses. I never failed to climb out to stretch my limbs, ever ready to catch a glimpse of the young belle above. But fate seemed to be against me, there was no becoming acquainted while she remained where she was.

At length noon came, and we stopped for dinner. In the bar-room I began a conversation with the young lady's brother, and made myself as agreeable as possible; but the young ladies did not appear in the dining-room.

When the stage was ready to start again, the three young people concluded to ride inside, as several passengers had stopped on the way, and took possession of the back seat. For a time they talked only to each other, but by and by the conversation became more general. I was far more lively than in the forenoon, and by degrees I directed my remarks to the daughter. Everything she said seemed to be appreciated by me, and when others were talking I did a good deal of squinting around the judge's shoulders toward the object of my attention. The judge had much to say of California; the old lady told of her travels; and when Caleb and I informed them that we were on a tour around the world, all seemed anxious to hear our plans.

We were now at Mariposa, the home of the judge, where everything was green and beautiful, and the crops, watered by mountain streams, were growing luxuriantly. Here we took supper, and tarried an hour for rest. The judge, who had stopped at his home upon our entering the town, came around just before our starting, to bid us good-bye. Most of our party were reluctant to part with him, although the acquaintance had been brief. But I remembered his shoulder had been in my way, when I conversed with the young lady and didn't regret leaving him behind.

Our carriage was now an open one, with three seats to be occupied by six persons, two on a seat, and as luck would have it the charming young lady and myself were put on the same one. What could be nicer?

Away we went over foot-hills, winding around and up the sides of the mountains, and I never was jollier. The young lady and I became quite intimate, and I wished we were to drive all night, instead of the twelve miles which brought us to our stopping-place for the night.

Never had I seen a lady who had so completely taken my fancy, and I felt that I would be happy were this stage ride with her to result in something more than a mere flirtation. For her sake I passed a restless night.

Next day we again occupied a seat together, and soon we were winding up the sides of the Sierras. It was splendid; and I felt that she who sat by my side was an angel of light. I enjoyed her smiles and words a hundred times more than I did the yarns and jokes in which the conductor began to indulge. As we were admiring some large trees, how uninteresting to have him remark :—

"They are nothing but hoop poles compared with the Big Trees. Six months since, a boy was started round one of these, and has not been heard of since."

And when Caleb questioned him in regard to their height, how very uninteresting to have him reply :—

"It's well known that one of them is so tall that it requires two men and one boy standing one on the head of the other, to see its top."

And when he came to that old, old story of Greeley's ride down these mountains, it seemed to cap the climax of all dullness.

We had wound round eight miles up a steep grade, almost to the summit of the mountains, and now began the descent of four miles to the valley between the Big Trees and Yo Semite.

Crack, goes the driver's whip, accompanied with a "Git, climb out of this," and the horses are on their heels. Down we plunge, around gorge, and point, and cliff, at break-neck speed, the road being barely wide enough in places for the horses. The stumble of either, the hubbing of a rock around a point, seemingly must dash us to pieces.

Soon we came to where the road was more level, and the horses moved slower. A thrill of happiness shot through me as I discovered that my arm was around my companion's waist, holding her in. However, it was reluctantly withdrawn before she was compelled to suggest its removal; but just then I would have been glad of another plunge down the mountain side.

Upon arriving at Clark's we at once made arrangements

READY FOR THE PLUNGE.

to visit the Big Trees, five miles to the south. The graded road had ended, and now we were to take ponies along a winding trail. My belle was not much used to riding, and I made myself useful in every way possible. I assisted her to mount, adjusted her riding skirt, and then climbed upon my own nag. As we followed the trail along its winding way among large spruce and pine, I always managed to keep close to her, and was ever ready to lead her pony over difficult places.

Look! what mighty forms, whose towering heads reach toward the sky! Only a glimpse we at first catch of them through the dense forests; then nearer and nearer they come like a new world moving upon us. Foliage thick and deep is beginning to hover above us, the light of the sun is disappearing, shut out by tree tops which seem to swim in the soft ethereal sky.

Now we approach the "Fallen Monarch," far up whose side many an insect man has climbed to carve his name. Ascending the ladder we stand upon its mighty trunk. How grand and majestic is the prostrate king, although his head, once towering so proudly above the surrounding forest, has taken its flight to earth.

Our party becoming somewhat scattered about this time I missed my belle, and looked here and there, listening to hear her voice and laughter, but could see or hear nothing of her. I put spurs to my pony and went galloping around to the

CALEB'S RACE COURSE.

opposite side of Grizzly, where I found her apparently waiting my coming. How beautiful her smile!

From Grizzly we soon came to another fallen tree, which, from the effects of the fire, lay in several parts, like great hollow logs upon the ground. Caleb undertook to ride through one of them; as the pony was in a hurry to get the job done he shot ahead, and on reaching the place where the opening was smallest, Caleb was brushed from his saddle, and the steed emerged from the farther end of the log, riderless.

Close by was the "Queen of the Forest," very tall, very stately, and beautiful, but I fancied that, like Elizabeth in her old age, she was becoming wry and gnarly from rejecting so many proposals of the surrounding monarchs.

The Ancient Couple stood so closely together as to fulfill the strictest law of union—especially in these days. They had weathered the storms of many a century, and now their garlands, though of evergreen, were faded; together they were tottering into their grave. My lass remarked,

"Surely they know by this time whether they are suited."

Longfellow and Whittier stood side by side,—both high and stately; but the former reached above his companion. These two gentlemen may trace their relationship back to Nero or Cæsar—yet even then these trees had peeped their heads above the sod.

In the cool of the evening, winding our way leisurely among the mountain scenery, we returned to Clarke's. It would be folly to say that I enjoyed myself during this ride, and that the attractions of my darling were more irresistibly impressed upon me than ever before. I thought her sweet, flowing words, her sparkling laugh, her attractions were perfectly angelic, and that it would be a Paradise to spend one's life wandering with such a lovely creature through the wilds of the Sierras.

When Caleb and I at our leisure, stepped to the counter to register our names, I glanced to where our companions' had just been written down by the son and brother, fondly hoping that the sister's name had been written last, so that I might put my own beneath it. I thought the two would look so well together. It *was* written last but judge of my consternation at finding that it was prefixed by a Mrs.! There was no mistake about it. One *Miss* and two *Mrs.*

comprised the ladies of our party. I crawled off to bed crestfallen; to sleep, perchance to dream.

Next day as we wended our way along the trail over the sides of the mountains, and occasionally through snow-drifts, it was much more awkward and tedious to be at the service of the young madam than it had previously been. After dinner at the Half-Way House our friends concluded to linger among the mountains. It was with a good will that I with Caleb passed onward into the valley.

CHAPTER VII.

SIGHT-SEEING IN YO SEMITE.

WE were approaching the Yo Semite Valley, and began to breathe the air from its mighty chasm. Skirting along its side we heard the waterfalls, and now and then caught glimpses of the opposite wall. Walking and creeping on an overhanging rock we reached Inspiration Point. Here a chasm seven or eight miles long, from half a mile to a mile in breadth, and from 3,000 to 4,000 feet in depth, opened before us in a mountain bed of granite. Hanging over the edge of the rock upon which we stood, and casting the eye perpendicularly down until the power of vision was lost in the depth below, the soul shuddered and shrank back.

In that lower earth we saw a valley, green, smooth and beautiful, through which flowed a silvery stream, skirted with trees, while Bridal Veil, on this side a short distance above, and Yo Semite Falls, on the opposite side still further up, poured over the walls their falling streams. Beauty, grandeur, sublimity, mountain, waterfall, cascade and precipice mingled their attractions. Art was surpassed a thousand fold.

Leaving Inspiration Point, we began to descend. Here, at the lower or western end, was the most favorable place for doing so; and even at this point we wondered how it was possible for a pony to make his way. But down we went along a winding trail, at times ready to shoot headforemost overboard, plunging under hanging rocks, around sharp points, and along the edge of precipices—till, thrown upon our ponies' necks, we were constrained to cry out, "Whoa! whoa!" Sometimes they did whoa, but more frequently brought up against a tree, or the side of a rock.

When we reached the level valley below it was coming on dusk, but the evening was clear. It was three miles or

BOUND FOR THE VALLEY.

more to the hotels, yet Caleb wanted to ride way out to Bridal Veil, and more, he was determined to do it—so the guide and I rode on, alternately receding from and approaching the foot of those towering walls; now in a grassy lawn, now in a forest, and again winding around gigantic rocks, fallen from that upper world just beneath the blue sky, through whose curtains the evening stars, like the eyes of angels, were beginning to peep.

At Ladick's Hotel I awaited for two hours the arrival of Caleb, but no Caleb came. I began to wonder what could detain him, and spoke to the landlord. He told me that there were some rough rocks about the foot of Bridal Veil, and that one might possibly meet with an accident. After waiting a while longer, I wandered far back on the trail, but heard nothing save the echo of my loud halloa, deadened by the thunder of distant waterfalls.

All at once a light gleamed along the summit of the northern wall. It was the rising moon. Sitting down, as in an enchanted world, I saw, as the moon rose higher and higher, the grotesque features and irregularities of the southern wall pictured on the naturally fantastic canvas of the northern one. Sometimes a black form, which I took for a cloud, floated along the bright upper part of the wall, while darkness and terror hovered, and curled, and yawned below. Finally the orb of night looked over into the valley, and upon the level green turf from which arose El Capitan to the startling height of four thousand feet, like a polished column, formed by a bold curve of the wall.

CALEB TAKING THE VEIL.

Startled by a loud boom of some waterfall, I thought of Caleb, and ran forward with affright. The further I went the more frightened I grew, until I espied something approaching, which proved to be Caleb. He had evidently found the falls, for he was some excited and considerably wet; and he related his adventures while we were going to the hotel, as follows:—

"From Inspiration Point the waters hung like a veil down the side of the wall, then rolled away in graceful vapors which lost themselves in gaudy mists far down the valley; but what lay beneath that trailing veil no mortal could ever have fancied. As I scrambled around their slippery forms, how the wind blew the water and mist into my face! while thundering tones, such as I had never heard, sounded in my ears. I did not feel like going up there all at once, so I stopped behind a large rock that broke off the driving mist. At last I cautiously ventured beneath the falls and beside that mighty jarring wall. I did not have the rainbow around me, for the sun had disappeared. Neither could I see distinctly the magic beauty of the veil woven by the lightning speed of sparkling drops, and crossed by threads of finest mist—yet I did not want to see. My soul was too full to see through mortal eyes; the thunders of the Eternal God filled my soul. How I got down from there I hardly know. I found my pony, and here I am. I have been in a dream ever since; but it is not a dream—this valley is a reality."

Next morning, as we were wandering up the valley, we saw a cavalry party approaching with their guide, who was showing them what they ought to look at, what they ought to admire, and when they ought to quit. But we were not taking lessons under him, and sat down on a stone to let this school teacher in nature and his pupils pass along. We noticed that some of the ladies had missed the mark in mounting, and were riding with a foot on either side of their steeds. But what of that—it was only woman's rights advancing; and the fashion made good progress, for before night all had adopted this style, and two lassies whom we had seen in the morning lingering behind through modesty, were now racing with their gallant lovers.

WOMAN'S RIGHTS ADVANCING.

Yo Semite Falls, in plain view on the opposite side of the

valley, pouring its immense body of water over a low place in the wall—only twenty-six hundred feet high—naturally attracted our attention; and as they proved to be rather above our vision, we hazardously climbed upward about a thousand feet to the point where the water strikes the wall. Here the scene was almost too terrific for mortals to behold. We looked above us sixteen hundred feet, to where a large stream of water leaped from the rock, dividing into huge bodies, which kept their distinctive shapes a hundred feet or more, their edges spreading into vapors, while the center of

ABOVE THE FALLS.

each shot down like a comet; still further down they expanded into a vast sea of vapor and spray, shifting, as the wind blew it, three or four hundred yards from side to side, beating into our faces and through our clothes like driven rain. The cascade was just at our side, and below us; at times its waters were almost hidden from sight by the spray, but we caught a glimpse of them as it angrily rushed and plunged onward to take the final leap over the lower precipice.

We beat a retreat out of the spray and into the sun, where we stood dripping and drying, and occasionally glancing at the falls; and happening to see a crooked tree which shot its roots into the crevices of the rock just beneath the summit, we agreed, and shook our wet hats in testimony, that if we ever visited the Yo Semite again we would sit on that zigzag tree over the brink of the falls, and gaze down and down into that awful chasm beneath. But we didn't expect to come again—at least for a thousand years.

We descended by a circuitous route, occasionally following a narrow path over precipices where it seemed one might commit suicide so accidentally as hardly to trouble his conscience, and at last came to a place which defied all our attempts to pass. Here we became separated, and I struck a narrow ravine in the wall, and on following it, soon reached the valley. After calling several times to Caleb, he replied from far up the side of the dark wall:—

"Go home, go home— I'll camp." I concluded to take his advice, and proceeded to our hotel.

From the window of my room I gazed out in the direction where I had parted from Caleb, and I

WATCHING CALEB'S CAMP-FIRE.

knew that the little fire which burned brightly at some distance above the level of the valley marked his camping place.

CALEB'S NIGHT ADVENTURES. 89

At early dawn I was out looking for the straggler, and soon, to my astonishment, I descried him squirming down a long pole which he had set against the face of the rock. I stood in silent dread as he removed the pole and placed it carefully in a lower niche. Again he descended; and by repeating the operation several times he at length stood beside me. As we walked to the hotel he related to me the adventures of the night. He had rested on a ledge not more than three feet wide, so situated that it would have been dangerous to roll out of bed; and he had managed to keep up a fire by breaking dry branches from a tree near by. He had not been the least afraid of bears, for he did not believe they could climb where he was, even if so disposed.

CALEB'S PERILOUS DESCENT.

CHAPTER VIII.

A CLIMB OUT OF THE VALLEY.

AFTER breakfast we passed far up into the valley, to where it branches into three deep, narrow cañons, and stood at the entrance to one of them between North and South Domes. Not a ripple had yet stirred the surface of Mirror Lake, which lay at our feet, picturing every color, streak and form of the mighty walls. North Dome hung beneath the left-hand inverted wall, a thousand times larger and more grand than the dome of our National Capitol, while, on the opposite side was South Dome, as perfect as art, but cut in twain from top to bottom, as by the sword of a mighty angel; and one-half of it had fallen into the lake. Either summit pierced a sky of richest blue, at a height thirty times that of the Falls of Niagara.

After floating out upon the lake and giving the trout a chance to bite,—of which they did not avail themselves,—we ascended the middle cañon through a dense forest of evergreen, winding around gigantic mossy stones which had fallen from the heights above; while on our left, a dashing rivulet, white with foam, splashed wildly into the air; and occasionally we passed under the spray that came floating far down that narrow cañon, as if fleeing the thunder of the distant falls. We met a party of ladies and gentlemen with umbrellas, who smilingly remarked:—

"Quite showery, to-day."

Quite slippery, thought I, as a couple of the party sat down rather suddenly on the drenched grass.

In their company, under the mighty arch in the right wall beside Vernal Falls, we stood and gazed upon a broad and beautiful sheet of water, falling more than three hundred feet without a ripple. Around us the chasing rainbows played; the grassy blades and hanging mosses decked themselves with diamonds; laughing faces, brighter than anything else, admired them; and the happy birds flapped their wings above the circling spray.

"QUITE SHOWERY."

The Cap of Liberty, a towering majestic column, four thousand feet in height, next engrossed our attention as we passed up the gliding stream, until we were aroused by the awful thunders of Nevada Falls, whose waters shot over a precipice more than twice the height of Vernal Falls. After approaching them as near as we could, we returned to the valley.

Many days we lingered in this beautiful vale, wandering through its sylvan retreats, picking strawberries and lying upon the grass in the shade of the trees. On one of these last-named occasions, our attention was called to Glacier Rock.

"Wouldn't it be grand, Caleb, to perch on that dizzy point, and at a single view take in all these scenes that have separately entranced us?"

"That's the height of my ambition."

"Look, there comes a guide—I know him by his broad-brimmed hat. Halloo! will you please tell me whether the point of that rock can be reached?"

"Yes, sir; by a twenty miles' ride on ponies."

"But is there no shorter way?"

"A few persons with Indian guides have hazardously scaled those rocks, but if *you* attempt it there will not be left pieces of you large enough for the buzzards to pick."

He rode out of sight, and we started for Glacier Rock. We were, of course, fools to do so, but one learns something by being foolish, if he survives the experience.

Over rocks that have fallen from the wall we scrambled, occasionally tumbling between them, causing us to feel a little fearful that the buzzards would have a chance to try us, after all. We made for a cañon,—or rather a fissure in the wall—where dreary darkness soon overtook us, and there we passed a gloomy, uncomfortable night.

At moonrise, about 2 A. M., we resumed our task, little dreaming of the difficulties which we were to encounter. Places that did not look very steep or high from below, rose up like mountains as we approached them; the rocks were crumbly, and the slip of a foot might have dashed us to pieces on the rocks below. But we pressed bravely on to where the gorge divided; and after vainly attempting to follow up the left-hand branch, we tried the right-hand one with better success. At this point the sun arose in all his beauty, and although surrounded by difficulties, our hearts drank in the joy and light that filled the valley.

At length we came to where the gorge was again subdivided into many branches, and here we were separated. I climbed up some very threatening rocks and reached a place which I named "Starvation," where I was captive a weary hour before I could escape. It was hazardous to proceed, but more so to return; so from niche to niche my feet followed my hands, until it seemed impossible to ascend further. The wall proved to be overhanging at the top, while it was nothing less than destruction to look down or attempt to retrace my footsteps.

Hark! what is that startling crash? I listen in awful suspense until the sound and echoes die away in the depths beneath, and then fear to call, lest no voice answers me.

A few minutes later and I hear another crash. Then I halloo, but almost fear to do so, lest the sound will loosen my frail clasp. I call and listen, but no answer. I call again, but only hear the echo reply. Fearful moments! had they not soon passed I should have been dashed to the bottom! But I heard a voice that seemed above me, and at once knew that Caleb had been in too precarious a position to answer. Presently he hallooed again, and I told him, as best I could in a word or two, my position, and that in a few moments more it would be either life or death, as I could not long cling to the wall! A brief pause and I heard his voice:

"Hold on, Wildair; I'll make a rope!"

Aroused by renewed hope, I sustain myself with more ease, wondering, however, where he can obtain material for

THE RESCUE.

the rope. Crash come the stones, dancing and bouncing above my head. I look up and see nearing me the end of a brush rope tied together with bark. Happy moment! it just reaches me. The thought of life, of a speedy rescue, imparts strength sufficient for the emergency, and I climb, while Caleb draws on the rope. A decaying tree against which he sets his foot, comes near brushing me off, but with increased effort the point is at length gained in safety. Long I lie upon the precipice and almost worship that rope as the means of my deliverance. Then wearily we resume the ascent, climbing on until past noon, when again we separate.

Our courses diverge more than we anticipated. I come to a place that seems to defy my power to ascend. I pause and soliloquize: If I get above this overhanging rock I must climb around to one side, along a ledge over a precipice, where, if a hand slips I shall be precipitated into a chasm hundreds of feet below me. I call to Caleb two or three times, but hear no answer. What shall I do? I have tasted no food since 4 o'clock last evening, and then but a small and insufficient quantity. My tongue is parched from thirst and I am exhausted from fatigue. I look above and see that I have nearly reached the top; if only I were above this I am sure I should have but little difficulty beyond. I cannot retreat; I must go forward, if but to my death. Reaching to the side, I pull myself around and hang dangling over the edge of the ravine. Have I, (with the slight holds for my hand,) strength to pull myself above? I make one mighty effort, feel my arms tremble, and my muscles begin to weaken; but I gain a better foothold now, and push myself up. At last I reach the rock and fall exhausted upon its ragged surface. Soon recovering myself, I begin to look about me.

But where is Caleb? Calling several times but receiving no reply, I presume that he has made his way up the rising ground through the brush to the trail, so I push on in that direction. My foot is caught between the limbs of a fallen tree and held fast; the branches tear my clothes; the dust rises from the dry limbs, and I almost choke with thirst. But I continue on, still calling to Caleb, yet receiving no response. Finally I strike the trail, down which I follow the Glacier Rock; but Caleb is not here as I expected. I sit down to wait.

After looking at the valley a few moments I creep out upon the overhanging rocks, only three or four feet wide at the point which projects over the precipice, here to look down the perpendicular wall to the valley below. My energies seem to have left me, and soon I fall asleep. After a while I awake startled. My brain reels! I shrink back! Almost before terror is banished from my mind, comes the anxiety for Caleb. I look up the trail. Joy! yonder he comes. We meet! Each is anxious to hear from the other. We waste no time in looking at the valley, but make straight for some snow banks we discern not far away, upon which we sit, talking, and eating snow until our lips are swollen almost as thick as our hands.

We now look down into the valley. We see the walls, domes and waterfalls, but catch no inspiration from them; their beauty fails to awaken any enthusiasm on our part.

We discern the grove and the grassy lawn, at the edge of which we had stopped to rest. We look at the guides and visitors riding past like specks, nearly a mile below us; then turn our weary steps along the winding trail of five miles to the Half-Way House, wondering that we are yet in the land of the living, and resolving in our hearts never to be so foolish again. The distance seems long and tedious. We pass near Sentinel Dome, but have no desire to ascend. We tarry for a few moments and gaze at the Sierra Nevadas, rearing their cone-shaped peaks as far as the eye can reach; some so sharp and jagged as to pierce through their snowy coverings, leaving their uncapped heads to battle with the fiercest storms; while to the east a few miles, the peak called "Cloud's Rest" climbs upward and upward, till its summit is lost among the clouds.

Again taking up our march; at length we reach our destination, and with our rude canes walk up to the log fire in front of the hotel, around which the guests are assembled to beguile the pleasant evening hours. All are amazed and look upon us with astonishment. We cannot answer their questions fast enough. Some have finished their supper,

AROUND THE LOG-FIRE.

and now it is prepared for us. For once during the evening we are natural and do justice to the meal. The landlord surely wonders if we have not camped out for a week.

After supper, we linger a few moments and review the various events of the day. Outside, the guests are laughing and talking. They are from San Francisco, New York and many other large cities of the East. Some have been to the valley, others are on their way. What a diversity of themes they have for conversation, and what a new phase of life for New York fashionables, to sit around a log-fire beside a hotel of log-cabins, beneath the wild deep forests of the Sierras. But we are exhausted, and punching a log-fire has no charms for us just now; so, weary and worn with our journey, we retire.

The next day we bade farewell to the matchless Yosemite, and resumed our travels westward.

YOSEMITE VALLEY, CALIFORNIA.

CHAPTER IX.

EXPERIENCES IN SAN FRANCISCO.

WHEN we arrived at San Francisco, Caleb was very anxious to see a certain young gentleman whom we had met in Denver. His personal appearance was very imposing, but when we made his acquaintance he was out of money. He thought he could do much better were he in San Francisco, but was out of means and desired us to assist him in getting there. However, he did not trouble me much. I could not imagine why, for I was quite willing to lend him aid in the matter, but notwithstanding this, he pressed the affair upon Caleb rather than myself, till I became somewhat jealous. He told Caleb that he had a brother in business at San Francisco, but he did not like to wait till this brother could send him the money, and therefore proposed accompanying us thither, if Caleb would secure his passage. As Caleb seemed inclined to be accommodating, I told him that the fact that the young man and his brother were strangers to us should not be considered; that all men were honest beyond doubt; that I was anxious to see the young man prosperous, and that, since he would not take the money from me, he (Caleb) ought to let him have it. Accordingly the fellow was provided for. We could not have him as a traveling companion all the way, however, as we stopped at different places along our route.

Being anxious to see our friend in his new position, we started forth with card in hand, bearing the address of his brother. Presently we came to the street, and soon found the number designated upon the card, looked anxiously at the sign, and inquired within; but, confound the gay deceiver, the result was not satisfactory to us or according to representations; no such person occupied the premises or had ever done so. We examined the city directory, but could find no one of that name in San Francisco.

Perhaps I ought not to have any unkind feelings toward the young man for not accepting my offer; neither should Caleb feel discouraged, but rather magnanimous, for the privilege of lending, without expecting to receive either interest or principal. From the way Caleb bore it I imagine he was trying to make the best of the circumstance, and practice the Golden Rule. But we were a little surprised that people to whom we told the story, did not seem to blame the fellow, but simply termed him "rather old-fashioned." When asked to explain that term, they told us that a few years ago it was the custom for a man, when "broke," to inform the first person he met, that the gold for which he had been digging was still safe in the mines, but that he preferred to have fifty or a hundred in hand for the present emergency. The generosity of these hardy frontiersmen, however, seemed likely to be developed to an undue extent, before it was discovered that some roughs had taken the "emergency" complaint in its severest form, requiring continued treatment and large doses.

The common hardships encountered on the frontier, and the hopes and uncertainties of gold-mining, tended to develop in the people of the West a combination of unbounded generosity and recklessness. The following incident connected with the early days of San Francisco, which I have read somewhere, illustrates these traits of their character.

The "*Nim de Oro*," a gambling saloon in that city, was, in 1849, the principal resort of the disbanded soldiers of the California regiments, and also those who had been engaged in the war with Mexico.

Behind one of the largest monte banks in the room, sat a

man who had won for himself honorable mention, and an officer's commission was given him for his bravery at the storming of Monterey; but, preferring the climate of California and its golden prospects to a northern home, he embarked for that country at the close of the war with Mexico, and upon arriving in San Francisco, opened a gambling saloon. The emigrants came in by the thousands, and two or three nights after his arrival, a young man entered the saloon and seated himself at the bank and staked various sums on the cards, until he lost nearly all the money he had possessed.

Excited by the game, and maddened with his losses, he accused the dealer of cheating; the latter replied sharply; harsh words were exchanged, and then the young man struck the dealer a severe blow upon the face. Quick as thought, the sharp report of a pistol followed; the gambler had shot his customer. The room was soon cleared of the spectators present, the door closed, and medical attendance summoned to aid the wounded man.

The gambler sat moodily over his bank, running the small monte cards through his fingers, and perhaps meditating of the deed just perpetrated, when the wounded man gave a moan of agony as the doctor's probe reached the extremity of the wound.

The doctor inquired what state he was from, and the wounded man replied:

"From Vermont."

The gambler raised his head. It had been a long time since he had seen a person from the home of his childhood, and Vermont being his native state, the mere mention of the name interested him.

The doctor next inquired the name of the place where his parents resided, if he had any.

"Montpelier."

The gambler sprang to his feet, his limbs trembled, and his face became pale as death, for Montpelier was the home of his youth, and perhaps the wounded man might have been his playmate in childhood; perhaps a schoolmate who knew his parents, his brothers and sisters.

A stimulant was given to the wounded man, and the doctor inquired if there was any friend in the city he wished to send for.

"Yes," he replied, "my wife. She is at the City Hotel. Tell her to hasten, for I am badly hurt."

A man was sent to inform his wife.

"Doctor," said the gambler, "save that man's life, and there is my bank and $10,000 in Burgoyne, and you shall have it all?"

The doctor shook his head in token of the impossibility of recovery.

The gambler sat by the side of the wounded man until the arrival of his wife. She came, accompanied by a few friends, and as heroic women bear their misfortunes, she bore hers. Not a word of reproach was uttered by her. Words of cheerfulness only, passed her lips, as tears coursed rapidly down her cheeks. To her inquiry as to the chances of her husband's recovery, the doctor assured her that there was no hope whatever. She sank down on her knees and invoked the mercy of a forgiving God upon her dying husband and his murderer.

The gambler knelt at the side of the wounded man, and asked his forgiveness, and also that of his afflicted wife, for the great wrong he had committed, which was readily granted.

"This," said he, "is the result of disobedience to the sacred injunctions of my aged father and mother. I have faced death a thousand times, and still I have escaped; the balls of the enemy have whistled past my ears as thick as hailstones, and the bomb has exploded at my feet. Still I have lived, oh God, and for this! High above the red tide of battle I have carried my country's ensign, and have won for myself upon the field, a name among men. When not one comrade was left to tell of the battle, I escaped unhurt. Why was I not killed with the rest? All that was pleasing to man I have had, and if I could recall this last act by living on husks, sleeping in a pauper's grave, and renouncing every glorious act of my life, gladly I would do it. I was born in the same village with that man; we were nurtured beneath the same roof, and—O God!—the same mother gave us birth! He must not die—he is my brother!" And the gambler sunk down in a swoon upon the floor.

The wounded man raised himself upon his elbows; his eyes wandered about the room, as if searching for some particular one.

"Mary," said he, "is my brother William here—"

THE BROTHERS.

The words choked in his throat, and he sank down upon his pillow.

The wife knelt again, but it was beside the dead, and invoked the blessing of God on his soul, and forgiveness for the murderer.

The gambler awoke from his swoon, staggered up to the wife, and said:

"Mary, would it were otherwise, for I have nothing to live for now; the dead and dying do not want anything in this world; take this certificate of deposit to our aged father, and tell our parents we are both dead; but oh, do not tell them how we died!"

But before the woman could reply, or any one interfere, the report of a pistol sounded again, and the fratricide had ceased to live!

On the hill near Rincon Point, were two graves, a few years ago, inclosed with a picket fence, and one tombstone at their head, with this simple inscription: "Brothers!"

But these early drinking saloons and gambling holes have in twenty-five short years, given place to the great city of San Francisco, with its vast machine shops, manufactories, wealth, commerce, and a population of 150,000 enterprising people.

The business streets of San Francisco and the buildings fronting upon them, compare favorably with those of any of the eastern cities; stylish ladies, gentlemen and carriages throng the thoroughfares, and evidences of wealth are on every hand. And such quantities of gold! In this land of gold-mining, where the circulating medium was the yellow coin, we saw men crouching like beasts of burden beneath their precious loads. We never before felt so inclined to bear another's burdens.

COUNTING IN THE GOLD.

Arrived at the bank, these men throw their bags upon the counter, and await their turn—then tumble out their gold to be counted. The cashier picks up a handful of twenty-dollar pieces, slides three and four at a time from hand to hand, with a rapidity that makes the head swim, until he has counted twenty pieces. Quicker than thought he slaps them down in a stack, and in a moment more another one is beside it. These rapidly grow into one, two, or three rows. He glances over the number of stacks, and at once arrives at the value of the whole lot.

Some of this money was tumbled out to us as carelessly as if it had cost nothing to mine it; but lo, when we arrived in China, they weighed every coin. Whether any piece was found too heavy, I cannot say; they were not particular about informing us, if it was. They also weighed our Mexican silver dollars, and banged them all over the floor and counter, to ascertain whether each had the proper ring. The result was, that on about one-third of them they charged a discount of from ten to fifty cents each.

Upon our first initiation into the State of California, the boys flocked around the train with boxes of strawberries, shouting:

"One for a bit; two for a quarter."

Thinking that we wanted two boxes—our eyes being very large—we immediately told one of the boys that we would take a couple of boxes, and paid him the quarter. Then I said to Caleb:

"What fools we are! why didn't I buy one box and you another? Listen; those boys are crying them off at one for a bit—two for a quarter. Watch; yonder man only gives a dime for one."

"The boys in this country are the biggest fools yet," replied Caleb, slightly enraged.

Although the Californians disregard the cents, some are none too conscientious about the dollars. While in San Francisco, I was one evening standing by the window of a jewelry shop, admiring the display, when a fine-looking young gentleman stopped beside me, apparently to do the same. Soon he pointed out to me a gold watch-chain, in the links of which were some slugs of quartz rock, containing particles of gold in its original state. Then he said:

"Up the street a block or so is a very elegant jewelry store; I suppose you, like myself, are out enjoying the evening, and if you say so, we will walk along to where it is?"

I began to have an idea regarding this young man, yet as I liked to see handsome jewelry, I accepted his suggestion and we walked along together. We arrived at the place and found it as represented. My companion then proposed that we should take a little walk through other portions of the city. I had an opinion of this young man, a decided opinion, and desiring to see if it proved correct I accompanied him. He told me that he was going East shortly, but that he had been out in the mountains, mining. I thought so, and returned the compliment by conveying the impression that I was traveling for pleasure and had plenty of money. He then became quite confidential, said that he sometimes took a fancy to a young man, and implied that in this case he had done so. I replied that I was very glad to know that I was held in such esteem, and was sure that it was reciprocated. Presently he spoke about taking a glass of wine occasionally, —anything stronger he did not approve of. To this I made no reply, and he was led to suppose that I would not object to indulge in something of a more fiery nature.

"Well," said he, "once in a while I don't mind taking something stronger myself; and as I am with a friend, tonight, let us have a drink? Up the street a short distance is a club-room where some of my cronies meet occasionally to have a friendly chat, and there we can find drinks suited to our tastes."

I thought probably I had carried the thing far enough, and hesitated as to going further.

"Oh," said he, "it's only a short distance; it won't take much time; come on."

I walked along with him as though it were all right, yet looking well to my steps. When, however, he turned up a side street, I pulled out my watch and suddenly halted.

"I have an engagement with an old chum," said I, "it is now past the hour, and I must be off."

"Don't go yet, it will only take a moment."

"No, he will wonder where I am; I must be going," and I started off.

But my acquaintance was not to be shaken off so easily, and before we parted he made me promise to meet him the next evening on the corner of two designated streets.

Then he bade me good evening, pressed my hand warmly, and again assured me that he had enjoyed my society very much.

At the appointed hour, next evening, as I approached the rendezvous, I saw him there anxiously awaiting my coming. He was very glad to see me again, and we soon reached the side street previously named. After passing down it some distance he stopped, and with a key unlocked a door which opened at the foot of a dark stairway leading—I don't know where. Here I came to a sudden halt, and said:

"Doubtless you think I am a fool, but I know that you are a rascal—too low to crawl with the worms of the earth — too mean to creep into the slimy hole of the serpent. It is well for you that I refuse to accompany you to your den. I have my hand upon my revolver, and would not hesitate to shoot you or your villainous accomplices at the first demonstration." He went sneaking up the stairs, and I started for a more congenial locality.

THE STOOL PIGEON.

I scarcely ever listen to yarns, but in camp or at hotels it sometimes becomes a moral necessity to do so. The following is a specimen of some of the many stories we heard related.

In one of the old and almost deserted camps near Virginia City, an unwearied miner, who went by the name of Plodding Joe, still lingered, carelessly blasting away among the stones in search of some undiscovered streak of luck. One day he had nearly finished drilling a hole when he heard a groan. He listened a moment, then resumed work again, and soon heard a shriek. Taking this for a good omen, he patriotically began to pour powder into the hole, but it came out again like the crack of a volcano, carrying Joe high in air.

"HERE I AM AGAIN!"

Well, Joe naturally came down after the space of about a quarter of an hour, with the crowbar still in his hands. With new zeal he resumed the drilling, but what was his astonishment when he heard tones more human than before his departure, and what was still more strange, upon hoisting his crowbar he found that the point thereof was of a sanguinary hue.

Plodding Joe wasn't sharper than common fellows, yet he formed an opinion that made him leave his drill suddenly behind him at the rate of two bumble-bees and a hornet on the course.

Running across some straggling miners, he and they evinced enough curiosity to return and hold a deliberation over the bloody crowbar. One thought Joe had speared the Old Fellow of the lower regions, which theory seemed to explain the blowing-up arrangement; another suggested that a rich miser might be caged up here as a punishment for extracting the gold from the rock. This was a happy thought — "Perhaps he has his gold with him;" so down went the crowbar into the hole again. But no human tone was heard. Yet upon lifting the instrument, fresh blood appeared upon the iron. Harder than ever they worked; but all was silence, save a jarring, grating sound produced by the fall. Now they reasoned among themselves and drilled other holes. Having completed six drills in the form of a parallelogram, they prepared for blasting, lighted the fuse and then ran away.

A tremendous explosion ensued, but as there were no supernatural results, they concluded that if it was the devil, they had surely killed him. So cautiously approaching, they peeped down into the excavation, and there discovered the body of an old miner noted for his untidiness of person, who had mysteriously disappeared some time previous. An inquest was at once held, and the written verdict was drawn up as follows:

"Whereas, our comrade laid down here exhausted with the burden of earth and stone dust which had accumulated over him to a frightful extent, be it known that it was found necessary to blast him out, though we sincerely regretted the loss of a brother.

Whereas, by his side lay a great bag of tobacco, nearly emptied of its contents, and in his mouth remained the stem of a pipe yet smoking, be it known that it was this pipe which discharged the first blast of powder, and might as well have killed Plodding Joe.

And as a memorial, we regret that he left nothing to his memory, and that we did not leave him to his own natural burying."

Of course we visited the Seal Rocks. Fast horses, stylish gentlemen and fair ladies, were continually sweeping along that drive of six miles leading thither from San Francisco. A cold, penetrating sea breeze blew sharply when we went, ending the pleasure of some, and rousing up the latent vigor of others.

Arrived at the Seal Rock House, we took our seats on the portico, high above the wild Pacific waves that ever dashed upon the worn rocks beneath us. Within gunshot were a score of seals, as safely protected from harm through the veneration of mankind, as are the pigeons of Venice. Leaping head-foremost from the rocks, tusseling with one another at various depths in the water, scrambling up the sides of the rocks, washed back by the next wave, contending for position, but finally rolling in the embrace of one another into the splashing waters, all the while roaring and yawning, like lions in distress, they enact scenes upon which thousands look with interest.

But their sleepy moods attracted my most earnest attention. Here came "Old Ben. Butler," as they called him, from his cold bath to the warm sunny bed that he preëmpted many years ago, the right to which he still seemed inclined to maintain. Some of the seals, sleek as moles from their late baths, made way for him to pass; while many others, in profound sleep moved not till Ben. raked his finny paws across their noses, or gave them a shower bath from his dripping hide. But Ben. now runs across an old sleeper that claims the dignity of being respected, and growling gives him to understand that he must not waken him. Ben. however, persists in telling him to get out of the way or he will climb over him. But the sleeper only roars and snores; so Old Ben. gives him a smack on the jaw, at which the snorer throws up his long tusks, opens his red, terrific mouth, and invites him to walk in. As Ben. accepts the invitation, they rake each other down with their tusks, as if climbing icebergs. They tumble over others in profound sleep, who in turn awaken, until the disturbance becomes general, and each one growls, or roars, or yawns, and complains of the ways of Providence.

In the distance, a score of miles or more, the jagged Forlorn Rocks rise from the water like the adamantine remains of mountains stormed by the sea. Over their steep sides, like spots on a leopard's back, were the nests of the sea gulls, thousands in number, on which sat birds of various colors.

CHAPTER X.

FIRE AND BRIMSTONE.

SOME people do not profess to believe in "fire and brimstone;" such persons, evidently, never saw the Geysers of California. Let the boldest person stand by the Devil's Chaldron, as black as night, and feel the very ground burning his boots, and breathe the stifling sulphur, and behold the vapor from a hundred fissures steaming about him, and if he doesn't inwardly exclaim, "Beneath is the fiery abyss ready to burn up the world and the wicked," he surely possesses a conscience serenely tranquil.

As we approached this interesting locality we plunged down the winding mountain path, and quickly arriving at the bottom of a narrow valley, gazed upon a wonderful sight. Behold! all over the lower slope of one side of the mountains, and for a short distance up a steep ravine branching off from the principal stream, dense vapors are rising. Here it seems is the great laboratory of Nature, in which are not bottles of chemicals, but hills and mountains of unstable acids which are set into heaving commotion by some unseen agency.

With stick in hand to feel our way, we follow up the ravine leading into the mountains. All around us are a thousand holes and crevices, each having a peculiarity of its own, yet from each comes a hissing and steaming as if a hundred machine shops were at work, a hundred furnaces in full blast. The ground is hot—our feet are burning—and each step seems hotter than the last. The earth shakes beneath us; the hot vapor rises to our faces; we are almost suffocated, and hurry on as fast as possible. In some places the water is clear as crystal, in others as black and thick as tar, and varying from luke-warm to boiling heat.

We are now at the "Witches' Chaldron," an opening six or eight feet in diameter, whose black, thick waters boil, heave, and bubble. Should Caleb and I fall within we would become the witch's soap-grease on short notice, and all that would be left to tell of our former grandeur would be a few brass buttons.

Further on up this ravine, not more than fifty feet from its boiling waters, under its shady trees we take a drink at a refreshing spring, cool and clear. Other parts of the Geysers, other than up this ravine, are similar, but less striking. From the floating vapors is deposited everywhere a thick coating varying in color from white to yellow. In places it has an acid taste; in others it seems to be pure sulphur.

Wandering down from the Geyser House, we chanced to run upon a bachelor's hall, where anyone of this persuasion suffering from dyspepsia, rheumatism, or disappointed love,

BACHELOR'S HALL.

could board at seven dollars a week, eat hard bread baked in the ashes, sleep on the floor, and bathe in the mineral springs, providing he furnished his own towel or agreed to dry in the sun.

We returned from the Geysers by a route which led down the Sonoma and Santa Rosa Valleys. For a couple of miles from the Geysers, the road wound along the side of the mountains, up one of the steepest grades. We followed for several miles the summit of a range so narrow that in places there was barely room for the coach, and so steep on either side that it was frightful to look down, it being several thousand feet to the bottom. Casting the eye along this narrow ridge, the winding road seemed like a long wavy thread floating in the air; other ranges on either side, approached till the chasm between was almost bridged over.

At Petaluma we took a steamer and sailed down the Russian River, and across the bay to San Francisco, having spent three or four days very pleasantly and profitably. On this trip to the Geysers we saw some of the finest portions of California.

The dry mountain air and the moist ocean breezes play hide and seek through San Francisco Bay, while sunshine and fog clap their hands over the great city. But in the long narrow valleys, between the Coast Ranges, bright spring prevails, though occasionally fog from the bay is driven far up their endless windings. These valleys repose between steep green mountains, over which vineyards are beginning to spread, like the picturesque hills of Italy and Switzerland where the mountain sides teem with villages, and prophesy the future of our own illimitable West, when upon her numberless mountain-sides shall be found the happy homes of peace and prosperity.

CHAPTER XI.

POETRY OF THE OCEAN.

WE became acquainted with the oldest inhabitant of San Francisco, at least he claimed that honor, and he looked as though his claim was as good as any other person to that distinction; said he, "I believe there are now but seven hundred who profess to have been the first settler; and as their powers of absorption must increase as their numbers diminish, why, it won't be long before this oldest inhabitant business will be done away with. Why, gentlemen, I have had nigh a hundred men try to make me believe they were here before I thought of coming; yes sir, and there were persons who believed them."

He lived near an over-hanging rock from which a view of the great bay could be obtained when it was not foggy. It was a beautiful outlook; and here we watched the ships enter and depart, longing for the arrival of the one on which we had engaged passage for Japan. The time would have passed tediously indeed but for our "first settler," who had a story connected with every point of interest about the bay. If a vessel carried the Spanish flag, it suggested to him some story of intrigue; if English, something commercial. But one day in the midst of a romantic story, he shaded his eyes with one hand and pointing towards a large steamer, informed us, that that was our vessel. We never heard the end of his story, but from that moment became absorbed in the preparations for departure.

To one who had never seen an ocean steamer this vessel

CALIFORNIA STEAMER BOUND FOR THE ORIENT.

was truly a wonder. We paced the deck and found it to be one hundred and twenty-five good steps in length, and twenty-five in breadth; looking down from its lofty side the people on the wharf seemed like Lilliputians moving like a colony of ants, amid heaps of barrels, boxes, and bales. On one side a huge chasm received twelve hundred tons of fuel for our outward voyage, and when the grimy men had completed their task of loading the coal, the keel of the steamer seemed only a foot or two deeper in the water. Day and night men and horses tugged at the freight, and yet there was room for more.

At length the time for sailing arrived. At the last hour two wagons laden with barrels came down to the wharf, while the crowds of Chinese reverently parted to allow the wagons to approach close to the side of the vessel. Then the barrels were hoisted on board, each one marked with curious Chinese characters announcing that *Sing Lung* or *Hum Po* might be found pickled within—at least so we were told by a very intelligent Chinese steward, who also informed us that every steamer carried back a number of these dead Celestials—the most darling desire of all of them being to be buried in their native land.

Finally the ropes which secured the ship to the wharf were cast off, the hugh paddle wheels revolved, and amid the shoutings and "God speed" of thousands, we passed down the bay and out the Golden Horn into the Pacific Ocean.

It was far from pleasant yet we charitably loaned ourselves to dissembling a little libel. "Isn't this delightful," said Caleb. I said "Yes; glorious." I referred to the fog, which was so thick we could not see twenty-five feet in any direction, which was a mercy perhaps, for had I been permitted to see the shore I might have attempted to try a long swim.

Some one suggested that it would be pleasant to sit near the warm smoke-stack; so we moved thither, and tried to enjoy the delightful views of the ocean. It was not our intention be it understood to try to drive away sea-sickness, though I am of the opinion that the breeze was capable of driving away anything else. Some of us liked our novel situation so much that we forgot to go down to tea. The deep bass of the sounding gong had no music for us while listening to the roar of the billows. Soon the darkness of the night closed around us, yet some two or three of us still lingered, talking of the grand old ocean, until the engineer on duty passed on his third or fourth round with his lantern, to oil and examine the machinery; soon after the bell tolled half past nine we retired to our state rooms.

The next morning when we came upon deck, the drunken vessel, the dizzy-headed spars before our eyes, reminded us of what we would fain forget.

Although the vessel was surging yet I managed to stagger toward the bow. Oh I was feeling delicious—just indeed like a sea-sick man, a condition which to be fully appreciated must be experienced. Meeting the first mate I said:

"Very rough!"

"Ah my friend we are having a smooth sea."

I staggered on, I didn't want to hear anything more from him; on reaching the pilot house, I looked in and innocently suggested:

"What an unsteady sea we are having."

"There's nothing rough about this," was the reply.

I turned my back upon the speaker at once, saying to myself: "He's a fraud and knows better."

Stepping forward I leaned against the compass stand. To and fro the third mate on watch was passing. He approached; I wondered if he was "another." I meant liar, but didn't say it. Catching his eye I remarked:

"Quite blustering this morning!"

"Ha! ha! things are rather on a calm."

I could scarcely refrain from telling him that he and all the rest of the crew were lunatics. I looked toward the Chinaman on watch at the extreme forward point of the vessel. I wanted to get his opinion, and if he didn't say it was rough, I felt I should throw him overboard. Just then the vessel gave a mighty lurch; I slipped, and tumbling upon the deck was splashed by a wave, all of which was a source of great merriment to the mate and Chinaman. As

"ONLY A RIPPLE, SIR."

I climbed up I cast an angry look towards the officer, whereupon he remarked:

"Ha! ha! these are only ripples."

I had felt indignant enough before, but to get ducked and be laughed at overcame my composure. So I said:

"Any fool knows this is rough;" and after saying that I quickly left the locality, and went staggering off towards Caleb. After relating to him what the wretches had said he thought their object had been to make it appear that they had been in some wonderful storm. This quite appeased my anger and we went down to dinner, but were only able to look upon the others enjoying the meal, ourselves not being just now in good appetite.

After dinner the conversation turned upon the voyage. I became quite animated, tried to look lively, and remarked:

"You don't generally experience such smooth seas?"
One of the officers unconsciously remarked:
"Oh, so far it has been rather rough."
"Rough! I call these only ripples."

Seeing their astonishment at my facetious replies I quietly walked away, the passengers evidently thinking meanwhile that the green seamen had run across an old sailor.

As day after day dragged slowly along we were unable to picture to ourselves such a thing as stability amid the endless world of water which tossed us to and fro on its capricious waves. "We're not sea-sic-hic;" oh no! but inwardly we had deep convictions that anything in the wide world would be a relief if we could but make any exchange of our feelings; so we drank slyly a quart or two of sea-water, which helped us to pour out our pent up griefs and woes upon the bosom of old Ocean. Each outburst of our sorrow gave a renewed hope of relief, and finally we were all right, a little weak in our nerves, but picking up in strength of appetite.

CASTING BREAD UPON THE WATERS.

To some extent the poetry and sublimity of the ocean at last was realized. To our surprise it soon became our delight to sit at the extreme end of the bow as it almost dipped the waters, then arose thirty or forty feet above the dancing waves. A shoal of whales which we passed the first morning from San Francisco had hardly attracted our attention although these cetaceous monarchs of the ocean were spouting water high into the air with every exhalation. Notwithstanding we then passed through hundreds of miles where the blue deep below was dotted thick as the stars above by blubber-fish, yet they hardly aroused our curiosity. But now we could sit for hours, watching the flying-fish as they shot out of one side of a billow, flitted across the chasm, then disappeared in the next wave; or tracing the course of some large fish by the silver wings that flew up along his track; or again watching with delight the foam-capped billows chase each other from where the deep blue waters seemed to mingle with the clouds above; thus days of rest faded unconsciously into nights of dreams.

Seen at a distance a shoal of porpoises leaping from the water reminded me of a drove of black hogs or buffalo ranting through the tall grass on our Western prairies. They were a common scene; but one morning as the sea was rolling high, we noticed from our window a very large scull of them near our vessel. We hurried upon deck to obtain a better view. Leaping from one wave and plunging into the next, playing all about the bow, they sported with the pursuing vessel. We looked far down into the water at their graceful motions, and as they swam they hardly seemed to wave; yet, when their fins, which were ranged like spears along their backs, came to the surface it was as though so many swords with the speed of shooting arrows cut the water. When our vessel touched some of their fins, they gave their tails a flap or two that sent them darting here and there with the speed of lightning. They were a species of the dolphin which chase the swift flying fish from the water, catching them as they light, whose brilliant colors in the sun-light, flash over varying tints of golden blue and green with every movement. But in death their rapidly changing colors render them still more beautiful.

> "Parting day
> Dies like the dolphin whom each pang imbues
> With a new color as it gasps away,
> The last still loveliest, till 'tis gone, and all is gray."

It was expected that we should meet one of the other steamers of the line and for twenty-four hours a watchman had been stationed on a spar of the main mast high above the light. Next morning as the sun mounted up the eastern sky, the expected steamer approached us from the west; it was the only vessel we saw during the whole voyage. A signal was given through our steamer, and every person sprang from his couch and hastened upon deck. Soon we could see the waving handkerchiefs, and read upon the steamer the name, "America." The captain of each vessel stepped upon the high stand over the side wheel and loudly saluted each other, "All's well;" the vessels halted side by side upon the broad ocean. Over the wave came half a dozen Chinese rowers, who, with even strokes, dipped their long oars in the sea that with every swell raised them aloft, then hid them from our view. Soon mails were exchanged; the little skiff rowed back; the pulley ropes hooked to its either end; and the steamers were again under way while the dangling oarsmen were assisting to hoist their boat up the side of the vessel.

Boom! boom! and either vessel trembled while the sound of the cannon's roar died away without an echo in that boundless space as imperceptibly vanished the forms on that departing vessel, strangers from far distant climes, with whom we had exchanged the welcome of friendship, meeting upon this wide breadth of water far from our homes. Soon the hull of their vessel dropped over the wave, the little sail glided down beyond the encircling rim of the ocean, and left us gazing vacantly in the distance, while our thoughts went out towards that bright land which contained home, friends, all the past, and like the "America" seemed to be passing away.

Only four trips more did this steamer, honored by the name of our country, make over the billows; for not long after we met her, the mountains and bay around Yeddo were lighted up by the vanishing glory of the largest of our Pacific Steamers, the ill-fated America.

CHAPTER XII.

A VOYAGE ON THE PACIFIC.

BY degrees we became accustomed to sea life, spending many an hour, that otherwise would have been monotonous, sitting on deck in the cool of the evening, listening to yarns of the deep. Nearly all of the score of European passengers except ourselves had been accustomed to sea voyages, and several had been officers on ship board; and as farmers love to talk about their pigs, corn, and horses, so these bold sailors never tired of relating incidents of wrecks, adventures, and narrow escapes. One evening, at our usual assembly, an old salt remarked:—

"I always noticed that when a missionary was on board our vessel we had a rough voyage."

"I see no reason for that," replied one of the passengers.

"It's even so," responded another seaman. "Once we had about a dozen on board, and I thought the vessel would go to pieces! 'Twas rough all the way. When our steamer was wrecked," continued he, "our cat was not on board. It was the first trip he ever missed, and he always seemed to know the hour when we were to sail. Even the rats scampered off; and seeing it, several of the sailors absolutely refused to go on board."

Then he went on with a long and tedious story, only the remnant of which we will relate. But we listened to it all patiently, because we had nothing else in the world to do.

"After the steamer struck the rock the crew and passengers escaped to the island near by As the fury of the waves increased, the thought occurred to me that if we obtained any provisions from the ship it would have to be done quickly. So I gathered half a dozen of the boys and started in one of the boats. The way we were tossed about was indeed frightful! But as one can not die until his time comes, we finally reached the vessel, and four of us climbed upon the deck. We chopped holes into the provision room, and took out just what we wanted, only the ducks and geese were all drowned. Then we went to the cattle stall, and lo! one steer had his head above water. After great efforts we chopped him out also, and then pushed him overboard. He went splashing

A STEER-AGE PASSENGER'S FIRST DIVE.

into the water with head and tail erect. It was his first dive, and a deep one too, but he rose and swam safely to the island. We followed, but I had ordered some of the boys, when we reached the shore with the provisions, to be ready with clubs, and to run in, knocking passengers and every one else out of the way. So as we came riding upon the sand on a tremendous wave I shouted, 'Now boys,' and on they rushed with their clubs. One gathered a sack, another a ham of bacon, and off we ran into a distant part of the island into the brush, and hid our provisions in the sand. I rather think we feasted then to our fill."

Then followed a long account of the killing of the steer,

and of various squabbles in all of which he was the hero; after which he concluded with the following:—

"Several days rolled by on the island, and the time came when another steamer should be along; finally we saw her in the distance and hoisted signals to attract attention, but on she went. When however all were just giving her up, we noticed she was turning, and knew we were observed. When she came up, the way I hurried the lean passengers aboard wasn't slow."

After he had finished his story, a gentleman who had some knowledge of him and knew he had never ranked higher than assistant engineer, wounded his vanity somewhat by remarking as if for information:—

"You were captain of the wrecked steamer?"

But he did not seem to know that an answer was in order, and said nothing.

Though living exposed to influences that are very demoralizing, sailors of all nations have an instinctive trust in the God of the waves and the storm. We were told by the engineer that once during a fearful Typhoon, the Chinese firemen deserted the furnaces to implore their god Josh, and that officers with drawn clubs were necessary to keep them at their posts of duty. Some of the Chinese passengers on our steamer would approach the side of the vessel during a storm, and scatter to the wind and the waves showers of paper—bank-notes of the priests to buy the favor of the gods of these elements.

As soon as the storm abated these same passengers would fall upon their knees, in groups, and commence gambling; while the Europeans, passengers and officers, staked money, as to the distance passed, more eagerly than on former days as the storm had rendered the speed more uncertain. A machine oiler told me how shrewdly he had pulled the strings by betting ten dollars with a waiter that they would not make under two hundred miles, and with a steward that they would not make over two hundred and fifty. "Now," says he, "if it falls on either side I lose nothing; if between, I gain both—do you see?"

One afternoon a strange incident transpired. In the twinkling of an eye we crossed the 180° meridian from Greenwich, and jumped from Saturday the 15th, directly into Sunday the 16th. In crossing this meridian in the opposite direction, they told us they were sometimes thrown from Sunday into Saturday, having then to pass through another Sunday. Dear knows they need to pass through half-a-dozen to learn how to keep them properly.

Next morning after this occurrence a Chinaman came wandering vacantly into the cabin. We supposed this confusion of the calendar had deranged his brain. The guard

A TRYING TIME.

soon ushered him out, and on following soon after we found him handcuffed to a post in a distant part of the ship. A crowd was collected around, laughing at his futile attempts to release his wrists. Soon along came the "tater-peeler" on his way to the cellar; to be very smart he went through the motion of unlocking the handcuffs. Seeing the absent looks of the crazy man showed nothing of suspicion, but rather of expectation, he tried his tricks still further, making signs that he was going to unlock his mouth; upon which the fellow opened his lips, to the great merriment of the bystanders.

But the farce was soon changed to what threatened to be a tragedy. There was a great commotion in the crowd, caused by a couple of Chinamen who were assaulting each other with knives in a most reckless manner. Luckily the

A QUEUE-RIOUS SEPARATION.

guards were on the spot in time to help them out of the difficulty, which they did by seizing them by their head-tails and jerking them apart in an energetic manner.

The Chinese are like sheep, gentle and patient, detesting and fearing to fight, but when once aroused, courageous and malicious, knocking each other's brains out at the shortest notice. I was told they never fight with their fists. They act on the principle that as fighting is horrible it should be done in the shortest way.

Down among the Chinese passengers were three Japanese, who had been picked up by our steamer on her last voyage to America. When three days out from Japan the attention of the crew was directed to an object on the horizon, which, by aid of glasses, was discovered to be a small boat far out on the broad ocean. As the steamer approached it and whistled, a hand waved a response out of the little window. One of the boats was lowered, and sent to the relief of its inmates, who were found near the last extremity of starvation, while one already dead had been fed upon by his surviving comrades. Driven out by the change of the monsoon, and losing their rudder, they had been drifting about in the ocean for three months.

After being fed and clothed in American costume by the Japanese consul at San Francisco, they were now going back home on the ship which saved them. Like all Japanese they were very polite. On making their final acknowledgement of gratitude to the captain, they bowed their faces to the floor of the deck and almost crawled into his presence. They were of the lowest class of Japanese, who wear scarcely any clothes in summer, and their re-appearance in such strange attire must have surprised their friends.

Among the cabin passengers were two other Japanese, who had been to America preparing themselves for interpreters. They dressed in our costume, wore kid gloves, smoked cigars, and seemed in every way ready to adopt American ways; while a Chinese commissioner, also a cabin passenger, deviated not the least from Chinese dress.

We all rose early on the morning of the 24th, and as the sun first looked down upon the surrounding scene the mountainous shores of Japan rose out of the depths of water. It was Niphon, the kingdom of the Rising Sun; and we imagined that his majesty never rose on a greener or more beautiful isle. Small sailing vessels, and smaller craft without sails, were in sight, and as our gigantic ship plowed by them, their crews looked up with wonder, while we, on the other hand, looked at them with equal curiosity. The dwellings along the shore, magnified by our glasses, presented the appearance of comfortable homes. Passing into Yeddo Bay, we were delighted by the moss-capped rocks and woodland hills that rose from the water's edge close on either side and rolled away into mountains and volcanic peaks in the distance, the most prominent of which was Fusyami, whose snowy cone arose in grandeur aloft to the clouds, though with us it was a hot summer day.

As the bay opened, we were not less delighted by the vegetation that covered the level valleys, and climbed away in terraces far toward the summit of the hills and mountains, between strips of forests left for fuel. Masts and spars lined one side of the bay, and Yokohama was in view. Soon the signal gun was fired, and the surrounding hills and mountains echoed their prolonged salute. Slowly our unwieldy, gigantic vessel steered up among ships floating the flag of various nations, and while we were coming safely to anchor the Chinese scattered gilded papers as offerings of gratitude to their god.

The American consul with his red sash, and other gentlemen were already on board to hear the news from far-off America; also an occasional Japanese to change money or sell strange curiosities; while the Japanese boats, like buzzards, were hovering around, sculled by men who at each stroke answered each other with barbaric sounds, like the hissing of so many warlike ganders. Stretching their necks upward they seemed to say, "Light down here and we will paddle you safely to the shore."

Here and there European gentlemen, and an occasional blushing lady who had not yet become familiar with Japanese dress and customs, were taking boats for the shore; yet awhile we lingered, gazing and asking ourselves, "Are these Japanese, and can this be Japan, at last?"

CHAPTER XIII.

SIGHT-SEEING IN JAPAN.

WHATEVER is novel in anything can be enjoyed but once in a lifetime; upon a second view it vanishes. The broad ocean had a novelty all its own; so when we found ourselves in Japan, our surprise and astonishment was complete. Nothing we had ever experienced seemed so strange and unique.

We felt the very blood thrilling through our veins as we stepped down the long ladder at the side of the vessel and were rowed away in a rude skiff toward the shore, while we watched the two oarsmen as though they were the inhabitants of another sphere; yet they looked as unconcerned as if they had rowed their little boat here ever since these hills first looked at each other across this bay. We paid them ten of their oblong copper coins with great square holes in the centers, worth about a cent each. At this they seemed highly delighted, and we were afraid one of the poor fellows would tear his gown with joy; being long and unfastened in front, it alternately covered and exposed his body with each swing of the oar. The other one, if I remember correctly, had none to tear. They claimed no interest in our welfare—no dimes as mementoes; but that, however, didn't lessen them in our esteem.

As we stepped upon the rock-paved shore of the Old World, every stone was charged with an electric thrill; even the air seemed fraught with the mysterious influences of the past ages, causing the very hair to stand on our heads like quills upon the fretful porcupine.

GOING ASHORE AT YOKOHAMA, JAPAN.

Next to the bay was a row of fine looking buildings, the homes of Europeans. The most familiar object to our American eyes was the Stars and Stripes, floating above the fourth in the row. It shadowed the home of the American Consul. A little farther on, another flag designated the office of the Pacific Mail Steamers. Near by floated the flag of England, above the home of the English Consul. As we walked the length of this row of buildings, we admired the curious tiled roofing, and the beauty and the elegance of the marble imitation walls, displaying finely the art of the Japanese in cementing. The yards were ornamented with semi-tropical plants, and they presented a somewhat strange but pleasant scene.

We next turned our course to the city. But our attention was soon absorbed by the strange sights along the streets. On one hand, rode a European on the trot or full gallop, and just before him to clear the way ran a Japanese bettos, his tattooed body and swift limbs covered with dragons, fish,

A FORE-RUNNER OF CIVILIZATION.

and figures of various shapes and colors. He accompanied the rider to hold the horse and render general service. In another direction a European gentlemen, or a gaily attired lady or two, drove a low carriage which was drawn by a Japanese pony. Beside the buzzing wheels ran a Japanese, his gown trailing, waving in the wind, or swinging on his arm; and anon he jumped upon a seat at the back of the carriage, to rest like an intelligent "dorg" behind his fair mistress.

But hark! from whence comes that wild barbaric noise, filling the air like the shrill war-whoop of the Indian. Have some of the natives with the most searching voices been employed to awaken the ears of their god of the sun? The sound

THE GREAT ORIENTAL EXPRESS.

neared, as up the street approached a great two-wheeled, awkward dray, piled with boxes from the wharf, and pulled and pushed by half-a-dozen or more broad shouldered, muscular Japanese, who, keeping time at each step, strained their terrific voices in proportion to the strain of their muscles. When returning, with no load, the flow of their answering tones, ha-ho-ha te-ho-ho ha-te-ho, was not unmusical. In every direction the Japanese were going each with a bamboo pole on his shoulder, to either end of which was swung some kind of a burden, like a pair of scales.

Here and there passed those whose labor was not muscular. Instead of being without shoes or simple grass-plaited sandals, they had small stools three or four inches high, loosely fastened to the bottoms of their feet, causing a nod and a clatter at each step—not a bad institution, either, in wet weather.

Wildair was puzzled to distinguish the men from the women, not being accustomed to seeing boys wear gowns up to the tender age of twenty-one, and then conclude it was too late to make a change, save to put on the suit of matrimony. With us even this suit is often exchanged for the suit of divorce.

However, we soon learned to distinguish the fair sex, not only by the paint on their cheeks, but by the flashy colors of their attire, which they wrapped around their persons so closely that from head to foot they appeared like diminutive lamp posts. But it was comical to see such figures assuming the Grecian bend on their stilted shoes; such short, mincing steps would have provoked a smile from Socrates.

When we observed a majority of the people passing bareheaded we naturally supposed it was an economical dodge, but after discovering that the men all bore the cost of shaving the tops of their heads as clean as a plate, making it necessary to carry a fan or parasol to defend them from the rays of the sun, we changed our minds. It occurred to me that there was no discount on baldness here. We did not entirely fancy the manner in which the rest of the hair was brought back into a tail and daubed thickly with paste.

It is quite natural in Japan not to fancy a married lady, her husband requiring her to blacken her teeth, pluck out her eyebrows, and in short, to render herself sufficiently hideous to repel all would-be admirers. I reckon she must have a false set for home use. When Wildair derided these people and called them a set of barbarians, I naturally halted before a shop full of boxes of lacquered ware, whose beauty, elegance and fineness of finish no other people on the globe could equal, and exclaimed, "What barbarians! how coarse in their tastes!" Then in a few minutes he would retaliate by calling my attention to half-a-dozen coolies carrying a single man swung beneath a beam.

In order to lay the foundation stones of a canal we saw them pumping out the water by means of rude wheels, one above another, trodden by men; while coolies were backing the stone from the quarry some distance off.

"See Caleb, these men turn themselves into pack mules."

"They go on the principle that eight men can do as much work as one horse and eat no more rice; therefore kill off the horses, let men take their places, work for what rice they can eat—in short, replace the horses with a more intelligent breed. And you see it has already worked well in China, for that country could not support such a dense population if every man required four or five horses and a large farm for his support."

"But please tell me why they don't transport these stones on wheels instead of their shoulders, or use steam to elevate this water; that wouldn't consume rice or anything men could eat."

I scratched my head by way of reply and we walked on, passing through a square full of men, women and even children, sitting flat on their feet, selling fish and vegetables, many kinds of which we had never seen before.

In the suburbs we ascended, by a long flight of steps, a steep woodland hill where were tea-houses—simply a row of sheds on either side covered with boards and boughs of trees, under which were furnaces for heating the tea. The young ladies stepped forward and saluted us "O-hi-o" (how are you), offering us cups of the beverage. Just as I thought Wildair was overcome with their politeness, I gave him a slight nudge to bring to his mind, "Barbarism." We drank our tea standing, in preference to sitting on our heels, after which we bade them an unceremonious good-bye, and wandered leisurely back into the city.

Presently we noticed three or four boys with hoods on their heads, full of showy cock-feathers, who upon seeing our attention called, suddenly spreading their hands and feet, rolled sideways, as a wagon wheel, at rapid speed up and down the street. Then two, splicing their bodies together, their heads in opposite directions, revolved rapidly over and over, striking on their feet. Again, one bending his body backward crept between his own standing legs, with head, hands and shoulders, until we were on the point of throwing down a penny and asking him to turn himself wrong side out, but were deterred by the unearthly crawfish thus creeping towards us on all fours. Meanwhile, another was walking around grotesquely on his hands, his feet thrown back,

INDIA RUBBER BOYS.

catching himself under the chin. We supposed the boys must have bodies constituted of whalebone and India-rubber, yet we failed to see how a man could spin a top on the edge of a sword, or on the limber end of a stick balanced on his nose. But the most astonishing feat, was the flying of paper butterflies, formed by twisting bits of paper into the shape of these fairy insects, and setting them afloat in a still air whose currents were controlled so perfectly by means of fans that all the graceful movements of the living butterfly were attained. The dexterity of the performer caused two of the mimic papilios to engage in innocent frolics and sports, then alight upon the edge of flowers and nod as if to sip their nectar sweetness.

We finally partially compromised by agreeing that their civilization and ours might be contrasted but not compared. As well attempt to compare an elegant and exquisitely finished vase with Niagara Suspension Bridge; or this Japanese who by means of a fan could cause a paper butterfly to advance, retreat, sip at flowers, and flit about as though alive, to a Franklin flying his kite amid the fitful lightning.

If the best definition for progress is a locomotive, the Japanese were surely starting on that road. They were laying a track for the Iron-Horse to connect Yokohama with Yeddo, the bay being too shallow for the gigantic vessels to ascend. It was completed in the beginning of October 1872. The Mikado—who for centuries had been regarded as divine, too sacred for the sun to shine upon his head, much less for mortals to gaze upon—rode down on the cars, and appeared before the foreigners and the vast public at the opening ceremonies at Yokohama. It was a new era for Japan, and vast multitudes thronged the ways leading to the city. Some prostrated themselves with their faces to the ground, others half bowed, while many were undecided what to do. They were evidently afraid they would approach too near Mt. Sinai or some other awful presence, and the gods would thrust them through and through.

But the Mikado was sensible; he wanted to have a drive behind the locomotive, and see folks; and I consider him quite excusable in his desire. The roar and clatter of the mighty engine on the road of progress, is waking up those old sleeping monarchs who have been dreaming, ever dreaming, of their own divine origin and absolute right to rule this lower world.

But think of these Japanese who had never dreamed of the railway far away over the ocean; to whom a man pulling another on two wheels seemed a strange upstart. To them it appeared according to the natural order of things that they should carry travelers swung beneath poles from Yokohama to Yeddo; only think of these jumping into houses with seats, and rolling away with the speed of lightning toward

Yeddo. Who can imagine how it must have lifted their souls out of their bodies, and transported them with joy ineffable!

Does anybody know how they endured it?

NEW JAPAN.

CHAPTER XIV.

A COUNTRY RIDE TO YEDDO.

CRACK! went the driver's whip above the heads of four wicked original ponies, and we were off at full speed, with our tattooed runner, as swift as he was spotted, ahead of us to clear the track, while the natives gazed at the carriage as if trying to find out what kind of a creature was passing by on four rolling feet. Soon a gathering cloud discharged a torrent of water which flowed down the streets and poured from both tiled and thatched roofs; the occupants of the open-front houses, with their friends seeking shelter therein, who were reclining on the matted floors watching the rain, gave themselves an extra stretch as we went by; and our runner who had taken refuge with us crouched on his feet upon one of the seats.

"Look there Wildair, that's the way a dog sits to a t-y."

"You mistake; no dog doubles his hind feet backward under him after that kind of style."

So I gave it up, and was about to rank him with the elephant tribe, but discovered a serious difficulty—he had a very short and stubbed nose. Soon the sun came out bright as ever, and he resumed his advanced position on the road.

We were now coming into the country, yet houses lined either side of the way; every half mile or so, an opening between them showed a grassy path leading into a grove to a wayside shrine, where the weary traveler is supposed to stretch himself upon the grass, and pray.

Coming out into an open space where a couple of rows of

shade trees took the place of houses, around us was a broad plain, as level as the surface of a lake, covered by a carpet of rice which hid the irrigating streams of water. We seemed to be crossing one individual farm, although there were hundreds of distinct cultivators. Here and there bowed each husbandman on his little plot of ground, carefully pulling out every stray blade of grass. The tenants paid their feudal lords half an average crop; all they could raise above that quantity was their own. No wonder each farmer wanted but little ground so that he might cultivate it well, since a poor crop left none for himself. In years of famine the lords of the soil got rich, for rice was high. In years of plenty the tenants made nothing but a living, for rice was cheap.

Earthquakes were so frequent in Japan that it was said they needed no cradles to rock their children in; and though we could see the contents of each house through the open sides, we saw no cradles unless the houses themselves were intended to answer that purpose. They were constructed of four beams without braces—just the thing to rock and never cease rocking from the end of one earthquake or typhoon to another. This was a convenient and safe mode of lullaby for young and old, as there were no upper stories to tumble down and disturb the sleeper's rest.

The floors are all covered with straw matting, and an elevated portion thereof in the centre forms the bed, the lounge, the table, the chairs, the desk, the counter—in short the furniture of the room. Upon it sat the tailor on his curled up feet, or the seamstress plying her needle, or the spinstress turning her busy wheel, or the damsel playing her guitar for the pleasure of her callers, who were also seated in this unmentionable posture, while her mother, we supposed, was in the kitchen. Upon this elevation sat the lady of taste and industry, painting the Japanese fans exported so extensively; and it was as often occupied by indolent people—the mechanic lying on his back with his head on his wooden pillow waiting for a customer, or the whole of a half nude family still resting their heads upon their wooden blocks as if they intended to sleep both day and night.

This elevation of the floor being considered as tending to degradation and as a promoter of laziness, has been recently abolished by decree of the emperor, who proposes to make his people sit upon chairs and quit taking it so easy.

The working man whom we saw treading down one end of a lever that the other end might fall upon the unhulled rice, at evening lay down upon the straw and enjoyed a good night's sleep with but few cares to keep him awake. In a

NATIVE SWEETMEATS.

few years he will have a modern machine to thresh his grain with, but will also have new wants to be supplied,—new anxieties to disturb his rest.

While changing ponies we refreshed ourselves upon the native sweetmeats. In the language of one who had traveled this way before us, "the landlady and her damsels overburdened us with their attentions, placing our chairs (for the special accommodation of foreigners) in the most convenient spot, wiping our shoes, placing cushions on our seats, and anticipating every want." Cakes, soup, rice, and sweetmeats were brought in succession. One laughing bright-eyed damsel knelt before me with a cup of tea in her hand; another in the same position offered sugar, and a third, from her lowly posture on the ground, held to my lips a boiled egg already broken and peeled, and seasoned with salt. With garrulous vivacity they anticipated every look, and vied in their endeavors to be the first to bring us their native dainties. When our wants were supplied they remained kneeling close to our sides.

But how was this kindness returned? Let my own eyes bear testimony to what they saw. Our genteel American

FOREIGN SAUCE.

companion who moved in the highest circles at home, having repeatedly insulted the ladies who brought us out tea at every stopping place, now, with the sneaking crook of his umbrella, tried to loop up the dress of one of these kind, genteel, heathen ladies, who politely resisted his efforts. We felt indignant, for he degraded our nation's honor in the sight of these people, and insulted every American citizen who loves the fair fame of his country. We felt indignant, for he disgraced our sacred Christianity in the eyes of these natives. Imagine what we would think and do if strangers, coming among us and professing to be far above us in knowledge, civilization and Christianity, conducted themselves in like manner toward our sisters! But if the Japanese or Chinese resist by force the brutal conduct of the Europeans they have to suffer. I say brutal, because we frequently saw them cuffed and kicked about like dogs.

To us it seemed strange, yet natural that our runner, who had forgotten his suit and left it at home, should make himself agreeable to all the girls, many of whom were pretty and nicely dressed; at each tea-house they remembered him with a cup of their beverage.

As we approached Yeddo, we were naturally on the lookout, supposing it lawful to inspect everything we could see; but involuntarily hid our eyes in our hands as we came upon a party of young ladies who were bathing in a nice

A SMALL WATER-PARTY.

little door-yard in the shadow of the house. But we forgave them; they meant no harm, and ablution is part of their religion.

OUR ARRIVAL AT YEDDO, JAPAN.

We had not the remotest idea when we came within the limits of Yeddo; we simply knew that for mile after mile the street became more thronged, until at last we could confidently say, "We know we are in the Great City." We imagined, from the crowds of persons of every age and sex, that they were having a Fourth-of-July on a grand scale. They may not have been, however, for we could discern no loose tongued orator upon a stand, reciting the thrilling deeds of their Washington. They only appeared to be enjoying themselves in a social way. It is true they had music at every corner; but it was not the stirring martial tones of brass bands, or fifes, or drums, nor even the singing of "Hail Columbia" by a choir of young ladies and gentlemen. The musicians reminded us more of organ grinders, but their instruments were contemptible little things that seemed squeaking their lives away, though eked out into an endless string, causing misery to our sympathetic nerves.

By and by however we came to some great character. We knew he was such by the thousand gilded ornaments and trappings which dangled about him. He was not speaking that we could hear, and had only been dead for two or three thousand years. He had been their Washington, or Jefferson, or some one else, who had achieved great victories for them; but he was a god now, and it was only his image which they were bearing aloft upon their shoulders.

Arrived at Yeddo, we "put up" at a European hotel. It was a large building, and a high one, which seemed strange, as the Japanese of every class never build high ones for their own use. We finally concluded it was intended originally as a trap to fall upon the heads of foreigners whose passport thither had been their gun boats.

The dinner hour was at 8 P. M., and the other meals were correspondingly late. This did not exactly please us, as we had been taught at home to imitate the birds at early retiring and rising if we would be healthy, wealthy, and wise. But at Yeddo, doing as other foreigners did, we imitated the owls, and "late to bed and late to rise" was our motto while there.

The table waiters, dressed in native gowns, were abundant but very slow. An American accustomed to traveling by rail could have swallowed two meals between dishes. Such a gentleman evidently sat at one of the tables. After disposing of the first course with amazing speed, he looked around and found that the others had only fairly begun. After sitting awhile in great suspense he discovered, to his astonishment, that they had stopped eating while yet three-fourths of the food remained upon their plates. Though he still felt very hungry, he was just drawing back his chair when along came waiters with new supplies. He now watched closely, through the corners of his eyes, the progress of his neighbors, and at the end of the sixth course felt himself to be master of the situation. Unluckily he now espied some near him pouring fluids of various colors from bottles, and, feeling thirsty, he reached for the nearest one and helped himself to a glass of its contents. The gentleman who had ordered and paid extra for the wine, looked somewhat puzzled, but said nothing as he saw that the innocent fellow was only trying to do as others did. Finally a bowl of water was set before him, and as he could see only one use to put it to he sent a portion of it after the wine.

DINNER AT YEDDO.

That unsophisticated fellow was long a subject for conversation with Wildair; he seemed to enjoy it, but I didn't.

On retiring for the night we found there was no lock on the door to our room; so Wildair set the washstand against it with bowl and pitcher thereupon. About the peep of day two or three of the numerous Japanese boot-blacking servants came round in search of their prey. Into our room they plunged, and over went the table with an awful crash. The frightened Wildair, with revolver in hand, at once bounded out of bed, and not discerning the mosquito-net

A BOOTLESS VISIT.

carried it with him. At this apparition the astonished servants forgot their boots; and the accidental discharge of the pistol brought Wildair to his wits and a crowd to the scene of action:

"What's the matter?" demanded the landlord.

"Burglars! Burglars; don't you see how they burst into our room?" replied the crest-fallen Wildair.

"I see this smashed pitcher."

"Well, that was them, and I was after—"

"Whose boots are these?"

"Mine."

"Next time set them outside the door."

"Well, I guess I will," scratching his head; and the landlord walked away.

CHAPTER XV.

THROUGH THE TEMPLES.

WE found Yeddo to be a vast city of almost indefinite extent. Now we wandered where thousands compactly lived and moved; then, with a suddenness that was surprising, we seemed lost in forests dense and wild where no sounds were heard save the screeching of owls, the cawing of crows, or some other doleful solitary cries. In one of these places we visited the imposing tombs of the Tycoon Dynasty, overthrown a few years since after a rule of more than three hundred years.

While the wild birds in their lonely hours were cawing their solemn dirges in this dreary retreat, we went from tomb to tomb and from temple to temple, each surrounded by mossy walls running through undergrowth so dense the eye could not penetrate its shades. The priests opened the massive gates beneath lofty arches, and as we entered these secluded regions they bowed their shaved heads to us, then conducted us across the paved courts to the doors of the temples, where they pulled off their shoes or sandals and motioned for us to do likewise. The altars were tastily and pompously ornamented, and every part thereof could be traced into the graceful shape of some animal or plant, while the whole shone as burnished gold. On the walls of one of the temples were frescoed various kinds of birds in life-colored plumage; and we imagined the winged tribes were ardently loved by the Tycoon there buried. In another were bows, arrows, hunting implements and animals, suggesting that a mighty hunter there reposed.

In one temple the priest with great solemnity, conducted us up spacious steps shining as a looking-glass. As he approached the altar we knew from his step he was nearing some sacred presence. Soon we discovered the august object. It was a monstrous bronze turtle upon whose back stood a gilded bird, with legs as long as those of the cranes I used to shoot for eating the corn and leaving us the cobs.

BEFORE THE HIGH AND MIGHTY.

Wildair had once in his life, when in swimming, been bitten by an uncouth turtle so that he was no friend of that animal. Just then the sober priest with great veneration and solemn dignity prostrated his sacred person before the crane and turtle, kissed the floor, and motioned for us to join in the devotion; as we failed to do so and showed unmistakable signs of merriment the priest doubtless thought our veneration had been sadly neglected; while we thought the crane might have traveled faster without riding.

Down the capacious avenue shaded by rows of majestic

trees, used to come the solemn royal procession to this imperial cemetery, from the now deserted Tycoon's palace. The walled terraces and broad moats of that palace still testify to the security of its position in former days when it was defended by swords; but it could make but trifling resistance to cannon, or even to the American rifles which we saw in the hands of the Japanese soldiers drilling in the palace grounds. Near by were the capacious grounds and palaces of the provincial princes, who were formerly required to live in the capital much of the time as hostages for the good behavior of their provinces. It was their traveling to and from the capital with vast retinues of retainers, that for centuries made it such a great centre and the Yokaido along which we rode to Yeddo such an important thoroughfare. Their two-sworded retainers were still around the half deserted palaces of their lords, looking with suspicion upon foreigners and on the soldiers drilling with rifles.

But there was one thing I loved in the Japanese, and that was their ardent admiration of nature—it arose to a passion. They possessed what I deem the prettiest country in the world, embracing from four to six thousand islands standing out of the ocean in moss covered rocks and snow-capped mountains, hiding an infinite number of woodland glens and dales decked in foliage of surpassing beauty. No wonder they seldom emigrate. But not satisfied with this affluence of beauty they helped nature into new forms. In dwarfing they excelled all other nations. We saw vases containing various kinds of trees which appeared to be as old as any in the woods, yet not so lofty as Tom Thumb. Ha, ha, Giant Tom with head above the forest trees! "The Big Trees" of California were yet in our minds, as we contemplated a bamboo, a fir, and a blooming plum tree, all growing in a box one might carry in the upper story of his hat. As a contrast the growth of others was so stimulated that their branches extended to a great distance supported upon props, while strangely worn stones and pebbles were piled in such positions as to present in appearance the bottom and moss-

A JAPANESE TEMPLE.

covered banks of streams, as if nature had been at work
destroying and restoring for ages.

It seemed strange to see these human beings who were
competent to teach us many things, taking the place of horses
between the shafts. As I saw their manly forms as they
drew us along, and witnessed their noble exertions, I looked
back at Wildair and wept. I thought they were our brothers,
the work of whose hands we admired but could not equal;
our brothers, whose hearts knew the warmest and sincerest
friendship. As they warmed up with the exercise, they
dropped their thin gowns lower and lower down, and finally
removed them entirely. My steed was not as large as Wildair's; yet with commendable pride he was bound not to be
outdone in speed or endurance, and the latter was something

THE LATEST INNOVATION.

wonderful. The two-wheeled cart was of new invention, a
grand step on the road of progress. Frequently we whizzed
by those still riding in the old slow style in a cramped
position swung beneath a pole borne on the shoulders of two
coolies, who carried props in their hands to hold up the pole
when they rested.

When we told our horses (for we did not guide them with
reins) to take us to Asaksa Kanou, they first ran home to
procure a few small coins to throw upon the altar, for they

did not feel like worshiping without a sacrifice. We found this to be the principal temple of Yeddo, but no aristocratic church where pews are sold. Here rich and poor alike might worship. Under its vast outer and inner arches ever came and went the thronging multitudes, among whom were pilgrims from the remotest parts of Japan. As they approached the altar they threw their offerings toward the altar, and as the coins went jingling down from apartment to apartment, they fell upon their knees, folded their arms, and muttered their short prayers. Sometimes half a dozen were bowed at once. It was easy to tell by their countenances those who were in earnest. Some bowed and said their prayers in a hurried ceremonial way. I noticed one poor lame woman who seemed to have traveled a long distance,

THE WIDOW'S MITE.

coming across the broad pavement in front of the temple. She rested twice upon her staff, and there was a tired but earnest expression on her face. Perhaps she had been praying or struggling long at home, and had come here to unburden her soul. As she approached she dropped in three little coins, doubtless all she had, and clapped her hands as she fell upon her knees, and turning her eyes toward heaven she worked her lips as if whispering her sorrows into the ear of Him who heareth every inward moan. She continued long with clinched hands as though unwilling to leave, and then went her way unhonored and unknown until the Great Day when many whom the Master knows will come from the East and the West and sit down in the Kingdom.

Within the capacious altar sat shaven-crowned priests vowed to celibacy, chanting in an unknown tongue their ritual of worship, which was answered by others. In their monasterial cells some sat muttering their formal prayers, one for each bead in their rosary. Here was one distributing prayers on pieces of paper, which possessed great merit because they had come through the hands of persons devoted to religion. Some of these prayers were for souls in an intermediate state. Occasionally the priests marched in procession to tinkling bells, or moved in their long gowns about the distant altars among the smoking incense sticks, or adjusted the candles so as to reflect the glitter of the images.

Outside the enclosure of the altar were pictures of ghastly figures—writhing men, and tormenting spirits, which seemed intended to frighten visitors to implore the gods of mercy. The sinner, as he approached the altar, appeased the wrath of the gods by burning incense. Each one passing dropped a little coin, picked up a pinch of some kind of herb looking like tobacco, and dropped it down the mouth of a horrible image, and in the smoke which rolled out of his mouth and nostrils the evil spirits of the worshiper ascended. I took it to represent the devil; but Wildair called it the Smoking God, or the God of the Smokers, and naturally enough he was one of the most popular gods there. I should not wonder if many worshiped him as such, for religion was awfully mixed. Everybody had a god to suit his own fancy.

But there was another image whose name or attributes could not be mistaken even by strangers. It was the Goddess of Mercy. She had no marks of distinction, no glitter of gold or pearls; but in places the image was much worn by the simple contact of hands that were afterwards laid on corresponding portions of their own bodies, or the bodies of children. Whether any limbs were made whole thereby or any diseases cured I cannot say, for her work was silent; all I know is that crowds came with apparently as much faith in her ability to relieve them, as those had who in earlier times strove to touch the hem of Christ's garment. They called her the "Queen of Heaven," the same appellation as is applied to the "Virgin Mary."

Three centuries ago Japan was almost a Christian nation,

TOUCH AND BE HEALED.

so forcibly did the wonderful story of the cross impress them. St. Francis Xavier, the great apostle of the Indies, was the first missionary to Japan. His spirit had caught the apostolic fire, and he hastened thither with the first merchant vessels. The Japanese have a warm, passionate nature, and could this missionary have stood on their mountains, and sounded out the glad and stirring news with an untiring tongue, they would have experienced a Pentecost on a grand scale—a nation would have been born in a day. He soon died from self-exertions and hardships, but still the glad tidings spread, and multitudes were converted and baptized—twelve thousand in two years. But soon the tide turned; they saw enough of foreigners to note many shortcomings and rascalities, and naturally wondered that Christianity as preached to them did not bring forth better fruits. The vessels which visited Japan went armed, and not unfrequently some turned pirates. No wonder such actions changed the feelings of the natives from love to hatred. About this time the Great Tycoon asked a Spaniard:—

"How is it that your king has managed to possess himself of half the world?" The unwise but true reply was:—

"He sends priests to win the people; his troops are then sent to join the native Christians, and the conquest is easy."

The result was an edict banishing the priests. Twenty-three were put to death in a single day at Nagasaki. But the government had a Herculean task. Although the native Christians were butchered and massacred year after year, and foreigners excluded, yet there are thousands of them still left. About the time we were there nearly a thousand men, the heads of families, were exiled from the sight of the world to work in mines and dismal pits.

Many people speak of all heathen profession in a light manner, but it either arises from ignorance or arrogance. Some missionaries go to them with the idea that all their doctrines, beliefs, and faiths, must be overturned; but nothing can be more erroneous. What is good in them—has that to be overthrown? By attempting such a course their indignation is naturally forever aroused, for many of the doctrines of their philosophers and religious teachers would hardly disgrace the most sublime and sacred pages of the Bible.

CHAPTER XVI.
SOCIAL PROGRESS IN JAPAN.

AMONG our friends in Yeddo were a young married couple with whom we had become intimate during our Pacific voyage. The bridegroom had resided in Japan before, and becoming weary of a bachelor's life had returned to America for the girl he left behind him. Certainly, he had no cause to regret doing so. It seemed strange to us that so many Europeans should here pass away their lives as lonely bachelors, or purchase native wives, when lovely creatures of their own race can be obtained so easily. The bride's modest cheeks were just becoming accustomed to native scenes. What a contrast between her and the fat water-carrier of the hotel whose chief garment was an old European vest which he wore more for ornament than use, and of which he seemed very proud.

About the time the Pilgrim Fathers landed their little bark on the savage New England shore, Japan drew herself into her shell to enjoy alone her superior civilization and refinement handed down from the dreamy past. Years slowly numbered into centuries during which, to Japan, the outside world seemed like a dream fast fading. But one bright afternoon, up Yeddo Bay came the Stars and Stripes floating above a squadron of screeching gun-boats. As the boom of the saluting cannon shook the surrounding mountains, it sent a thrill of mingled amazement and horror through the country and awakened the emperor in his seclusion. Startled, he learned that an embassy had arrived from some nation that had sprung up like a mushroom in an unknown quarter of the world. He turned to the history of his country and read how the Portuguese, three centuries before, had come to these shores and sold foreign articles at enormous

"GETTING USED TO IT."

prices; bought up their vast treasures of gold with silver; secretly conspired against their government; and how the Japanese finally drove the invaders away with sharp steel.

He now asked:—" Who are these American foreigners demanding intercourse?—and was about to say, " No, no! get away; let us alone;" but as he turned his eyes toward the stranger fleet, each vessel he saw seemed to wear a frowning aspect, and thereupon he reluctantly said, " Yes." But no sooner were they gone than the English fleet came and made similar demands; then the French, the German, the Russian; and before he had time to consider, the United States were renewing their demands for trade and intercourse.

Less than twenty years have elapsed since our first treaty

with the Japanese was effected by Commodore Perry, yet no other people on the globe are to-day more eager to introduce our modern improvements than they. Fire arms are particularly interesting to them and many thousands have already been imported. Foreigners have been hired to teach them military drill, for which they show a decided taste; and even Wildair

WILDAIR'S WARRIORS.

was one day importuned to act in that capacity, and evoked the applause of an admiring crowd by the masterly way in which he handled his file of incipient warriors.

After the drill was concluded, Wildair entertained a crowd who had gathered around us, by showing them pictures of Japanese in a guide-book we had brought with us. They looked at each other and laughed; then at the pictures again, and manifested much delight at the thought that they had a place in American books and literature. We then showed them a map of the world and pointed out the relative position of the United States and Japan, and thereby greatly enlarged their ideas of geography.

Although this is an age of startling events, yet such progress in civilization as the Japanese are making had never been dreamed of. Their school system has been adopted after

the most careful examination of our educational system and
that of other nations, and covers every grade from the college
to the common school, being expressly intended to benefit
every child, rich or poor, male and female. The press, yet

WILDAIR AS A GEOGRAPHER.

in its infancy, has begun its work of scattering the news of
the empire and of the world to the masses, who can generally
read. The liberty of the press is now a reality, and already
public sentiment is being formed which will soon prepare the
people for voting, at which time they are to have a voice in
the government. Railroad lines, telegraph wires, and mail
routes are being established throughout the country. How
wonderful the Providence that has possessed the minds of the
feudal princes with such a love of our institutions as to cause
them to lay down their regal powers, untold wealth, and
separate armies, through pure love for their country, abdicate
the birthright of twenty centuries, to make themselves citizens
by the side of their serfs who had never known or dreamed
of any thing but service! When we were there many of the
princes yet retained their territories nominally, and their two-
sworded soldiers, but shortly after these were all nobly surrendered. We saw many soldiers or retainers still wearing

their two swords wandering about idly, hardly knowing what to do now that their masters and support were gone. They were born soldiers and knew nothing else. It was curious to see many of the little boys of this class still wearing their diminutive swords; but the little fellows would soon have to throw them aside and earn their own living. We saw on one occasion a party of boys of this rank playing "blind

SOCIAL EQUALITY ILLUSTRATED.

man's buff," and were glad to notice that two boys of a lower grade—one with only one sword and the other with none at all—had ventured to join them; for it foretold the downfall of the military aristocracy. The two swords that have been in families for hundreds of years are being thrown aside; even the regular soldiers, policemen, and government officials, carry our arms and wear French uniforms.

To see how fully aristocracy and castes have been swept away, I need only to state that the Mikado, who from the time of the gods has lived in divine seclusion, never eating twice from the same dish, and never leaving his seclusion excepting in a closely curtained cart drawn by snow-white bullocks, has lately visited the despised tanners who were below all castes, and revoked the stigma. More, he has even received European ladies and taken them by the hand.

The government has recently ordered the adoption of our

Christian Sabbath as a day of rest to take the place of irregular holidays; instead of twelve hours the day is to have twenty-four; our months take the place of the Chinese hobgoblin lunar months; the year is to begin with the first day of January, and Christmas is to be observed as a holiday in memory of their first emperor, whom they hold as divine.

OLD JAPAN.

CHAPTER XVII.
FROM JAPAN TO CHINA.

IT was south-westerly along the coast of Japan that we two pilgrims were sailing. To us, there was something attractive in the white-sailed fishing junks of these good natured rascals of the island, as they floated among the high rocky promontories of the coast; in the mountains cultivated in terraces almost to the summit of the highest peaks, and in the whole country, mountains and valleys, so beautifully green. Occasionally we met a ship, or beheld one in the distance, whose full, white sails looked as robes dropped from heaven upon the waters, but were only wafting cargoes of tea, for American speculators. As we passed a fortification several miles away, the Japanese flag was seen ascending and descending a pole, while the American flag at the stern of our vessel gracefully glided up and down its standard, and thus the two governments which they represented saluted each other.

One afternoon, when we were near the southern part of Japan, we passed a strait, then another one, where the land divided, and the channels of the water wound around the bases of mountains. Towards sunset and till night began to throw her shady mantle about us, the scene was almost enchanting. We were sailing between the mainland of the island on our right, and a number of small islands at our left, sometimes shut in between high walls, and again obtaining views of the volcanic islands to the south as they rose one after another far as the eye could reach like peaks and light-houses from the bosom of the ocean. Around the summit of one close by, the smoke was hovering densely, while occasionally a blaze shot up, scattering its rays over the heads of other volcanic peaks, which now lay slumbering in the broad ocean till again aroused by the fiery elements beneath.

The dark bases of these peaks seemed a fitting abode for malignant beings; and it is here that pirates hold their nightly carnivals. They watch for their prey as the hyena

THE PIRATES' DOOM.

for the wounded deer, and attack every vessel which is wrecked or becalmed within their reach.

We were told that a sailing vessel, delayed by a calm not long previous, was stealthily approached by these pirates, who threw a burning substance upon the vessel, the smoke of which choked and stupefied the crew. Then the pirates boarded the vessel, killed all within, and carried off the cargo. A man-of-war hearing the news, sailed for the place, having first taken in her guns and painted her ports to indicate that she was a merchant vessel. Upon arriving she raised a signal of distress, and all parties went below. Soon the pirates cautiously approached. When close by, the crew ran on deck and opened fire upon the surprised wretches, killed several, and captured the rest, nearly all of whom were afterwards hung.

As the eastern coast of Asia is frequently visited by typhoons at the time of year we were sailing over its waters, the passengers were frightened at every change of the weather. Only a few days before, one of these terrible storms had visited the shores near Nagasaki, wrecking several vessels, and landing one or two high upon the beach. When a vessel is caught in the centre of one of these hurricanes its destruction is almost inevitable. The storms are occasioned by the change of the monsoons, which blow six months from one direction, then six months from the opposite. At the time of year this change takes place, there is a shifting of the winds, which sometimes blow from different directions towards one centre, soon beginning the whirl that terminates in the typhoon, the dread of the mariner.

As we neared the coast of China we passed thousands of small fishing crafts with their little sails. The inmates were naked like so many barbarians, yet they all retained their braided queues. As they shifted their sails to get out of our way, they looked up in surprise, and I fancied with awe. The Chinese returning home on our vessel were now allowed to come on the hurricane deck to look at the fishermen, and behold again the shores of their native land. Seemingly they were much delighted as they gazed around, yet might they as well have hunted for a lost pebble upon the sea-shore as looked for an acquaintance among these thousands who to us appeared as near alike as so many peas. Toward evening there were indications of a typhoon, and a hurrying shoreward of the fishermen, near and far. How their sails bent before the wind, and their small boats keeled far over on their sides as they mounted the waves, and again disappeared in the hollows of the sea. But the expected typhoon did not come off, much to our disappointment.

One morning as the sun arose from the bosom of the Pacific, we were entering a channel between the British island of

Hong Kong and Oriental China, with rock-ribbed hills standing high up on either hand. Soon the city of Hong Kong appeared in view, its streets rising conspicuously one above the other on the mountain side. The signal gun was fired, and we were soon dropping anchor in the middle of the channel among vessels whose flags represented many nationalities, while hundred of sampans, small boats ten or twelve feet long by three or four in width, in which whole families passed their whole existence, were paddling here and there through the water, and swarming about our vessel. Their inmates looked anxiously up at us, making signs, and jabbering in broken China, to impress it upon us that we ought to go ashore, and that they wanted to do the job for us. So we accepted the solicitations of a couple of sprightly looking girls who had an oldish looking mother and three or four small brothers and sisters to support. They took hold of our arms, helped us into their sampan, showed us to the best seat, and paddled us ashore. How they paddled, and how the mother and children smiled—for they expected something with which to buy a dinner. We had been told the customary price by the officers of our vessel, and paid them about twice that amount, but still they wanted more. So we gave them a little more; yet they were not satisfied, and followed us ashore. We desired to be liberal, especially toward girls—but it would not do; we must bluff them off, else they would follow us all day.

However, in a moment after we reached the shore that was done most effectually by other parties. The males, with chairs to carry us to the hotel, swarmed around like bees, pushing and scrambling; the girls were crowded back to their boat, while we would have prayed, had it been of any use, to have been again cared for by them, instead of this rabble that wanted to shove us into a hundred different chairs at once. Luckily we succeeded at last in getting into only two of them, and were carried a short distance up a crowded street to the hotel.

CHAPTER XVIII.
ADVENTURES IN HONG KONG.

WERE I a Chinaman, I would vote to keep all foreigners out of my country; for they must be a constant reminder to the Chinese that they were somehow neglected when their turn came to be created. Perhaps some journeymen had the job when all the best talent was on a strike; this is the only way I can account for the existence on this earth of some 450,000,000 moral vacuums, at least 99 per cent of whom are striving in their own benighted way, to determine how small an amount of nutritious aliment is necessary to support a given bulk of animated matter. Not unfrequently they shave the thing a little too close; then the solids give way, and a "Celestial" fungus is erased. They began 4,000 years ago to speculate about what reason there was for their existence, and what was to become of them when they ceased to be an incumbrance to this earth; and their foremost philosophers came to the conclusion that they were mere excrescences on this mundane sphere; they sprang up, flourished, departed, and that was the last of them. And it is to be sincerely hoped they were correct if they carry into the next world many of the traits of character they have in this.

But there were some things in China which we liked, and among them were rides in the chairs. Our first excursion by that mode of conveyance was to the Government Gardens, and it was one of the most memorable. We jumped into a couple of chairs whose owners looked sprightly, to contribute our quota of polish to their bamboo contrivances, some of

STREET SCENE IN HONG KONG.

which seemed to have survived the rack of centuries. When
we desired to turn to the right, we tapped with one hand
on the right pole, when to the left, on the left pole, and
a tap on both poles at the same time was equivalent to saying
"Whoa." We met other foreigners in chairs taking it as
lazily as we, as they were carried along by their panting
fellowmen, some smoking or reading newspapers; or perhaps
two abreast—usually a lady and gentleman—were talking with
each other as they traveled along. I think this style of riding
would not afford the best accommodations for a couple of
lovers. We also met some of the wealthier class of the Chinese
who rode in the same style. In fact it is a very pleasant way
of riding, if one can keep it out of mind that he is making a
horse of his fellowman.

As the day was warm we bought a couple of great hats
made of pith and covered with white satin. They looked

STARTING UP THE LEADER.

like immense white turtle shells, and were so arranged by
bands and braces as to keep them from touching the head;
the air circulated beneath, and was cooling to the brain.
With these *generalissimo* hats Caleb looked heroic, and I
felt just as he looked, and proposed that we should have a
race. To increase the speed of my team, I first swung my

handkerchief at them, which produced but little effect, as they did not know exactly what it meant and were somewhat frightened. I now shouted at them, which proved too much for the sensitive ears of the leader, who immediately dropped his end of the shafts and ran off. This change in the programme I had not anticipated; Caleb thought I might have had more sense, but still enjoyed my disaster. A few kind words from him brought my chairman again into the traces, and at a fast walk we proceeded on.

We now passed among tropical trees and foliage, along winding roads running between yards whose limits were well defined by cuttings in the side of the hill walled up by rock. Rising above these walls, yards of rolling green reached on to stately mansions owned by foreigners of wealth, and beyond these were the Government Gardens. They were very attractive indeed abounding in the richest flowers, shrubbery, trees and paths winding among shady nooks.

Just outside of the Gardens we espied a long string of English convicts, who were handcuffed, and watched over while at work on the road by Indiamen and men from other southern climes, almost as dark as Africans. I once had an idea that all English evil-doers were transported to Van Dieman's Land or Australia, but like many other of my juvenile fancies it has been dispelled. Here in this great city where labor is so cheap that men perform the work of oxen on account of economy, the British Government finds it to its interest to send whole gangs of these convicts to work the public roads and build stately edifices dedicated mostly to mammon,—for what could induce the noble Briton to forsake the island of his idolatry, with its proverbial "roast beef and plenty," but the allurements of a more tangible god? One could scarcely believe but what these self-exiled English were the upper class of the Chinese, separated alike by their wealth and inclination from the common herd. Contact with the western nations has in turn sunk these heathens, whose sole claim to enlightenment seems to be a power of imitating every vicious habit, and ignoring every moral principle, into depths of depravity, of which in their seclusion they never would have dreamed.

On our way back to the city we saw an army of washermen standing in a brook and beating the clothes they were washing against the stones, many of which, from continued use, were half worn away. Frequently after that, not only in China, but also in India, we understood full well how it happened that our shirts buttons came home in halves, and sometimes not at all.

At one time the chairmen were carrying us with the poles

A DOWN GRADE.

on their shoulders, as was more customary than in the hands. Thought I: "They played a nice trick on me as we were coming up, but now I have them—they can't let me down, and run off." Caleb was a little in advance of me, and as it was a down grade I thought it would be a good time to overtake him. So I again swung my handkerchief, shouted "Hip, hip, hurrah," and very imprudently kicked at the leader. The consequent acceleration of his speed was all I could have desired. We flew rather than ran, and quickly passed our companions. But at that instant my lead horse stumbled, and went sprawling upon the ground—headforemost I tumbled upon him. As I struck, smash went my "*generalissimo*" hat; it was forever ruined. As the frightened Chinaman was scrambling from under me, Caleb condoled me by saying:—

"It's good enough for your foolhardiness."

"Foolhardiness," I replied, "why didn't you catch them? The rascals were running away with me."

I was now somewhat recalled to a sense of my situation. I must reconcile the fellow or walk back to the hotel. So I said," My friend, I fear you have mistaken my nervous anxiety for personal violence directed toward you; nothing of the sort was intended, I assure you; and as an earnest of my good feelings I here tender you a token of her Majesty Victoria Regina, value one shilling,"—and threw him a coin. Thereupon he returned to his duties but kept an eye on me for the balance of the trip.

When again in the city we stopped at two or three shops to buy some curiosities. Upon pricing them, I thought they were quite dear. However, I bought two or three articles, but soon found I had been terribly taken in. Every time we started to leave, they lowered their prices, until by degrees they had fallen to about one fifth of what they had first asked. It was so in regard to a certain beautifully carved ivory card case which was fairly worth two or three dollars. I felt somewhat vexed, and pulling out a brass coin worth about one eighth of a cent, offered that for it. As a general thing the Chinese countenance is dull, and void of expression; but this Chinaman rolled up his oblique eyes, stared at me in astonishment, muttered something in Chinese, seized his card case and put it away, while we walked out.

Upon our return to the hotel we paid our chairmen fifty cents for each chair, which was good pay for them, yet they were dissatisfied, and my leader afterwards took delight in revenging himself on us, and especially on me. Whenever we walked the streets, he was sure to meet us, and to throw off his pigeon-English sarcasm, "American walk! American walk! Coole! Coole!" At the same time, he would have been very glad to have carried us again.

Whenever we started out for a stroll, it was almost impossible to get through the crowd of chairmen who hovered around the door. All through the city, "Chair! Chair!" continually greeted us. As but few foreigners walked, they thought surely we should not, and blocked our way at times until we were obliged to treat them like dogs.

One morning as we were upon the portico of the second floor, these chairmen so obstructed the door of the hotel that the landlord came out with a club, apparently frantic with rage, and made an indiscriminate attack upon them. Some tumbled headforemost over their chairs, and came sprawling upon the ground; the rest shot off like rockets, a hundred pig-tails streaming in the air. Then the landlord kicked and knocked the deserted chairs about till he was exhausted, and returned triumphant from the field.

ABATING A NUISANCE.

CHAPTER XIX.

MORE ADVENTURES IN HONG KONG.

CALEB is a philosopher, and feels that everyone should have something like his proportion of this world's goods; and whenever he sees one of his fellowmen worse off than himself, the first thing which suggests itself is an attempt to restore the equilibrium. On one occasion a beggar, without any special claim to distinction, asked an alm and of course got it. The consequence of Caleb's rashness was that we were obliged to leave Hong Kong sooner than we had anticipated, for a report soon got around that two American travelers of unbounded wealth and generosity were in the city, and our peace of mind was at once destroyed. Wherever we went, beggars thronged around us.

When a Chinaman of the lower class is not working, or smoking, or begging, he is gambling. Sometimes this assumes the form of a cheap lottery; but far oftener small groups might be seen sitting on the floors or pavements with little piles of money besides them, from which they slapped down one or two small coins, the ownership of which was afterwards decided by the throwing of dice. The dice boxes used on these occasions are owned and shaken by an outside party who receives a certain commission on all sums won.

The Chinese generally smoke tobacco in a pipe, but are beginning to learn to use cigars; as yet they have not learned to chew. When an aristocratic Chinaman assumes airs in the way of ventilating a smoking engine he does the thing properly. He procures a furnace to which he attaches a pipe that reaches from the floor to his mouth. Having filled the boiler beneath the furnace with cold water, he puts a small pinch of cut tobacco in the furnace with one hand, and with the other applies a stick of slow-burning pith to the fuel.

GAMBLING.

After taking a deep inhalation he adjusts a tube which changes the current of air, and blows out the whole contents of the furnace, although yet barely ignited. As the smoke is curling from his mouth and nostrils he arranges his apparatus a second time, and so continues, never taking but a single puff at each firing up of his engine.

The "opium smoking houses" are found all over China, and are the curse of the country. At our first visit to one of them, we beheld a well-dressed lady sitting close to her husband who lay upon a "kang." There were unmistakable evidences of sadness in her countenance, and well there might be, for this was the commencement of her sorrows. Her husband had entered here on several former occasions, but on the previous evening he had inhaled the poisonous drug more freely than ever before. It had worked its customary result, and he lay all night stupid, in fact insensible, and in the morning she had gone in search of him to find him in this horrible den. She well knew that it would not stop here; that it was as the first glass to the drunkard's lips, and it was all she could do to refrain from sobbing.

We visited several of these places and were horrified and disgusted by what we saw therein. Some of the inmates sit upon the floors or counters and stare at us, while others lie senseless, or are too far overcome by the drug to take any notice of strangers.

Some are preparing the opium for their pipes by means

THE FAITHFUL WIFE.

of small iron wires, one end of which they heat in a lamp burning near at hand. When the wire is hot they put it into the opium gum, twist on a little lump, convey it to the lamp, heat it until it swells and begins to run down, but keeping it on the wire by means of whirling it about. When properly heated, they run the end of the wire into a small hole in the bowl of the pipe. As the opium cools it sticks to the bowl, enabling them to draw the wire out by giving it a quick twist, leaving a hole in the opium through which to draw the smoke. Now they lie down upon the matted floor beside the lamp, put the pipe to the blaze, and puff away. For a few moments it seems to exhilarate, though scarcely noticeable; then follows a quiet languor. Still remaining upon their sides, they adjust the opium a little, probably pushing another hole through it into the bowl of the pipe. In fifteen or twenty minutes they are ready for a fresh supply.

By the time two or three pipes are smoked, and occasionally sooner, they begin to lose all activity. It seems to benumb the sensibilities, and take away all life, and they lie apparently lifeless. Those that are habitual smokers become enervated in both body and mind—their limbs are withered, their ankles and wrists appear like pipe stems, their eyes are sunken, and their features pale and ghastly. Here they lie, their lungs having become so completely saturated with smoke that it comes curling out at their nostrils for some time after they have ceased smoking.

The Chinese are now learning to cultivate the poppy, and manufacture its juice into opium themselves; but the great amount of this drug is imported from India by the British, even to the amount of from 12,000,000 to 15,000,000 lbs. per annum—an increase of fully twenty fold during the present century, and this notwithstanding the government of China, knowing its pernicious effect, has continually opposed such importation. The Chinese, having once come in contact with it, have been wild with a desire for the drug; while the English, to their shame, be it said, have assisted in smuggling it into the ports of China, and have pressed the permission for its sale upon the Chinese government with unwarranted means, even by arms, so that now its importation is legalized.

As an offset to this vice of opium smoking, it may be said that the Chinese do not use intoxicating liquors of any kind; tea and weak spirits made from rice, being their strongest drink. I never saw a drunken Chinaman; and I suppose they would be as much astonished at our drinking propensities as we were at their opium smoking. That they are occasionally amused thereby is certain; and while we were in Hong Kong an American gentleman who, when sober, was qualified by nature and education to move in the best society, greatly amused the natives by sitting down in the mud, under the impression that he was taking a seat in the "chair" which he had engaged for a ride.

The Chinese are justly noted for their great imitative powers. This faculty, together with their incredible patience in application, renders them a very skillful people, to the truth of which their many beautiful carvings and other works of art will attest. Let any object no matter how intricate and puzzling, be placed before one of these Orientals, and he will accomplish the reproduction of it even to the smallest and most insignificant particulars. This imitative power has been

AMUSING THE NATIVES.

the origin of many yarns. Probably you have heard how an American took an old pair of boots to a Chinaman as a model by which to have a new pair made. In a few days he went for his new boots, but to his surprise one of the toes was adorned with a patch similar to that on one of the old ones.

The story related by Bridget illustrates in a laughable manner this faculty in a Chinaman employed to assist her in the kitchen.

"You're aware yersel' how the boondles comin' in from the grocery often contains more'n 'll go in anything decently. So for that matter I'd now and then take out a sup o' sugar or flour or tay an' wrap it in paper, an put it in me bit of a box tucked under the ironin' blanket, the how it cuddent be bodderin' anyone. Well what shud it be but this blessed Sathurday morn the missis was a spakin' pleasant and respectful wid me in me kitchen, when the grocer-boy comes in an' stands fornenst her wid her boondles, an' she motions like to Fing Wing (which I never could call him by that name nor any other but just haythin)—she motions to him, she does, for to take the boondles an' empty out the sugar an' what not where they belongs. If you'll belave me, Ann Ryan, what did that blatherin' Chineser do but take out a sup o' sugar an' a handful o' tay, an' a bit o' chaze, right afore the missis, wrap them into bits o' paper, an' I spachless wid shurprise, an' he the next minute up wid the ironin' blanket and pullin' out me box, wid a show o' bein' sly to put them in. Och, the Lord forgive me, but I clutched it, and the missis sayin' "O Kitty" in a way that 'ud cuddle your blood. "He's a haythin nager" says I. "I've found you out," says she. "I'll arrist him," says I. "It's you who ought to be arrested," says she. "You won't," says I. "I will," says she. And so it went till she give me such sass as I cuddent take from no lady, an' I give her warnin' an' left that instant, an' she a pointin' to the doore."

One day as we sat in our room at the hotel, a Chinese barber entered seeking employment in his profession. After he had shaved Caleb satisfactorily, I concluded to have my hair cut, and that pretty short, as it was in a hot climate. The next thing was to make the barber understand how I wanted it done. My chin whiskers had grown out an inch or so, while those on the side of my face were four or five times as long. By stroking my chin whiskers, I tried to make him understand that I wanted my hair cut about so short. He looked astonished; so I again rubbed my chin, and told him with considerable emphasis that I wanted my hair cut to same length. As he still appeared astonished, I became vexed, and told him to go to work; whereupon he nodded his head, and began to clip away at the top of my head. I thought it rather a singular commencement and looked round at Caleb who appeared to be busily engaged reading. A moment later however he burst into laughter, and I rushed to the looking-glass. Stars!—The barber had cut a furrow from forehead to the crown of my head like a swarth through a field of wheat. He was evidently trying to make the hair on my head correspond to that on my face.

As I gazed on the Chinaman's handiwork, a wild frenzy seized me, and I looked at him in a way which overcame his serene composure and caused him to retreat to the other side of the room, while his spectacles fell from his nose. The ridiculous appearance which I presented proved his salvation, for I laughed so loud and long that I was powerless to harm him.

We three then held a consultation, as to how I could best get out of the scrape, and as a result, the barber was invited to persevere in the work he had commenced; he did so with a will, and soon relieved me of nearly all the hair I had on my head. For a full month after, I was a perfect scare-crow, and the laughing stock of all the guests at the hotel.

A BARBEROUS BARBER.

CHAPTER XX.

THE LAST OF HONG KONG.

SOMEONE says there are 300,000,000 Chinese in the world, and I suppose he must be correct. I would not contradict a man who has counted 300,000,000 of anything, much less Chinese. I am willing to believe there are twice that number rather than dispute even with a man who has suffered so many Chinese to rest on his mind. We saw only about 5,000,000, and thought we had seen all we could conveniently remember; in fact their presence became quite monotonous.

The fashions of China are at a standstill like everything else, and although a stranger is very much interested for a while, the sameness soon becomes wearisome. Every Chinaman has a single tuft of hair left on his otherwise cleanly shaven head, and this hair is plaited and lengthened out with pieces of black silk until it dangles almost to the ground. Very loose trowsers, a garment half shirt and half jacket reaching below the hips; shoes made of straw with wooden or felt soles, or more frequently no soles at all—these are the habiliments of over one third of the human race. Their hats are studies of absurdity and are as varied as the caprice or wealth of their owners. A beggarly sedan carrier may be obliged to put up with a discarded sailor hat, but a patrician rat dealer feels more dignified under the shade of a broad brimmed palm leaf. Others suggestively adorn their heads with a covering resembling a candle extinguisher; and large numbers go without anything in the shape of a hat.

The women of the lower classes dress nearly the same as the men, but select more showy colors for their garments. A blue cotton stuff is the prevailing material, but silk and linen

A STUDY OF HATS.

are worn by the upper classes. The women retain all the hair they can, and among the more refined the method of dressing it is very good—in effect at least; they comb it neatly back, flute it on either side to resemble wings, and do it up in a large mass on the back of the head. All the poor women go without shoes, and their feet are moderately large; but the nobility bind the feet of their children in infancy, thereby preventing their growth though their ankles are of the natural size. The unfortunate victims of this fashion seldom walk; but when they do, go hobbling along leaning for support on servants. The corset is as yet unknown in the country. They have in China an infallible way of discovering who are gentlemen of "elegant leisure" and who are not.

Every man who has nothing else to do, spends his time in cultivating his finger nails. It is considered a great mark of beauty to have long nails, and some even go so far as to wear small bamboo sheaths on their fingers at night to prevent their being broken while sleeping.

From the balcony of our hotel—which faced so that we had a view down four streets—we observed, morning, noon and night, passing crowds of Mongolias, each seeming intent on some object, ever wondering at their ceaseless industry, and the poverty resulting therefrom. Here and there were sedan chairs borne by stalwart men regardless of all in their

MISTRESS AND MAID.

course, who violently jostled the yielding throng that never thought of resenting the indignity. Venders of soup, gamblers plying their nefarious profession, tinkers, each and all on the streets, working along as stolidly and incessantly as though in some private shop where no one could interfere.

What a motley group we look down upon from this balcony

of ours! Here two partners in a venture sustain their united capital stock in a huge basket hung to a pole, and shout their jargon above the din of competing venders of vegetables, fruits, or curious wares—each traveling merchant presenting the appearance of a pair of walking scales. Across the way is a bookseller; next to him is a fishstand; then comes a barber.

SIDEWALK ARTISANS.

The principal person of one group shakes from a little cup a number of small sticks, looks intently upon each one, and pronounces his customer's destiny.

One day a native ran by our hotel at the top of his speed, followed by a gaunt Indiaman in the garb of a policeman. Down the street they went, but the policeman rapidly gaining on the runaway at length seized him by his pigtail, compelled him to carry the bundle he had stolen back to its owner, and then dragged him away for punishment. Soon after, down the widest street came a funeral procession preceeded by a band of weird musicians playing upon their instruments, which sounded as though each man was playing a different tune as his fancy dictated. Close behind them came people carrying food and ornaments to be left at the tomb as is the custom, that the deceased may not fare badly before he becomes ac-

A POLICEMAN AND HIS VICTIM.

quainted in the next world. The coffin was made of two hollow logs, which, slung on poles, was borne along by four men on foot. Then came the hired mourners dressed all in white. What a noise they made! I believe one good healthy Chinese can make more discord on a gong than any hotel waiter ever dreamed of. The only cheerful thing about the procession was the ringing of the bells, which was kept up incessantly by boys who seemed striving to drown all the other performers.

Just outside the city away from its noisy turmoil is another —the City of the Dead. The ostentatious display of wealth in every direction, contrasts strangely with the oppressive silence that is broken only by our echoing footsteps as we wander from house to house paying our respects to the mute occupants, who, deaf alike to our curiosity or compliments, sleep on undisturbed. As the lengthened shadows of declining day creep across this chamber of the tomb in which we are standing—a tomb more beautiful than all the rest—a vague sense of terror comes over us. On a raised platform

12

covered with an embroidered velvet robe rests the coffin of a high Mandarin. With an appropriateness suggestive of his bloody career, the trappings of this dispenser of Chinese justice are all red. Cruel, unrelenting and purse-proud, there came an hour when neither wealth, pride, or power availed him; custom, and family pride for a little longer maintain this empty show of power, but it is only a parody on life and soon another lifeless body will thrust him from his hollow throne.

We went to a wedding, and saw the presents which the bride was to receive; there was a substantial look about them which was refreshing. They consisted of pieces of household furniture, baskets of ducks and geese, and two pigs. We moralized considerably over the ostentatious display; but our landlord told us that most of the presents were hired or borrowed for the occasion. A man when he marries a wife in China takes her sight unseen, for he never sees her until after she is brought home to his house in a covered sedan chair.

This is the time of year for religious processions from Canton, and we are frequently drawn by curiosity to look over the railing of our hotel veranda as they pass, and watch them as long as they are in sight. We do not understand them; and doubt very much if any earthly being does—not even the Chinese themselves. Here comes one! It is late in the morning, yet some in front are bearing torches. Now comes their hideous music. Following, are parties carrying images, such as dragons, scorpions, lions, serpents and gods, while behind them are others dressed in strange uniforms, hand in hand, keeping step, noticing nothing, but appearing downcast and looking toward the ground. In the rear are carts containing little pale-faced girls, with each standing on one leg—the other one being tied up so that it cannot be seen. Thus they stand the livelong day, and at night they are completely exhausted.

Our stay at Hong Kong was full of interest, and our landlord, an American, did everything possible to make it pleasant for us. The hotel was run in the European style, though somewhat modified to suit the Chinese taste. At meals we had seven or eight courses of dishes, including two or three plates of soup. The waiters, and those who pulled the great fan that hung from the ceiling over the table, and the servants who blacked our boots in the morning before we were up, were all natives. As their labor was cheap, they were numerous about the hotel; one to do this, and another that, without our being charged extra for services as we were in Europe. Still our bills in Hong Kong were, upon the whole, larger than they were either in Europe or America, as the vegetables which suited our taste were scarce, and much of the flour was brought from San Francisco.

The Chinese restaurants were simple and primitive beyond anything we had ever seen. Here and there along the sidewalks were Chinamen with little fires kindled, upon which they were boiling kettles of soup, and occasionally dropping therein something which resembled small apple dumplings. Around these restaurants were the guests; each one received a bowl of soup or a dish of the dumplings, and ate in a standing posture or while squatting upon the ground like a monkey. Sometimes little rolls of sweet cakes might also be bought at the more stylish of these establishments. We purchased some of the cakes, out of curiosity, and tried to eat them; but they had a sickening sweetish taste which we could not appreciate. The soups and dumplings we were not brave enough to try, but we had the audacity on a certain occasion to take a meal at a Chinese hotel. It is seldom you find these hotels anything else than mean and dirty, and the one we patronized was no exception to the general rule.

The dining table was set with two or three small plates and saucers for each guests, while other delicate dishes of China-ware were scattered here and there over the table; each guest was also furnished with a "China spoon," and a pair of "chop sticks." These sticks were slim and round, and generally six or seven inches in length, and took the place of knives and forks. Of course our tea cups were filled with tea, as this article is universally used, the tea-plant ranking first in importance of all the products of China. We were fully supplied with rice, this article ranking next in importance to tea; it is to the Chinaman what bread is to the American—in fact many almost live on it, at a cost of not more than five or six cents per day. The Chinese eat rice with their chop sticks with the greatest ease; but we made bungling work of it. Then something else was brought in.

No person except the cook could tell what it was, as he, by grating, or hashing, or rendering into soup, nearly always disguises the original shape of the eatables—especially meats. All we could tell was, that it resembled a slimy and glutinous soup. For this kind of soup they beat the world; and as it is generally made from sea-weeds of all descriptions, blubber fish, the roots and tender shoots of plants, bird-nests, insects etc, we didn't know exactly whether it would be safe to try it or not. It tasted about as might be expected from its looks; but we ate it all, and could not even then decide whether we liked it or not.

After finishing the soup we were ready for something else, and a bowlful of what might be hash was brought in and passed around. The guests dove into it with their chop sticks, and we finally managed to get a little onto our plates. What was it? It could not be beef, for this is never eaten by the Chinese. It did not look like pork, although this is consumed in great quantities; nor did it look like fowl, notwithstanding poultry is their favorite meat; nor fish, yet many almost live upon this article of food. Tortoise, turtles, and frogs are frequently cooked, but we were not so well acquainted with those kinds of meat. We knew snakes, puppies, cats and rats are sometimes eaten, but hoped it was not any of these. We must not judge by appearances however, for that would throw us out of our Chinese dinner, as it looked as much like dog meat as any thing else.

A taste however satisfied us that we did not want any more; and at the same moment Caleb, staring at his spoon, declared that he had found traces of a defunct puppy. On looking at the mysterious "fossil" I became of the same opinion, and was incited to a closer inspection of my own dish, which resulted in the discovery of an eye-lash of a rat. One seldom sees Caleb angry, but this was too much for his serenity. His eye kindled; blood shot through his cheeks, and he exclaimed:—

"It's a mean dirty swindle! I shall have my revenge on these heathens yet!"

They all stared at us, but we jumped up and walked toward

OUR FIRST RAT-SOUP.

the cashier, who was astounded and frightened, and seemed anxious to run away. Throwing a few coins down before him, I shouted:—

"Take them, and run your rat shanty into the ground!"

As we walked out, a dozen pig-tails collected around our dishes to see what had so mysteriously wrought upon the feelings of the "foreign devils" as they called us, and in fact call all foreigners. For some time this dinner haunted us; and I think it must have been a full week before Caleb prayed again for the "heathen Chinese."

Our American host informed us that had we remained to finish our dinner there would have been twelve or fifteen changes of food, all similar in appearance, generally insipid to our taste, but with only a few repulsive dishes.

CHAPTER XXI.

UP THE CANTON RIVER.

AS we steamed away from the British harbor of Hong Kong for the vast city of Canton, my blood naturally ran cold upon discovering that we constituted two of the four Europeans aboard. We glanced with suspicions at the hundreds of Chinamen huddled around on the floor gambling for small iron coins. "Will not they, imagining that we have gold, conspire against us and divide the spoil?" I did not say it aloud, but thought it.

Soon however our attention was drawn to a fellow on the lower deck pillowing his head on a bundle of hay. Accidentally, as it seemed to us, his cranium slipped from the bundle which, thereupon, rolled overboard into the water. The patient Chinaman endured his loss by meekly replacing it with another. By and by this suffered the same fate as the former one. Caleb suggested that had this Celestial possessed any inventive genius he would have made it fast with his pigtail. Finally, upon his loosing a third bundle, we concluded he was softening the hay for greens. But I confess that secretly I did not believe in this supposition, as I had never seen a Chinese horse, and consequently *horse greens* could be of no earthly use;—besides we observed that a boat happened along and picked up each bundle before it had time to soak much. We had heard of opium smuggling, and naturally formed an opinion. As the principal officers of the steamer were Europeans, of course they did not see the trick. The sale of opium was increased, and the Chinese government was minus the duty—that was all.

Soon after this another European came aboard our vessel. He had been in China so long that every other word he used had lost all traces of the English ring. We consoled ourselves with the idea that our random responses to his questions were as unintelligible to him. However, after great difficulty we comprehended that he was a Chinese detective employed by that government to board all vessels passing these waters. It struck us that were there five hundred such detective offi-

OPIUM SMUGGLING.

cers, smugglers might hide their boats among the numberless islands that crowded both the open sea and the mouth of the Canton river. We seemed to be sailing among mountain peaks projecting boldly from the water, yet under terrace cultivation.

Our fears of the native passengers subsided as we steamed up the river, past fort after fort, and village after village,—walled cities in fact—and beheld the cannons dismounted, and the walls more or less broken down, during a former unpleasantness, by shots from the European gunboats. The whole of the interior of the forts was exposed to view, for instead of the walls crowning the summits of the hills they were bravely built along the bottom, so that the retreat of the inmates when attacked had been rendered impossible owing to the steep banks behind them. The English and

French troops went round to the rear of the fortifications and rolled stones down upon the heads of the innocent inmates, who had never thought of this device and considered it a dishonest trick. "Inglis fits no far; he snaks round on rere an' hurl rock an' shell onto us back!"

The principal object of the English, especially in destroying these forts, was a disreputable one, namely, the flooding of China with their opium from India. As early as 1793, an embassy from England was kindly received at Pekin; but on account of its efforts to introduce opium, another embassy which was sent in 1816 was not admitted into the presence of the emperor. Afterward, severe prohibitory laws were enacted against the use of opium. This exasperated the British who then tried to frighten the Chinese by certain military demonstrations in Canton, which were however without effect.

At intervals ever since they have continued these demonstrations, and at times have even bombarded forts. Occasionally they have gained some advantages, and in 1842 the island of Hong Kong was ceded to them. In 1856, a crew of Chinese who were carrying on the smuggling business under the British flag, were captured by the Chinese authorities at Canton. The British demanded restitution, which was haughtily refused. The English resorted to force, and were joined by the French as an ally. The Americans in Chinese waters, to the surprise of many, were rather inclined to take part against the natives. About this time an American ship was fired into, probably through mistake, and at once the United States frigate under Commodore Armstrong bombarded and captured four forts with numerous guns below Canton; but it is only fair to state that this act was not approved of by our government. The English by bombardment destroyed the principal government buildings at Canton, and gained some advantages; but in the latter part of the year the Chinese populace made a demonstration, and many Englishmen fell victims to their wrath.

Early in 1857, the English destroyed a squadron of Chinese

junks, and in September the Chinese government declared war against her enemy. Upon this the English, with France as an ally, pushed forward more vigorously than ever. Fort after fort was taken. The Chinese sank thousands of sampans loaded with stones to check the progress of the gunboats, but on they pushed until opposite Canton, which soon surrendered, although the gunboats were few in number, and Canton was much larger than New York, and surrounded by a wall many feet thick. Since that time the Chinese have thought it useless to defend these dismantled forts along the river.

After capturing Canton the invading forces threatened Pekin itself, and toward the middle of 1858 approached to within a few miles of that great city. The emperor becoming alarmed entered into a treaty respecting opium,—thus legalizing suicide, and paying the other side for it

Why will a thousand Chinamen permit one European to rule over them? Some answer, they are weak and feeble; but a couple will carry an European through a town at a speed faster than he can carry himself. Is that feebleness? Others say they are cowardly; I think so too, but could never fully understand why in a quarrel they will bravely face each other with the most deadly weapons. The secret of the matter is, I believe, they have no self respect. I have frequently read that they are proud; but it seems to be in the sense that a dog is at times proud. The masses have been so accustomed to that old Confucian idea of childlike obedience to superiors of every grade and rank, and so cowed down into their respective spheres of littleness for thirty centuries, that their canine dignity has become a second nature above which they never aspire. We observed that if one of the natives on board our vessel happened to be trying to find out how a Chinaman would fit an European chair, he would vacate it when we approached, as meekly as though he had been shot at and missed, causing us to rather appreciate his deference than to fear his force.

The river banks were now low and level, dotted here and there by a city, between which there was not a single habitation. Vast fields minutely but imperceptibly divided and subdivided, were covered with Chinamen. Here they were bending among the rice, hoeing and pulling out the weeds; there half a dozen in a square rod were using sickles in a harvest field; while not far away were others threshing a field of grain; and still others near by more brisk than their neighbors, were setting out their second crop of rice on ground that had lately been scratched over by a wooden plow drawn by a

PLOWING LIKE HIS FATHER.

buffalo that moved just slow enough for a Chinaman unanimated by the presence of a foreigner or his half dollar. As their fathers have plowed before them for centuries back so plow they, nor sigh for innovation or improvement.

The emperor has a habit of plowing one furrow and sowing rice therein every year, to impress upon his imitative subjects the importance of agriculture which is the chief industry of China. In their slow way they elevate water in buckets over their fields, and what a Chinaman will not con-

AGRICULTURAL SCENE IN CHINA.

descend to do in the way of enriching the soil no other being can do. He is content to cultivate a small piece of ground above the graves of his ancestors, thus drawing sustenance from their bones.

THE GUARDIAN PAGODA.

The pagoda was the striking feature in every landscape, within sight of which generation after generation were born, lived, and died, happy in the thoughts that they had never been beyond its guardian vision, that they had worshiped the ancestral idols in each of its stories —especially those in the ninth or highest—and that they had looked once each day at its highest balcony, prefiguring their hope of a home in the highest heaven after numerous transmigrations and punishments here for their evil deeds.

We were now coming among beings who lived in a single spot—but that was a moving spot—I mean the occupants of sampans. In this boat, ten or fifteen feet long and three or four feet wide, the whole family resides; and many of the children never set foot on dry land until they have entered on their "teens." When they "go a courting" they simply step to another one of the myriads of boats swarming in the river. But they find no parlor nor any piano—excepting they tread on the toes of squeaking babies. The strictest economy requires every inch of space for washing—though little of that is done—cooking, eating and sleeping, especially if the family be numerous.

Near the centre of the boat there is a curved covering large enough to shelter five or six persons, but so low that the adults have to go down on their hands and knees as they enter. It was an interesting sight to witness the father and mother, and eight or ten children, gracefully seated round a dish of fish and greens, diving into it like so many greasy, yellow-faced monkeys. The baby has no cradle, but it has the floor; and a bamboo joint is tied round its waist so that it cannot sink when it falls overboard into the water. I have the impression that this buoy is attached only to the boy-babies, for girl-babies are considered as a misfortune; and "they are so unfortunate" who have them.

"ROCK ME TO SLEEP MOTHER."

Look at that mother with a child strapped upon her back, rocking it as she rows; or, when she rapidly skulls, flapping its head from side to side. Thus has she wearily toiled on from day to day and from year to year, till six children have climbed down from her shoulders to roll, tumble, frolic, and thump each other in the bow of the sampan. Were it not for her garbless and guileless progeny, there would be no epochs in her life for noting the countless number of times she has swung her monotonous oar, while her lazy husband impeded their progress by cooling his feet in the current as the old homestead floated along.

We became interested in observing the junks sailing up and down the river, with the oblique eyes of the Chinese sea-god

painted upon their unwieldy prows. But our fears were
again aroused when we saw small cannons pointing at us from
some of the decks. I had heard of the scum of society, and
now believed I had actually found it floating on these waters.
400,000 outcasts were here engaged in fitting up piratical
boats to infest the coasts of Asia; in rearing rats, mice, ducks,
dogs, and other animals for the epicures of Canton; or in floating out swarms of females to entice the inmates of European
and American vessels.

We were now approaching the great commercial city with
its ten or fifteen hundred thousand struggling souls, where,
by a foreigner, novelty and wonder are found perched upon
every object. According to travelers competent to judge,
Canton, located upon rising ground on the right bank of the
river, presents, as it is being approached, the most imposing
appearance of any city in the Orient. We could readily
believe it. What did we see? We may not know the exact
limits of a tornado, yet all recognize that something mighty
is at work; so we knew that a mighty city lay off to our northwest, although we could not apprehend exactly what it was.
Yonder among the tiled roofs, and spires, and temples, towered
two pagodas as if keeping eternal watch over the city with
its thronging myriads below.

The sampan owners were posted in regard to our anchorage in the middle of the stream and were on the lookout for
us. As our vessel neared them, a shower of lariats were flung
at different parts of the steamer, many taking effect. To these
lariats, and to each other, clung sampan after sampan, until a
fleet of these little boats was being towed along by our vessel,
and soon we all came to a halt.

Then began a crowding, and a scrambling, and a running
into each other of these small boats, each trying to get next to
our vessel to secure the passengers, which would have seemed
comical to a brigade of clowns. The runners were soon aboard,
but passed by the Chinese pilgrims to throw the full force of
their attack upon us. Their battalions seemed to have been
recruited from the gentler sex—and all seemed to be recruits

—so we were calm, though they caught us by the hands and tried to lead us away as prisoners. Some very fine Chinese ladies drive these chariots of the water; so when one with captivating looks and ways seized my hand, I said:—

"Caleb, I'm going to surrender."

As we passed over several other sampans to reach the one presided over by our fair enslaver, others of the same sex laid claim to honor of the capture by attempting to march us off by the coat-tail, and seemed likely to carry away the defences

AN ATTACK IN THE REAR.

of our modesty if they did not ourselves; and another one ran off with Caleb's fan, holding it up as a trophy of victory to lead the way. We might have respected her claims to an interest in our welfare by following her, had we been at liberty; but finding that those in the rear having made a serious breach, appeared likely to carry my last defences, I opened upon them with my heels and voice in such an energetic way that they beat a hasty retreat, and my nearly sundered coat again dropped into position.

Our original captor, the bright eyed lass, who had defended us to the extent of her power, now politely led us forward by the arms till we reached her boat, assisted us to enter it, and then rowed towards a prison for which she was acting as a sort of scout. Her father, a stupid fellow, was lounging upon his side under the canopy of the boat. He was bare-footed, bare-headed, and grasped in his sleep the opium pipe whose fumes had evidently overcome him, so that a package of fire crackers exploded at his feet would not have sufficed to arouse him. We thought at first that he had set something on fire as smoke arose around us, but on looking for the

THE GENTLE ROWER.

cause thereof we discovered an idol before which was set burning incense-sticks and some provisons.

At length our mermaid safely delivered us over to the custody of the jailor—I mean a Portuguese hotel-keeper, who tormented us awhile with his Portuguese-English largely adulterated with Chinese, and after dinner undertook the task of setting us to punching billiard balls.

CHAPTER XXII.
THE CHINESE METROPOLIS.

WHEN a man settles down among a lot of people five thousand years old, he is apt to feel so juvenile as to adopt many of their customs. I became acquainted with some foreign residents of Canton who, unwilling to appear to set themselves up as better than or different from their neighbors, had each purchased a pretty Chinese girl, and in a joint stock sort of a way boarded them all together at a hotel just out of the city. There were in all seven Chinese girls, with thirteen improvements on the maternal stock whose acquaintance with the English and Chinese languages will perhaps, at some future day, be of benefit to the commercial world. When I saw the little semi-celestials they were engaged in "playing horse," and had utilized their pigtails for the occasion. One of them climbed on my knee and called me papa!

These children were happy, their mothers were contented, and their fathers were testing a new feature of the social evil on the co-operative plan, at an annual expense, I was informed, of about one thousand dollars, exclusive of the first cost of the females which would be about five hundred dollars each. I was curious to know how these gentlemen's lawful wives liked this sort of thing; but strange to say we found on inquiring that it was a subject not often spoken of at home. So these martyrs to improvement secretly conduct their co-operative industry without the smiles of women of their own nationality. We thought it a trifle selfish in them not to tell their wives; but theirs alone be the glory and theirs the shame.

The natives of this country will generally sell you anything they possess in this world—or the next—if you offer them enough. They decoy you under the most childish pretences

IMPROVEMENTS ON THE RACE.

into their dens, and then offer the whole family to you, one by one, stating the price of each. If you are a Chinaman you cannot get a sight of the party you think of buying; but if comparatively youthful and possessed of plenty of money, a man not to the manor born has an opportunity of examining his purchase before paying for it. When a father finds one of his daughters blooming into beautiful womanhood, he hies him to the foreign quarter and beguiles some connoisseur in females to invest from three to six hundred dollars therein. This does not look quite right to us, but it may fifty centuries hence; I hope it will not any sooner.

The foreign suburbs of the city is comprised of about four

13

acres lying west of the wall, and just back from the river. A part of this is laid out in beautiful walks, and planted with flowers, shrubs and grass; the remainder is covered with fine dwellings, factories, and stores, from the roofs of which flutter the flags of several nationalities.

We noticed that American and English women do not seem to thrive well in this climate. They look unnaturally pale, yet they are seldom really sick. They seem to be too weak to walk; but perhaps the contrast between foreign and native ladies makes them appear more delicate than they are. The Chinese ladies, when in full feather, put such an extravagant amount of paint on their faces, as to completely change their

A FIRST CLASS RAT-SELLER.

appearance and make them resemble dolls. This is no fiction. I wonder they have any vermilion to export, so generally is it used and in such quantities.

One night, during the celebration of a festival, we visited a floating city, made by fastening thousands of small boats together and placing boards from one to the other. Our landlord went with us in his sampan, or we should never have ventured through the endless maze of restaurants and shops of every kind which, lighted up by lanterns of all colors, appeared more like some glittering theatrical show than real life. Here in all his glory was the rat peddler, delicately exhibiting his rodents, and soliciting customers, while impecunious celestials gazed with longing at the dainty morsels, which could be bought alive, if suspicions of their antiquity haunted the customer; but live ones were high in price, and buyers did not appear to regard decomposition as an unfavorable adjunct.

In one of the saloons where we stopped, I had some conversation of a very entertaining kind with a young woman. She spoke Chinese; I English. I was pleased with her remarks, and smiled approval; she reciprocated as far as she was able. What might have been the result of our interview, had it been prolonged, I cannot say; but just as we were in the midst of a discussion, I was invited by our guide to accompany him on a voyage of discovery further into the interior, and had to leave abruptly.

THE GUTTER SNIPE.

There was a class of persons roaming about the floating dwellings, who are worthy of mention from their saving proclivities. A Chinaman is a wonder of economy, particularly if he is poor; still there must be a waste somewhere, or how could the class I refer to exist? They are met everywhere, plying their vocation with an amusing indifference to every thing else. What in the world they found worth picking up and carrying off we could not imagine.

I shall never forget our first ride through the streets of Canton, when all was new and novel. We had procured a Chinese guide, and three chairs, with four coolies to each. We started with the guide in front; sometimes Caleb was second, but generally I was. I wanted to be in the middle, you see, so that I could show my bravery. Were we to be attacked in the front, or rear, I should be ready to assist at either end.

We were carried for hours through innumerable winding streets, only five or six feet wide and covered over at the top to keep out the hot sun. The rocky pavements were damp and slippery from the proximity of sewers. The trash, and dirt of the city with all its produce and merchandise, were carried to and fro, as in a pair of scales, upon the shoulders of men. Our chairmen continually hallooed to the noisy throng, warning them to hug the walls as we passed; and teeming myriads of people from their numberless little shops, looked out and stared at us. Pig-tailed boys pressed their way among their pig-tailed sires, and children were as ants struggling among the inmates of a bee-hive. During a whole day we never saw a human being except these half civilized Orientals. We lost our bearings entirely and almost our individual identity, and seemed to be moving in a new and strange world.

At times we dismounted from our chairs, and visited the shops near by. Or again the guide would send the chairmen off down a street without us, and then lead us along narrow foot-paths where not even the chairs could pass, to visit shops far away in the interior of a block, or round a court or under a corridor. Emerging at length, we knew not where, we always found our chairmen waiting for us at the designated place. "Out West," a cat when blindfolded, taken miles into the

A COVERED STREET OF CANTON.

woods, and turned loose, will find its way home again. These chairmen seemed to be equally sagacious.

Here and there and everywhere were bright ornaments and curious trinkets; and vast quantities of porcelain or Chinaware. We passed through buildings where were being stored millions of geese' and hens' eggs, for transportation to different parts of Asia. There were many shops where ivory, silver, and gold were carved into card-cases, boxes, images, and various strange and beautiful figures, a few of which we bought as mementoes of our visit. The most remarkable of these was an ivory ball containing eight or ten smaller ones, one inside another, and all carved from the same piece of ivory. Each of these, as far in as we could see by shaking them about, was covered with beautiful figures. It seems wonderful how these inner balls were reached to be thus touched into exquisite design.

The Chinese lacquered ware is much the same as the Japanese japanned ware. Occasionally we watched as the finishing touch was being given. When the box or other article has received numerous coats of varnish, the last few being of the finest quality so that the surface shines like a looking glass, they take a piece of paper which has been flowered and figured by the piercings of a needle-point, and placing it upon the box rub a white powder over its surface. Then with a pencil dipped in varnish, the design is run out as indicated by the powder. While this penciling is still moist, gold-dust is rubbed over to gild the figure. Finally, the whole is touched over with a light varnish, and the surface has then become exquisitely beautiful.

The Chinese weave their silks in looms, throwing the shuttle just as our own countrywomen used to do years ago; but to me it was surprising that they could do such nice work by this process. With all their manufactories and facilities the Americans and Europeans cannot equal the Chinese in the manufacture of the superior qualities of silk.

Did you ever visit a penitentiary? If so, doutless you saw criminals who were imprisoned for life, from whose countenance all the light of hope had disappeared; no more were they to enjoy the smiles of friends, or the endearments of home; nevermore to come and go at will, never more to be free. But this is a humane mode of punishment as compared with the methods adopted by the Chinese. We passed men who, as a

POKING FUN AT HIM.

punishment for stealing, were wearing the *canque*—a broad heavy board for the neck—and chained at the door where the crime had been committed; while the boys of the neighborhood amused themselves by tantalizing them—even poking sticks into their ears to make them squirm. Occasionally we saw a man undergoing the bastinado. He was dragged down upon the ground, while his countrymen piled upon him to thump and beat their victim. They seemed to look upon this as sport too, and engaged in it with a joy akin to that of gambling.

At the police-stations and prisons we noticed several men in cages. Sometimes their heads were stuck through the sides or out at the top in such a manner as to oblige them to stand day after day on tip toe. In other instances they were fixed in a bending position, unable either to kneel or to stand upright. We even saw one victim hanging by his feet with blood-shot eyes and distorted features. Upon his noticing us he seemed to revive. We could see it in the expression of his features, though we could not understand his words. He

"THEY SEEMED TO LIKE IT."

had entreated his countrymen in vain ; now he thought that we might be able to assist him. We could not endure his entreaties, and as we withdrew he shrieked with agony and despair till our blood ran cold.

Through a cheerless street we went to visit the place of public executions. It was a dark gloomy spot surrounded by a stone wall, where the heads of men are severed by dozens at a time. Often delays are made that a number may be executed together.

During our stay in Canton we ascended the wall in the rear of the city, to obtain a view. At the top, and on the outer edge of the wall, was a rim, five or six feet high, and about the same in thickness, pierced with port-holes for small cannon, while inside of this rim was a fine promenade. From this elevation the two great pagodas, the spires of the temple, and the red flag-poles in front of the mandarins' dwellings, showed to good advantage; but it was almost impossible to distinguish the streets, as they were narrow, and covered over so as to entirely conceal from view the crowds who thronged them.

From the highest part of the wall the country northward presented a scene of beauty and novelty. It was a far-reaching plain covered with broad fields of rice, studded with groves of small trees and innumerable villages, and silvered by winding streams, which were tapped at short intervals by countless irrigating channels, forming a net-work of water communication unequaled in any other country. Along these watery veins were thousands of junks, whose gilded masts seemed to walk through the land, and were mingled with the spires of the pagodas that stood, one beyond another, reaching to the horizon.

It was toward evening when we stood upon the wall, and the views of the city and the world around were so interesting that we tarried long, almost forgetting that we were several miles from our hotel. As we passed down through the walled city, night came on, and darkness prevailed in the narrow streets. The dim lights glared into the faces of those within the shops, and we passed by ghostly forms between the close walls. We knew that Cantonese had murdered many a European; and that of all the Chinese, they probably were the most hostile to foreigners: and the thought did not reassure us.

Our passage through the city was very tedious, and seemed to occupy many hours; we hurried our men, as we knew it was the custom to close the gates at 8 o'clock. It was now past that hour, and half an hour more elapsed before we reached the grim iron barrier that prevented our egress. The gates were closed, and we were locked in.

We were most anxious to get out, and urged the guide to do his best to pass us through the gates, for we feared that violence would be offered to us if we remained where we

"THE GRIM IRON BARRIER PREVENTED OUR EGRESS."

were long, as no European is allowed to remain within the walls after the gates are closed for the night. The guide went to find the gate-keeper, while the crowd stood staring at us. We almost expected every moment that they would fall upon us, if only for the sake of our money, which would have afforded them a fine feast for a few days. Before long, however, relief came. The gaping throng parted—our guide had returned; and, better still, he had found the gate-keeper, who after a little persuasion opened the gate, and we passed through, glad to leave behind us those gloomy walls and the ugly crowd within them.

CHAPTER XXIII.
AMONG THE "GODS."

ONE morning, while wandering along one of the principal streets, we noticed that a great crowd of people had gathered round a certain large box, in which they seemed to take great interest. The scene reminded us of election day in America; so we formed in line and advanced towards the box, but on drawing near were startled to behold within it what appeared to be a corpse. Looking closer we saw that the creature—whatever it was—was alive, for its glaring eyes were fixed upon us with a horrible expression, and riveted us to the spot. The idea at once flashed across our minds—the inmate of that box was a criminal, or had offended the authorities. He might be innocent, but we could not help him; so with a word of pity we passed on.

Returning later in the day we found that the throng had vastly increased; and soon after our arrival the padlocks were unloosed from the box, and the man removed from the iron spikes which had penetrated and lacerated his swollen feet. At this sight the feelings of the crowd became intense, and the box was broken up and sold as relics; pieces of the bottom, in which were the nails, bringing large prices.

We took special pains to inquire into the meaning of this scene, and were informed that a priest from some distant city, having been unsuccessful in raising money to build a temple, had a few days since shut himself up in this manner as a means of procuring the funds.

On the whole we were not favorably impressed with the

religion of the Chinese. The scorpions, dragons, serpents, lions, and other animals, ranged upon the curving eaves and roofs of their temples, awakened a feeling of horror rather than devotion; while the burning of incense-sticks before scores of idols in the darkness within cast gloom over the mind, which was deepened by the monotonous music and the continual beating of tom-toms by the priests as they recited their incantations. At times these priests wandered vacantly about in their long gowns, above which projected as many closely-shaven heads, on which grew not a single hair; indeed their principal property seemed to consist of razors.

THE MYSTERIOUS BOX.

They manifested great interest in showing us that they were not too poor to own an alms-bowl; but they did not importune us for a donation, as almsgiving is considered to be a greater blessing to the giver than to the recipient. I imagined that they passed their lives in celibacy, as they were all well-provided with needle and thread as if for an emergency.

The most cheerful sight we witnessed was the bringing in, by the patrons of the temple, of some roast fowls and pigs, which were waved before the idols by the priest. A very small part thereof was then burnt as incense; and the remainder was set before the idols to satisfy their appetites until the priests became hungry, which they were before long; for as we passed out, we noticed them in an adjoining room enjoying a feast of fat things.

This absurd farce on the part of the priests was not so

ridiculous as a custom that the people have of burning before the statues and pictures or at the tombs of their ancestors, paper representations of hats, shoes, garments, money etc.,

FRIEST WITH ALMS-BOWL.

which they purchase at a high price from the priests, imagining that their ancestors, who are now gods, will kindly give them credit for the real articles. We noticed, too, that by far the larger number of sacrifices were offered to the gods of evil, in the hope of appeasing their wrath; the favor of the good gods being considered as a matter of course. The following is an example:—

Upon inquiring the reason why a number of people were burning incense on the pathway, we were informed that on that spot somebody had tripped his foot and had smashed a basket of eggs. At once the place where the eggs were broken was supposed to be the abode of an evil spirit whose wrath must be appeased by incense or even by sacrifice. We suggested that the unlucky owner of the eggs should have offered a basket of those articles in a stale condition as the most appropriate incense for an evil spirit. But a Chinaman would never do that, or anything else, unless his ancestors had done exactly the same thing. Those ancestors were great people according to their ideas. In the temples we saw the bronze statues of many of them; they were fifteen or twenty feet high, and sitting at that. Their size was in proportion to their position in life and the estimation in which their descendants held them.

We observed a Chinaman approaching one of these images upon all fours, rapping his shaved head frequently against the floor. This particular ancestor had rather a long nose, and carried his trunk with him; he was, in fact, a facsimile of a Buddhist god.

The Chinese religion is a little mixed. Ancestral worship and the Buddhism of India are so joined that it is difficult to tell whether it is one of his ancestors or an elephant that a Chinaman worships. The white elephant is very sacred to Buddhists. They believe that innumerable Buddhas have appeared from time to time to save the world, and that finally Buddha Sakyamuni descended from heaven as a white elephant in the sixth century B. C., took the form of a man, and at once solemnly proclaimed his mission.

A LONG-NOSED ANCESTOR.

Buddhism in India arose in opposition to the much older worship of Brahma, which divided the people into castes—a system which at that time had become almost intolerable. Many bloody struggles resulted from the introduction of the new religion—Buddhism—which, however, continued to gain the ascendancy until it became the established religion of the country. Alexander's invasion of the far East gave a great impulse to its spread, and about A. D. 66, it was introduced into China, and by degrees spread over the Orient, carrying the civilization of India to many a savage tribe, and among others to the inhabitants of the island of Japan. Buddhism did much towards abolishing caste; and in this sense, at least, it proved itself a blessing wherever it was introduced.

But by-and-by there came a reaction, and in the seventh century of the Christian era, Buddhism was rapidly losing ground in India, and many of its temples were crumbling to ruin. A century later, and it was almost entirely exterminated, and the laws of caste under Brahmanism re-enacted more rigorously than ever; but in the Island of Ceylon, lying immediately to the south of India, Buddhism has maintained a strong hold even to this day.

The essence of Buddha's teachings was that all is deception and illusion save spirit and mind; and that the final object of man is to be delivered from all pain and illusion. This is to be gradually accomplished by dispelling every passion from the mind—even the desire of existence. After death, this refining process will give the soul birth in a more refined body, and by continuing to tame the passions and by contemplating the good and true in the vastness of the abstract, the soul will be finally delivered from illusion, and from all further change by being merged into God.

Among the Chinese, swine are held sacred, and worshiped. In an enclosure connected with a temple we saw two large white sows, kept for that purpose. They were fat, clean and thrifty, and on the whole, seemed to be respectable beasts. They were also intelligent; for when the Chinese bowed and made signs of worship before them, sometimes even going down on all fours, the animals grunted as if in approval.

When a boy in the wilds of Western Iowa, I knew a swine of the gentle sex that would have stood no such tomfoolery. I used to plague her sometimes when she was in her pen, but she never seemed to like it. On one occasion while she was asleep, I reached through a crack of the pen and pulled the tail of one of her offspring until it squealed. As she sprang up and towards me, I withdrew my hand, but that didn't satisfy her. She reared up against the side of the pen, and, giving a terrible spring, was over and after me before I could get far away in the direction of the house. She gained on me, and was right at my heels, when just in the nick of time I saved myself by jumping into a friendly wagon which stood in my path. Baffled thus, she stood gazing at me for a while with frothing mouth and standing bristles, and then trotted peaceably back toward her pen. The moral was not lost on me, and I never again ventured to pull the tails of the pigs.

A PIG-TAIL EXCITMENT.

In one costly temple, entered only by the wealthy, the chief statue was an impersonation of longevity. Round the altar of this gigantic god were ranged numerous votive offerings inscribed with the names of wealthy citizens, who had placed these costly tokens here to amuse the god and secure to themselves long life. Our Chinese guide politely bowed, smiled, and courteously wished us the blessings of this god and a safe return home. He was a sensible man and a kind one too; for he told our fortunes though we had made no donation either to him or "Longevity." Having taken a box into his hands containing a score or more of nicely-painted sticks, he shook them until one fell upon the floor. This he took to a priest who, glancing at the characters painted upon it, referred to the similar figures in his Chinese bible, and thus read our fortunes, which were duly translated to us by the guide.

TEMPLE OF THE DRAGON.

A man is always considered fortunate when he buys one of these oracular boxes. On the pavement opposite our hotel sat a man engaged in selling them, and ever into our window came the dull dead sound of the pegs striking against the sides of the box as he shook it to attract customers. Occasionally some one, tired of life, or out of employment, halted to have his fortune told, imagining probably that the fates could make it no worse; at any rate he was willing to risk a penny on the chances.

We visited the "Temple of the Dragon;" before its horrible image, parties entering into mutual contracts burn copies of their agreements seasoned with incense. Chinamen, like other men, are sharper in business than in anything else; so they have a living snake as a witness, lest the dragon with eyes of bronze should fail to see their engagements, or prove forgetful of them. They are not always very polite to their gods; for on one occasion when there was a great drought, they dragged the god of agriculture out of his temple and over the parched sands, in hopes of moving his conscience; but to no purpose—their god was as helpless as themselves.

SPECIMENS OF CHINESE ARCHITECTURE.

CHAPTER XXIV.

THE EMPIRE OF THE CELESTIALS.

THE Chinese Empire comprises nearly one-tenth of the habitable globe and supports two-fifths of its entire population. The surface of the country is varied, being generally rough and uneven near the coast, but soon becoming more level inland. Towards the interior it again becomes uneven, and finally rises in the background into the snow-capped peaks of the Yun-ling. Timber is scarce in the more populated districts, as large forests are found only on the mountains; yet the trash picked up here and there, together with the groves that are grown, and the beds of coal that are worked in many places in the empire, afford the people a sufficiency of fuel.

Some of the finest rivers in the world are to be found in this country. These afford good facilities for inland navigation, and the same may be said of the numberless canals that are used for the double purpose of navigation and irrigation. No people understand the excavation and working of artificial canals and irrigation better than the Chinese. The Imperial Canal,—the largest in the world—connects Pekin, the capital, with Hang-chow; it is seven hundred miles long and from two hundred to a thousand feet wide. In some places it is carried over low regions between thick and high embankments. The tow-path is also carried over many smaller canals, by means of bridges; and from these smaller canals extend numerous arms or branches, until at length they form a complete net-work of navigable highways, or of smaller streams for the purposes of irrigation.

The inland commerce of China is immense. It is carried on almost exclusively by means of this great net-work of canals, and is supposed by some to equal that of all other nations combined. Her foreign commerce, although insignificant in comparison to her inland, amounts to about one hundred million dollars annually, and might be many times increased were not the exclusive policy so pertinaciously clung to by the government. The principal articles of export are tea, silk, both manufactured and raw, nankeen cloth, and mats; besides some minor articles such as fans, fire-crackers, sea-shells, gold-leaf, etc. Her principal imports are opium, rice, raw cotton, cotton fabrics, tin, lead, and iron; besides jewels from India, and birds' nests, as an article of food, from the Indian Archipelago.

The Mexican silver dollar is the principal coin of China, and they seldom pass out of the country when once there, it being the policy of the government to retain them. To this end they are bored full of peculiar holes, which are a kind of official stamp. No paper-money is in circulation, and they have no gold or silver coin of their own. The gold and silver coins of England and America are current, and all kinds of money can be exchanged at the offices of the principal brokers. They have a brass coin of their own, the value of which is about one-eighth of a cent. It has a large square hole in the centre that it may be strung on a grass string and carried on the arm.

The form of government is monarchical, yet strongly tinctured with the despotic. It is true the emperor is bound by certain ancient laws and customs which he could not disregard without danger, nor could he totally disregard the remonstrances of his ministers; yet his subjects must bow themselves, ko-tow, or knock their heads nine times against the ground, and literally creep in the dust whenever they approach him. When he appears in public he is preceded by two thousand constables, and surrounded by a large body-guard of five thousand chamberlains—eunuchs, of course—who are connected with his palace. It is customary for the emperor to have one legitimate wife, two inferior ones, and as many concubines as he may desire. The retinue of concubines belonging to the present incumbent is not yet very great. He succeeded his father in 1861, when a small boy; was married in 1872, and passed from under the united guardianship of his uncle, mother and aunt, on the 1st of February, 1873.

BEFORE THE THRONE.

The emperor selects from among the sons of his three wives the person he desires to be his successor, but keeps his choice a secret until his death, lest the favored one should become reckless, and unworthy. The other descendants of the emperor fall lower and lower in the scale of nobility until the seventh. Then they lose the title of prince, are classed among the masses at large, and of course are not supported by the national revenues. However, there are many offices to be filled, and every subject may become a candidate for office. There is no place where education does so much for one as in

China. Schools are established throughout the empire, and the people as a whole are educated sufficiently to read, write and keep their own accounts. In fact, many are very quick at figures. Books are general among all classes, and many of the wealthy have very fine libraries. The press is to a great extent free, but the publication of licentious matter is severely punished.

The officers of the empire are called mandarins, and are divided into the civil and the military. The official status of the former is marked by wearing in the hat one or more peacock's feathers, according to rank, and that of the latter by a ruby or sapphire on the top of the cap.

A MANDARIN.

The empire is divided into eighteen provinces, each having a particular administration, army, and finance. Each of these provinces is sub-divided into districts containing an average of two millions of inhabitants. These districts are again divided into departments, and the department into circles. The provinces are ruled by governor-generals, appointed for three years by a board under the direction of the emperor, who examine the qualification of applicants for office. The power of these governor-generals is checked by a cabinet. The various minor officers are appointed in a similar way, even down to the mayors of the principal cities; but the officers of the small cities and towns are elected by the people. The cabinet of the emperor, consists of four chancellors, two assistants, aided by the most renowned scholars, and attended by about five hundred clerks. The emperor himself takes an active part in the labors of this cabinet, his edicts being published in the *Pekin Gazette*. The laws of China are collected into a code which is revised every five years. It seems to be of little importance whether these laws are good or bad, as the various officers often overreach their authority. Edicts by the provincial officers are frequently issued upon matters already provided for by law, and cases of collusion of the police with thieves, and corrupt judges, are not rare; in fact, a large proportion of the men in authority make their offices pay double or treble its nominal value, by some underhanded means. In these things the Chinese officials act much like many of our own men in authority at home.

The military organization of China consists of about 600,000 men, besides about 200,000 Tartars who are at the disposal of the government. The whole 800,000, however, would not withstand the charge of a few thousand disciplined troops, for the Chinese are great cowards, and their army is little better than a mob. In times of peace the soldiers are quartered here and there in cities and villages; or they farm little lots of government land, and make a living as best they can. They are poorly paid; the foot soldiers only receiving from three to four dollars per month, and the horsemen a little over five dollars. Their arms are of the most primitive kind. The infantry carry clumsy matchlocks, spears, bows, swords, and bucklers. The cavalry are armed with shields, helmets, bows and knives. The cannon of the Chinese are also very inefficient, but they are beginning to cast heavier guns, and are also making improvements in their other weapons.

The Tartars, a warlike race, inhabit the country to the north of China-Proper. Their incursions in former times were so frequent, that the Chinese adopted the expedient of building along their entire northern frontier that enormous wall which has become one of the wonders of the world. It is fifteen hundred miles long, and thirty feet high, and wide enough to admit of six horsemen riding upon it abreast. Brick towers, forty feet high, are erected at intervals, and are well-defended by native soldiers. But this wall is no longer of any service; for in the year 1279, after repeated efforts, the Tartars succeeded in placing their own king upon the Chinese throne, and they maintained possession of the empire until A. D. 1368, when their power was subverted by a revolution headed by a Buddhist monk of low birth. In 1615, exasperated by the assassination of their king by the emperor of China, the Tartars took part in a civil war which was raging at that time among the Celestials. They united with the defeated party, overturned the ruling Chinese dynasty, and again, after years of internecine warfare, succeeded, in the year 1664, in making themselves masters of the empire. Since that time the nobility of China have all belonged to a foreign race, which however, even to this day, is hated by the native population.

When upon the wall near Canton, we saw some of the Tartar soldiers, and our guide turned away in derision. We noticed that they were of a lighter complexion than the Chinese, had more beard, and their countenances bespoke greater intellectual powers.

From the very first the policy of China was an exclusive one, but there has been some excuse therefor. In Europe, it has been impossible for any one country to avoid holding commercial relations with the other. Wars have also been frequent between nation and nation; and with them the improvements and more advanced thoughts of the one have been spread over the other. But in China, from the vastness of her territory, war, excepting the war with the Tartars, has been mostly intestine. This vastness of territory, where so many people are united under one system of government, has prevented China from seeing the advantage of intercourse with other nations, and has made her feel proud of her position; especially so, as many of the improvements of modern times, such as the compass, porcelain, paper, gunpowder and printing, were crudely used by the Chinese many centuries before they were known to Europe.

Toward the middle of the sixteenth century the Portuguese began trading a little with the neighboring Chinese islands; and in 1583, the Italian Jesuit Riccé was permitted to preach Christianity to the Chinese, and by partially conforming to the doctrines of Confucius, he succeeded in making many converts. A little later the Spanish and the Dutch sent a few trading vessels to China, but met with poor success. In 1653 the Russians were permitted to trade in the northern part of the empire. In 1671 the emperor had the whole of his territories surveyed and mapped out by Europeans.

At different times, treaties have been made in respect to the toleration of missionaries, and the opening of commercial intercourse with western nations; but on account of the hatred with which foreigners have been hitherto regarded, these treaties have remained little more than a dead letter, until within the last few years. Nor was the hatred of the Chinese altogether without cause. The importation of coolies into the island of Cuba and a portion of South America, especially Peru, was a disgrace to every nation engaged in that infamous traffic. Foreign agents, to secure their end, have scattered abroad by the thousand hand-bills in the Chinese language; have gone to the opium and gambling-houses, and every other place accessible, seeking out those that were in debt, and in fact, any that could be duped; they have offered such unfortunates a few dollars to begin with, and so much per month for a certain number of years after arriving in the country to which they were to be taken.

When a gang was ready, they were packed in such close vessels, that many have died on the voyage, and others have committed suicide. Upon arriving at their destination they have been bought and sold, and treated worse than slaves, and at the end of the term of years for which they were hired, it was pretended that they were in debt to their owners, and must work out a new term. Thus they were kept in perpetual bondage, till they cursed the day on which they were born. Who can wonder that the Chinese hated their

Christian brethren? However, by the interference of their own government, and those of other nations, the coolie traffic, in this form, has now almost entirely ceased.

By the treaties of 1858, the Chinese government agreed, in substance, to allow foreigners to travel in China, to recognize resident consuls accredited by foreign powers, to tolerate Christianity, to protect Christian missionaries, and to open four more ports to foreign shipping. Since that time, these treaties have been pretty faithfully observed, various amendments have been made, and several other ports have been opened to commerce.

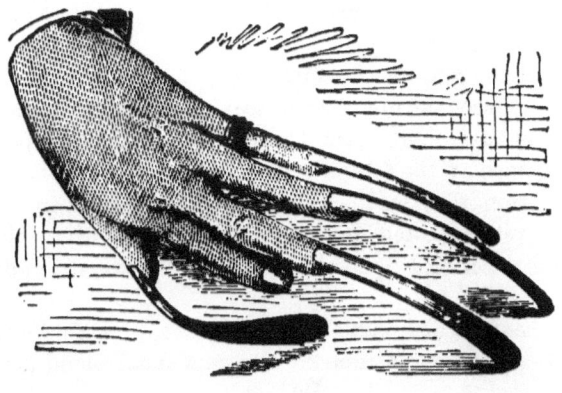

CHAPTER XXV.

OVER THE CHINA SEA TO FARTHER INDIA.

IN due course of time we paid a visit to Macao. This is a Portuguese city, situated near the mouth of the Canton River, at the extremity of an island ceded to the Portuguese many years ago as a reward for their assistance in expelling a Japanese pirate.

There are a few fine buildings in Macao, but the greater part of the city is built in the Oriental style; about fifty-five thousand of the inhabitants are Chinese or half-breeds, and the other ten thousand though mostly Portuguese represent various nationalities.

We were now restless for new scenes and new adventures, and again set out on our travels. There were two steamship lines from China to Europe, owned respectively by the English and French. For the sake of variety we chose to patronize the French line, and took passage on one of their magnificent steamers.

The signal-gun announcing our departure from Hong-Kong was fired at noon, and, leaving the city behind, we were soon steaming down the channel, and out upon the wide expanse of the China Sea. It was not without some apprehension that we had embarked, for we were to sail through waters visited at that time of year with typhoons, and then to set foot upon shores unhealthy and often deadly to foreigners.

For twenty-four hours the uneven coast of China was still in sight, and now and then we passed a small island near the mainland. The sea ran high, and the vessel rolled so badly, that although most of the passengers had been at sea before, several of them became sea-sick, and even Caleb's dinners did not agree with him.

We soon began to feel at home, and wandered about, prying into this, and that, as though we were the exclusive owners of the vessel and all that it contained. We were not long in discovering that there were five grades of passengers on board. The accommodations of the first and second classes were about the same. No reasonable man could complain of either. The great promenade on the deck, running the entire width of the vessel and from the stern to midship, was canvased overhead to keep out the sun, and was occupied alike by these two classes. The French language preponderated in the first; the English in the second; and although there was more of sparkle, gesture and smile among the former, yet as regards intelligence, good manners, and good dress, the second-class passengers (among whom were Caleb and myself) were fully their equal.

The accommodations of the third-class passengers were greatly inferior to those of the first and second; and when on deck they occupied that part of the vessel round and near the hot smoke-stacks. Among these were Portuguese—who took any kind of passage to save a little, in order that they might more effectually flaunt their ribbons and sparkle their jewelry when they reached their journey's end; Germans with their boisterous laugh, rough language and slouchy appearance; and a few Dutchmen, fat and jolly, with pipes forever in their mouths.

Chinamen, Indiamen, a few Portuguese, a Dutchman or two, and some French soldiers going to Saigon, made up the fourth and fifth classes, huddled away at the prow of the vessel, there to subsist on what was left after the other passengers had been fed. They passed their time away among monkeys and tropical birds, and boxes containing fowls and other live stock to be killed on the voyage. As we went steaming along, the music of the geese and ducks was mingled with the

grunt of the swine, the low of the buffalo, the chattering of
the monkeys, the screeching of birds, and the laugh and clatter of the different races of men.

THIRD-CLASS PASSENGERS AT DINNER.

As we wandered about the vessel, from time to time, some
things struck us more particularly than others. About the
hot boilers, among the third-class passengers, sat from day to
day, a couple of missionaries with their families. All were
dressed to a great extent after the Chinese style, excepting
that the pig-tail was not worn. The parents were always
busy, either talking, reading, writing, sewing, or hearing the
children recite their lessons. They were returning to England, there to spend the remainder of their days.

Not very far from the missionaries sat a young German
lady, who was nicely dressed and very pretty. I marveled
that such a fine-looking lady should take a third-class passage.
Caleb felt rather sorry for her, as she sat in the heat without
any lady-friend with whom to converse in her own language,

and he several times expressed a wish that he understood German, so that he might talk with her. I noticed too that she frequently glanced at him as though his acquaintance would be very agreeable to her. Caleb was a religious young man, and perhaps she would be glad to talk upon some religious subject—it might be that she was a missionary. His sympathies for the lonely lady were fully aroused, and there is no telling what he might have done had not an acquaintance of ours informed him that she was not a missionary, but was bound for Saigon, (the place where we were next to stop) and that her moral character was not quite so good as it might have been. Caleb thereupon concluded not to learn the German language on ship-board, but he ever afterward insisted that the lady had been cruelly slandered.

STATE-ROOM VISITORS.

Among the second-class passengers were a couple of very handsome and richly-dressed French ladies, one of whom had a little dog of which she seemed to be very fond. One day as this lady was passing our state-room, while we were within, the little fellow poked his nose under the curtain in the doorway and came in to make us a call; his mistress immediately came in also—to search for him we supposed. Caleb is very polite to the ladies, so he picked up the little darling, and smiling, presented him to his fair owner. She expressed her deep gratitude in French, and then walked hesitatingly away.

Subsequently these ladies received many attentions from some of the first-class passengers. One gay young French-

"THE CAPTAIN FREQUENTLY HOVERED NEAR THEM."

man in particular was much attracted toward them, and when seated beside them on deck during fine evenings would treat them to cigarettes, which they smoked with much grace. Even the captain seemed to be wonderfully pleased with his fair passengers, and frequently hovered near them.

It is surprising how many stories of scandal circulated through our steamer. We were even told, confidentially, that these French ladies were also bound for Saigon, and that their characters were no better than was that of the lonely German girl.

On our voyage we occasionally espied a solitary vessel far out upon the waste of waters. It was like meeting a friend in a distant land. Had it been later in the season we should have seen thousands of small Chinese boats, sailing with their exports to the islands of the Indian Archipelago. As there are but two monsoons in a year, these boats only make the round voyage once in twelve months, sailing south during the latter part of the southern monsoon, and north during the early part of the northern; in this way having about half the year to remain at home.

THE BANKS OF THE SAIGON.

Early in the morning of the fourth day from Hong-Kong, land was in sight to our right; it was the coast of Farther India. Toward noon we were sailing up the Saigon River, bound for Saigon, in Anam, in a latitude of about ten degrees north of the equator. The surrounding country was very low, so that the river, as it approached the sea, divided into several branches. As we sailed along we noticed that the under brush of tropical growth was so thick as to form a dense jungle, which the eye was unable to penetrate. In many places in the midst of the jungle arose large tropical trees, among the branches of which we saw birds of rich and gaudy plumage, and monkeys jumping from limb to limb, hanging first by one paw and then by the other, or swinging by the tail.

Nearer Saigon the country was not quite so low; and to our delight the growth of bushes and trees now opened, giving us glimpses of little bamboo houses and villages, and of the people who inhabited them. Endless battalions of ducks marched along the muddy paths leading from the river to the huts. Small patches of rice, cotton, sugar-cane, indigo, and tobacco were to be seen; but they had lost their pride, if ever they had any, and agriculture, the principal pursuit of the people, seemed here to have lost all its attractions.

At length we reached Saigon, which is about fifty miles from the sea, and anchored in the middle of the stream. Looking down from the deck, we saw numerous natives in their little boats, and many others on the banks of the river.

CHAPTER XXVI.
FUN AND ADVENTURE AT SAIGON.

AS we contemplated Saigon and its surroundings from the deck of our steamer the prospect was dismal enough to cause our accustomed cheerfulness to become for a while overcast; but the jovial remarks of a good-natured acquaintance soon put our gloomy meditations to flight.

While waiting for the heat to abate before going ashore, we passed the time on deck gazing at the natives, who paddled around our vessel jabbering to the passengers, and occasionally we pelted them with oranges. Larger boats, bringing betel-nuts, stick-lac, elephant hides and bones, rhinoceros bones, etc., were also rowed to the ship, and received in return the flimsy blue cotton fabric which, when made up into loose trowsers and a sort of gown, is the dress of both men and women. The people had high cheek-bones, yellowish-brown complexions, and black bristly hair. They appeared to be abominably lazy, as they lay stretched on their backs on the bank of the river, in striking contrast to the more industrious Chinamen, whose tall pagoda, towering over the city, indicated that their numbers here were already by no means small.

Close to the shore were some fine foreign dwellings, the navy-yard, the arsenal, and the citadel; and a well-walled canal took its course inland, connecting Saigon with the Cambodia River twenty-four miles away.

Towards evening the soldiers who had disembarked from our steamer were seen drilling under the shady palms, to the sound of martial music, and things looked more inviting on shore. So just as the sun was sinking from our sight we decided to visit the city, and were accompanied by a couple of young Englishmen who were acquainted with the place. They were old chums, and called each other "Dot" and "Dillion."

The natives were on the watch for us, and as we stepped down to the water's edge, there was a crowding and pushing among the little boats to secure our patronage. Dot began to use his cane, striking two or three of them across the shoulders, and then pointed out a certain boat whose services he desired to secure; while the rest of them scrambled out of the way in a hurry. As soon as we were ashore, we secured a couple of small cabs, one pony and a native driver to each, Caleb and I riding in one, and Dot and Dillon in the other.

These two gentlemen suggested that we should take a drive through the suburbs of the city, and to this we readily agreed, little thinking what a droll adventure awaited us. We had not gone far when the two friends suddenly halted. Caleb and myself drove up; and then what an extraordinary sight met our view! From yonder huts issued scores of girls who came rushing towards us! On they came to the front cab. They gathered round Dillon first; some grabbed his hands, some his arms, some his coat-tail. As they pulled and tugged away, he swayed to and fro as a sapling in the wind. I could not conceive what their object could be, or what was the cause of all this commotion; but I subsequently learned that it was the custom of the women and girls, whose quarter of the city this was, to capture any strangers who intruded upon their domain, and to hold them in captivity until they paid ransom.

Dillon was soon taken prisoner. Then all these hungry wolves were after Dot. He was dressed from head to foot in white linen, and he continued to wield his cane to keep the horrible creatures at bay. They drew back. Again they closed up, growing bolder and bolder, until one, darting in from the rear, seized him round the waist. Others immediately followed suit, and he too was at their mercy.

They were now at liberty to attend to Caleb and myself. In a moment their eyes were upon us. "Heavens and earth! they are coming down here!" said Caleb. It was too true. By the dozen they poured down toward us! Closer and closer they came. Whither should we run? Before a second thought could enter our minds they were upon us. They

ASSAULTED BY AMAZONS.

tried to creep into our cab. We beat them off. Before we knew it they were crawling in at the rear. Caleb scampered out toward the front in such hot haste that one would have thought a tarantula was under him. There, he was stormed by others. They had almost overpowered him, when suddenly a bright thought rushed across his mind. Snatching up the driver's whip he seized one of the Amazons by the hair of the head, and the others fell back afraid. By this time a she-Hercules had caught me by the coat-collar, and was pulling the very life out of me. She leaned back, and see-sawed—I heard my coat beginning to rip, and bent forward. I looked to see the whole collar ripped asunder the next instant. Now she gave a mighty surge as one at the rear was lifting at my heels, and I came tumbling out upon the ground! It was growing serious. To be jerked about this way by a petticoat—especially such a scanty one— would never do. I scrambled up with a clenched fist; when just at the right moment came Caleb with the driver's whip. With a few vigorous strokes he scared my enemy away, and I was free. We entered our vehicle again and drove off without delay, and this ended one of the fiercest battles I ever fought with the gentle sex.

Dot and Dillon soon overtook us. We blamed them for bringing us through such a quarter of the city, knowing, as they must have done, the odd custom of the natives. They pleaded, however, that they had had the worst of it, for they had been forced to pay ransom, while we had escaped with a few scratches.

After this rare encounter, we were driven into the center of the city, and a more squalid or more repulsive looking place we had not seen in all our travels. Some of the inhabitants in the streets were selling fruit from their dirty little stands; some were sleeping, and many others though awake were doing nothing. Dogs and cats, ducks and geese, crows and buzzards, were everywhere to be met with in the streets, and about the doorways; and as darkness came on these animals, and as far as we could judge many others, made the evening hideous with their cries.

After dismissing our cabs, we took a stroll through the city on foot. The women seemed to engage in every branch of labor known to the Anamese, and we could readily believe, from appearances, that they were slaves to their husbands. We noticed every now and then a small Chinese shop, the inmates of which looked like kings in their palaces in comparison with those around them.

But before we expected it the lights of the city began to

disappear, and we started at once for the vessel. It was not long before we found ourselves in a dark street which had no outlet. Dot had pretended that he could speak the native tongue, and Caleb and I were now anxious that he should enquire the way to the vessel; but he said the streets were so crooked that the people would be unable to tell anything satisfactory. We groped our way along to another street, when suddenly our two leaders tumbled headlong into a ditch, but quickly extricated themselves. As Dot, who was one of them, still neglected to enquire the way, I naturally concluded that he was a fraud and no linguist.

We now tried another street, and as Caleb and the linguist would take the lead no longer, Dillon and myself led off at a good speed; but before long we stumbled over something and went sprawling to the ground, and Caleb and Dot came

AN ADVENTURE IN THE DARK.

tumbling after us. As we regained our feet, Caleb, who had sprained his wrist in the fall, said in a ruffled tone:—

"I should think these natives might know better than to sleep out doors in the streets."

The men or women whom we had stumbled over were awake by this time, and at once suspected us of conspiring against their huts and worldly goods; and Dot, too agitated to remember their language, if he ever knew it, cried out:—

"We are lost!—can you tell us the way to the river?"

But they could not understand, and many others who were awakened by the noise came flocking round us.

I now seriously requested Dot to ask them in their own language the way to the river. He promised to do so, and shouted:—

"*Reing na kong krowl sonk?*" Then he paused for a reply, but none came that was intelligible to Dot. So he tried again:—

"Don't you understand? *Krowl*, the river, *sonk reing*, the steamer, you cussed fools; have you forgotten your mother tongue?—can't you tell us the way to the steamer?"

The vicinity was now alive with angry and threatening natives who supposed their huts were to be burned, or at least ransacked, without delay; so I said:—

"They *have* forgotten their mother tongue, and we had better get clear of them. There is no knowing how many brickbats are about to be hurled at our heads!"

The advice was acted on promptly, and we got away without being molested. Soon, however, we came to a dark unearthly-looking place which appeared to be a suitable abode for hobgoblins and ghosts. Another retreat was precipitately made, and at last, luckily, we got on to a street which led down to the river. We aroused some natives who were asleep in their little boats, and in a few minutes afterwards were safely on board our steamer.

Our steamer was to leave the next day, and as I wanted to buy a pair of gaiters Caleb and I started for the city early in the morning. Proceeding to the French part thereof, we entered a fashionable shoe-shop, and were gladdened at finding that we were to be waited on by a handsome young French lady—such a one as had been for years my ideal. She was in fact all that my glowing imagination had ever pictured.

She could talk a little English, and graciously asked me what size I wore.

"Number six," was my reply.

In a moment I was trying on a gaiter so numbered, but it was smaller than that size usually is, or my foot was larger; anyway it didn't go on. I was about to ask for a larger pair when she smilingly said:—

"YOUR FOOT VERY SMALL."

"Pull on ze shoe a leetle. Your foot very small."

I had been pulling; and I knew my foot was not small, but I did not feel like contradicting it, after such a compliment. So I concealed my efforts as much as possible, but tugged away with the strength of an ox. I noticed the shoe ripping slightly on the side next to Caleb, but he did not see it and it was almost on. If I had paused for breath the reputation of my foot would have been forever ruined—at least in the lady's eyes.

'Zere," she said when the shoe was finally on, "what did

I telz you? I knew your foot was small. Try on ze other; ze difficulty much less."

I was beginning to think my foot was really a small one, but still I doubted the expediency of putting on the other shoe, and for a moment I hesitated. Noticing this she remarked:

"Zere no difficulty wiz your foot; at first I noticed your foot very small."

I hesitated no longer; but soon discovered that the fit was to be closer than the other one was, and soon saw that the shoe was beginning to tear. Caleb noticed it at once, and was just going to speak when I gave him a sly wink.

"Zere no difficulty," said the lady, "just pull on ze shoe a leetle. When zay fit tight, ze foot look bootiful."

I was so hot that the perspiration rolled off my forehead in beads, but nevertheless I tugged away as earnestly as before. Rip went the elastic, enlarging the opening so that with another effort the shoe went on. Without waiting for another compliment I asked the price, for I wanted to pay it and be off before the lady discovered that my feet were large enough to tear her shoes.

Bidding her good morning I walked away as carefully as possible, but was aware that my shoes were tearing at every step. As I closed the door I caught a parting glimpse of the lady and from the way she shook with repressed laughter I really believed we had in some way greatly amused her.

"I really never noticed before how small your feet were," said Caleb as we reached the street.

"What homely things those French women are anyhow; I always supposed some of them were good-looking" I replied.

Just then one of my feet popped out at one side, and rested partially upon the ground. There was no going any further with those shoes on, so I sat down upon a large stone, pulled them off, flung them upon the ground, and put on my old boots.

"Your feet are growing smaller every day," said Caleb; "At one time a number six was tight for you, but now you wear it without any trouble."

I paid no attention to him, but pulled out my pencil and a piece of paper, and wrote a note, which I put into one of the shoes; then I wrapped them up, and started for the shop, Caleb walking along by my side. When opposite the door I tossed them upon the steps, and walked on; but Caleb, glancing back, saw the young lady come to the door, and pick them up. The note ran as follows:—

Madam:—I always admired a small shoe, and never felt well in one that was broad and loose. "My foot iz very small," and I cannot wear these shoes. Please sell them to some one with a large foot.

Yours, "Wiz a small foot."

It was now too late to think of visiting a second shoe-store, and we hastened back to the steamer, reaching it but a short time before all was ready for a start.

Farther India is divided into three divisions—Anam, of which Saigon is an important town, Burmah, and Siam. Siam is the largest of the three, and has a population of eight millions. It is watered by several important streams, one of which passes through the birthplace of the celebrated Siamese twins. The valleys of the rivers equal the Nile in richness of soil, and yield abundant crops whenever cultivated.

The dwellings of the Siamese consist principally of huts the sides and roofs of which are covered with leaves. The wealthy natives live in palaces covering several acres of ground, and built of white brick, ornamented with gilding, carvings, pictures, gold, silver and glass. These palaces with their apartments for wives and servants, are surrounded by high walls, within which are charming grounds with flowery beds, and shady walks. Among the common people few have more than one wife; but the rich bring to their palaces scores, and even hundreds. The first wife is the mistress of the house, all the rest being subject to her authority. The wife is seldom seen out in company with the husband, and even then is always kept in the background. Nor does she dine with him, but, as a servant, waits upon him crouching on her knees and elbows.

Social distinction is represented by numbers. The lowest slave receives the number five, as the representative of his social position. The next above him is numbered ten, and so on to the second ruler, or viceroy, whose number is one hundred t h o u s a n d ; while far above numerical representation is the king on the throne, before whom all crouch and crawl in the dust. To him an annual service of three months is given by all his subjects, and it has been estimated that one-third of the population a r e his s l a v e s, either by capture, birth, redemption from the penalty of the law, or on account of debts contracted by gambling, or otherwise.

A SIAMESE PRINCE.

Villages of thousands are composed of t h o s e c a p tured in war, and the chains of convicts are continually heard clanking in the different cities; while the men frequently sell their wives and children, and even themselves. The only relief to this gloomy life is found in sports, plays and holidays, which all seem to enjoy.

The most honorable mode of disposing of the dead, is by burning; while their mourning emblems are the shaved head and the wearing of white robes.

In general appearance the Siamese bear a strong resemblance to the Anamese. They are indolent, dishonest, and ignorant yet peaceable, and respectful toward the poor and the aged. They stain their teeth black, and sometimes serrate them.

The males shave the greater portion of their heads, only leaving a stiff tuff on the top, which they allow to grow to the length of two or three inches. The ladies wear their hair short, and frequently uproot a narrow line encircling the head.

Burmah lies to the northwest of Siam, and although the British have taken possession of its most fertile portion, and its only sea-coast, yet in many places the natural productions are abundant, and the forests are fine and flourishing.

Agriculture is yet in a very primitive state; garden vegetables, fruits, and crops, are cultivated with little or no skill, and the people live chiefly upon wild fruits, the young shoots of trees, and the succulent roots of various plants; mangoes, oranges, pineapples, custard-apples, figs, the breadfruit, the papaw, and the plantain, grow almost spontaneously, and answer as a substitute for bread.

The circulating medium of the country consists of gold, silver, and lead. These are used in their native state, it being necessary every time they change from hand to hand, to have them weighed by bankers. As the weighing costs three-and-a-half per cent of the value of the article in question, many are driven to the necessity of barter and trade, rice being exchanged for cotton, and cotton for tobacco, etc.

The government of Burmah is one of the most despotic of despotisms. It is even worse than that of Siam or Anam. The king dispenses justice according to his will, even to the infliction of the death penalty. Under him, however, is a court which frequently tries cases, thus saving him the trouble. This court charges ten per cent of the property in question as fees; consequently trials are seldom brought before it.

The prevailing religion in these three divisions of Farther India, is Buddhism. In Anam, however, but few profess this religion, the masses of the people caring but little for a worship in which the most abject superstition preponderates. In Siam and Burmah the old doctrines of the Buddhist religion have been kept more free from admixture with other religions than in China, yet missionaries have made better progress.

THE TEMPLES OF SIAM. 251

The special object of worship among the Siamese is the white elephant.

The temples of Siam equal in beauty and splendor any that can be found in Asia. Amid parks and groves their great white walls loom up, and from their serrated roofs rise wondrous domes and spires, inlaid and gilded with glittering designs of various descriptions, while continual music from air-rung bells comes floating out upon the breeze from unseen recesses in the roofs and domes, filling the whole atmosphere with mysterious sounds. One of these temples contains nine hundred images of Buddha, the most noticeable of which is in a reclining posture. It is of the extraordinary length of one hundred and fifty-eight feet. The whole form is beautifully inlaid and adorned with pearls and gold.

AN ANAM ARISTOCRAT.

CHAPTER XXVII.

VOYAGE TO THE LAND OF THE MALAYS.

WE left our anchorage at Saigon, and floated down the river towards the ocean; the motion of the stream being so gentle that during the night we were hardly conscious of the movement of the vessel.

Next morning the first objects that attracted my attention when I opened my eyes, were my old boots. They had received a good polishing, and seemed dearer to me than ever. I rose at once and made my way towards the bath-room, where a Chinese attendant stood ready to minister to my wants. Everything in this department was kept in as perfect order as the most fastidious could wish.

Having taken a dip in the sea-water which came spouting in through the mouth of a bronze-headed sea-gull, I stepped on deck, where a number of European ladies and gentlemen scantily and airily clad in their long Chinese night-gowns, and with nothing on their feet but low grass slippers, were slowly promenading, or lazily reclining on the long sedan settees.

Suddenly there is a hurrying to and fro, a hasty putting on of more closely-fitting garments, and a general preparation for using knives and forks. The breakfast-bell has sounded, and we prepare to enjoy our morning meal.

After breakfast, and occasionally when conversation lagged and jokes became heavy to all except their authors, six or eight of us would break the monotony by a game of "frog." This game consisted of pitching quoits at a curious-looking metal frog which was perched upon a box on the deck. His mouth was wide open, and he stared at us with his green eyes, which never even winked as the missile approached him. Many a drub did his countenance receive, and once in a great while he succeeded in catching and swallowing a quoit; but the feat was a rare one, and whenever one was

PLAYING "FROG."

heard rattling down his throat, he was greeted with shouts of applause from his audience.

Then we amused ourselves by watching the children playing "log." Many a mother was minus her spool of thread on account of that game. Thus it was played:—Having attached a cork or piece of paste-board to the end of a string they threw it overboard, when the speed of the vessel rapidly whirled the spool which they held on a knitting-needle. When all was unwound, a motley group of European, Chinese, and Malay urchins formed in line with the thread on their shoulders, drawing in the "log"—those from the front continually running abaft to form in the rear.

I never was in any place without taking a fancy to some lady or other. There was a suitable object of interest now on board our vessel. But, unfortunately for me, she seemed to prefer Caleb's company to my own. I could hear it as she sang her Italian songs, I could see it in her glances, and in her preference to promenade with him at evening. Sometimes when it was quite rough, and they went staggering along the deck together, I tried to convince myself that *I* would not on any account be troubled with lady-company at such a time; but I never quite succeeded. It amused me to watch them; Caleb seemed to have taken a fancy to tread upon his friend's dress, and I expected every moment to see him tear it from her waist, while she seemed rather to enjoy balancing herself against him in a most tantalizing way. I cannot say that I should have shed many tears if they had both rolled overboard together.

DOT WINS THE NIGHT.

About this time Dot, who was still our fellow-traveler, had some trouble with his room-mate—a fat German. The latter wanted the window of the state-room closed one night, but did not say so, preferring to get up and shut it when he thought Dot was asleep. Dot, on his part, persisted in opening it, giving his friend to understand that he did not know how it came to be closed and that he suspected some one was playing a joke on them. Finally Dot, after opening it for the fourth time, seized the water pitcher and vowed he would pour its contents over anything or anybody who undertook to meddle with it again. He carried the day, or rather the night, and the window remained unmolested.

On the fifth morning after leaving Saigon, just as day was breaking, we passed through the group of islands on the Malayan shore. They presented a charming spectacle,— fresh with the richest of tropical verdure, and alive with the songs of birds. To our left were islands near and far; those in the distance, from the smoothness and soft blue tint of the waters around, appearing to rest upon the clouds. As we sailed through these placid waters, upon whose face not even a ripple was to be seen, or passed immediately by the shore of one of those green islands, or caught sweet glimpses of others in the distance, we almost forgot that these were scenes of earth and that we were earthly beings. It was a vision that we could never forget.

Later in the morning we sailed up the channel—in some parts only half a mile wide—between the Malay Peninsula and the island of Singapore, which belongs to the English, and is the great *entrepôt* between Europe and the East Indies, as well as between Europe and China. "Look!" cried one; and immediately all eyes were turned to the right of the vessel's prow where a tiger was swimming across the channel. From our speed we seemed likely to head him off; but he was a good swimmer and put forth all his strength. We could see his great, fiery eyes as he passed immediately in front of us. At last he reached the island, shook his wet hide, and disappeared in the jungles. We were told that at times the animals swam across to the nearest islands in such numbers as to defy the weapons of the natives.

It was not long before we reached the English port of Singapore, where vessels of almost every nation were loading and unloading cargoes of coffee, tea, nutmegs, spices—in short all the riches of the richest countries of the world. Here the white man, the yellow man, the brown man, and the black man frequently stood together, giving ample opportunity for the study of the various nationalities of the earth.

Thronging upon the shore, were the brown Malays selling to the passengers, animals, birds of splendid plumage, and shells beautiful and endless in variety; and all going as cheap as dirt. We contented ourselves with merely buying some corals for bouquets to adorn our state-room. All around in their little boats were these same Malays, diving after copper coins as they were thrown into the water by the passengers. As a vessel departed, scores of them buzzed along in its wake darting after an occasional coin until the steamer left them far behind. A coin from our steamer was

A METEORIC SHOWER.

thrown far out on the water, and a score of boats started for the place where it would strike. A collision seemed inevitable, but down went the divers, head-foremost, three or four at a time, reminding one of a great meteoric shower. Pretty soon, up popped one of them holding the coin out between his thumb and finger, and the others shortly followed him.

Two of the divers in a tiny boat came close to our vessel motioning for us to throw over a coin; and one of them climbed on deck by means of a rope. As he perched on the railing he gave us to understand that he would dive down if sufficient encouragement was given him to do so; thereupon a coin was pitched into the water. Instantly he placed his hands together above his head so as to cut the waves, and plunged head-foremost from the ship. He was under the water longer than we thought he should be, and a feeling of uneasiness, then of suspense was evident among the passengers. But he came up all right at last, with the coin between his teeth.

CHAPTER XXVIII.

EXCURSIONS IN SINGAPORE.

WHEN Mr. Darwin gets through with his descent of monkeys or ascent of man, I wish he would impart some useful knowledge by tracing the origin of the genius who drive people around in vehicles for pay.

You see that race in every part of the world; they all evidently spring from one common stock, and take to their profession as kindly as young ducks to the water. They are white in one part of the world and black in another, but always as innocent as doves. I think I cherish toward them a feeling akin to that which I hold toward other land-pirates. I avoid them as much as possible, but when fate throws me into their hands, I close my eyes and resign myself.

I was about to say that we hired one of these guileless creatures to convey us from the landing-place to the city of Singapore; but on reflection I think it must have been a sort of copartnership, in which we were to do the suffering and he receive the pay. When we offered ourselves as his victims quite early in the morning, he understood English and could speak it fluently. Soon he showed signs of relapsing—like a converted Hindoo—into his original condition, and like the Hindoo could only be spasmodically reclaimed by a periodical reward for his faithlessness.

When we had bargained with him and obtained an honorable adjustment of all our differences, he carefully loosened every weak part of the harness, and then started off with us, cracking his whip; but no sooner had we passed the few houses skirting the shore than our troubles began.

Just as we were entering into a jungle of high cane, snap went one of the traces. The poor driver looked at the broken leather, wringing his hands, and exclaiming piteously that he must pay full damages out of his own wages. We consulted together, and agreed that if one rupee would mend the matter we would sink that amount more than we had originally intended to. He took the money on the spot, for fear, as he said, that it might be forgotten later in the day, as his own memory was bad. He was so grateful, as he tied up his harness with strings which he happened to have at hand, that we felt the pleasure of one who does a good deed.

ON THE ROAD TO SINGAPORE.

We were soon passing along the road which bordered the river; the banks on either side were covered with luxuriant vegetation, while along the road a constant stream of ox-carts slowly wended their way, bearing to the steamers coal and other products of the island.

At last we reached the city of Singapore and found that it

lay upon both sides of the river, some three miles from where our steamer lay at anchor. One portion was almost entirely inhabited by Chinese, who gained a livelihood by selling edible bird's-nests, spices of all kinds, cocoanuts, bananas, and other tropical fruits. The Europeans lived in one quarter by themselves, residing in beautiful mansions fitted with every convenience. The Chinese huddled together in miserable little shanties, while the Malays, who also lived by themselves, did not consider any habitation necessary.

I was told, that when a Malay deliberately washes himself, his friends make ready for his burial—because they know he is going to commit suicide. How true this may be I cannot say, but we judged from appearances that cleanliness formed no part of their religion. In the matter of wearing clothes they seemed very independent. Some had on a sort of bathing-dress fastened by a flashing girdle.

While hunting up our driver, who had dismounted from his seat and gone off without asking leave, we had an opportunity to see the inside of the Malayan houses. As we entered one of them the ladies of the hut were preparing themselves for a promenade, which they did by throwing a sort of blue veil over the face, so as not to frighten the opposite sex—I suppose—by their ugliness. In another residence we saw a Malay barber pulling the hairs from a customer's chin with a pair of tweezers. If two or three had not been ahead of us, we might have listened to the proprietor's blandishments and been denuded also.

In a third hut sat our cabman gambling away the rupee of largesse which we had bestowed upon him. His knowledge of English had forsaken him with his money, and nothing short of the redemption of the coin by us seemed likely to restore his peace of mind. This done, he bowed reverently, put it in his pocket, and then led us forth to a feast of intellect in a larger hut where a great crowd had assembled to witness a cockroach-fight.

As we pushed our way after our champion, his voice was loud and he held his rupee defiantly aloft. He grew reserved however when he had again lost it by betting, and slowly walked off toward his horse. We followed him, but his startled looks when he came in sight of the animal made us feel uneasy. Striking an attitude, he slowly approached the beast and bending low before his head, smote his own breast, and began gnashing his teeth. He then opened the steed's mouth, and beckoned for us to come and look down his throat.

"HE IS HUNGRY."

"His throat looks all right," said I, after examining it.

Then the man fell to the ground and acted like a horse with the wind-colic. On recovering his senses again, he informed us that under no consideration could he allow his animal to proceed unless we devoted the sum of one shilling for provender. It was hot and we could not walk; so we made a virtue of necessity, and yielded. It was weakness, nothing else, that caused us to surrender, for we knew well enough that the rascal would go off immediately and waste the money upon himself.

We followed him again, and this time caught him sitting beside a small wooden platform betting as before on the result of a fight between two cockroaches. Ever and anon an owl-faced Malay drove the two roaches together, until each seemed possessed with the conviction that it was to the other that he was indebted for his evil day. Strong and gamy fellows were these roaches, and not less than three inches in length. It was impossible to determine from appearances which was the better roach; but favoritism was bestowed on one which by some mischance had been deprived of a leg. This apparent disadvantage seemed to improve his chances, and the death of his antagonist justified the faith reposed in him by his backers.

"GO IT YOU CRIPPLE."

At the close of this strange encounter, our driver, who had added to his shilling by betting on the victorious cockroach, offered to show us a lizard fight for the paltry sum of half a crown. This favor we respectfully declined.

The darkening sky, as we emerged from the shed, admonished us of the necessity of obtaining shelter in the European quarter from a coming storm, but our tormentor insisted on feeding his steed before we started. While waiting, we were rewarded for the delay by seeing a woman practicing the prevailing custom of flattening her children's noses. She had two children—both little girls; the oldest not exceeding the tender age of eighteen months. On the face of each, a flat piece of wood was bound over the nasal organ by a string which was tied at the back of the head.

We felt no small amount of disgust when our guide prepared himself for the storm by divesting himself of his clothing which he carefully placed under the seat in the cab. Just as we were comfortably seated he remembered his money, and had to overhaul his garments for the treasure, which, when found, he placed in his mouth for safer keeping. We justified his lack of confidence by throwing his garments overboard with our canes, and no entreaty of his could persuade us to reconsider our action. We had stipulated that no one but ourselves should occupy that vehicle inside, and we were firm in the maintenance of our rights. Our driver, however, could not be brought to regard matters in a proper light. He closed the door violently, muttering anything but blessings as he did so.

Simultaneously with the banging of the cab door came a sharp flash of lightning, then a loud clap of thunder, and after the thunder a torrent of rain which seemed like a second deluge. The crowded squares, streets, and alleys, became mud pools and open sewers through which the accumulated filth swept in torrents, while the inhabitants dispersed with rat-like celerity into their thatched burrows.

Long before the rain had ceased pouring upon the earth, we had reached our quarters, and were inwardly rejoicing at being finally rid of our troublesome driver whom we trusted we should never see again. In this, however, we were mistaken; for the next morning as we left the hotel to make an excursion into the country plantations, foremost among the hackmen was that troublesome Jehu. To save his feelings and our own we jumped into the very first vehicle that came in the way, which to our infinite disgust we found, when too late, was the one belonging to the enemy. He did not give us a chance to escape, but instantly leaped on to his seat—crack went the whip, and we were off! "Bismillah!" we exclaimed—it is the will of heaven—and then we closed our eyes and resigned ourselves to fate.

This resigned state of mind however was not of long duration, for Jehu soon had us among the plantations of cocoanut trees, bananas, pineapples, etc., and was busying himself in pointing out all that might interest us, when suddenly he halted beside a great pile of cocoanuts, and persuaded us to alight from our carriage, break open some of the fruit, and drink the delicious milk. He was still extolling the sweetness and goodness of these nuts, which he said were free for anyone to take if they pleased, and we had just begun to taste the milk, when suddenly a pack of dogs, followed by a native with a huge club, mysteriously issued from a hut close by. The moment Jehu saw them, he exclaimed with much gesticulation:—

"Me a rupee! me save you!"

We needed no argument, but hastily tendered the money, without a word. Immediately our honest friend drew forth a much smaller coin, tossed it to the native, and in an instant, as if by magic, the dogs forgot their wrath, and the man his anger, and we were left alone. We saw at once that we were again the victims of an abominable swindle.

With child-like simplicity, and with all the appearance of having just performed a virtuous act, Jehu now attempted to persuade us to take a drive out to see the monkeys sporting among the trees, adding that it was good fun to get cocoanuts from those eccentric creatures. All the stratagem that was requisite, he said, was to throw stones at them, when they, in return, would aim cocoanuts at our heads; and all danger could be avoided by a little dodging on our part. We agreed to go, but no sooner had we done so than our extortionate friend announced that it would be impossible for him to conduct us to the abode of the monkeys unless we first gave him a little pecuniary encouragement. After much confabulation this difficulty was at last adjusted, and we were once again in motion.

We rolled on through forests of cocoanut trees, which were nicked up the sides to enable the natives to climb them. Thousands of the fruit lay scattered upon the ground, and we learned subsequently that the monkeys had clawed holes in the "eyes" of these nuts, in order to get at the milk inside, as they had seen done by travelers and others passing through the forest.

At length we espied something moving among the branches of the trees—it was evidently some creature trying to conceal itself. We guessed at once that it was our friends the monkeys, but did not care to appear too near them in a hurry. Presently we saw one little hairy head, and then another, peep out from among the branches. We waved our hats, and made grimaces, and threw a few small stones at the little rascals, who chattered and grinned, and then ran farther up the tree; but not a single nut did they throw down.

At first we supposed that they took Jehu, who did not look altogether unlike them, for one of themselves, and were afraid of hurting him if they threw down the fruit; so we sent him back to the cab. Then we yelled, and roared, and hurled sticks and stones up into the trees with all our might, expecting that now the nuts would fall; but all in vain. The monkeys in some things are almost as shrewd as men, and we came to the conclusion that this trick had been played upon them so often that at last they had seen through it, and did not care to waste their supplies.

When we returned to the cab I desired Jehu to drive us to the outskirts of the island, as we wished to see something of the natives living on the coast. He accordingly did so, and we were very much interested in what we saw. We found the people living in a state little advanced beyond barbarism, doing no work, and caring as little for to-morrow as the monkeys we had left behind us in the forest. They subsisted chiefly upon roots and herbs, and moved from place to place as the stock of food was exhausted.

We also examined their boats. They are used as much for places of abode as for a means of transit. From end to end they measured about twenty feet. At one end was a fire-place, and at the other a sort of awning made of matting, which served as a sleeping-apartment. There the whole family of six or eight persons, with the dog, the cat, or any other live stock that happened to be there, were accustomed to repose; while in the middle of the boat were stored the various domestic utensils. How blissfully lazy, how happy and contented they seemed, living thus upon the bounties of nature and drifting aimlessly over the smooth waters, fanned by the soft breezes of an eternal spring!

BOAT LIFE IN MALAY.

Here and there we espied some boats, larger than the rest, and different in appearance. We were informed that these were pirates; and not wishing to be in too close proximity with them, we returned inland. Piracy, however, will not long be known on that coast, for the settlements on the larger islands are working radical changes; and English gun-boats are teaching Mohammedan pirates that the time is past when they could commit with impunity those deeds of cruelty and rapine which have gained for them such an unenviable notoriety.

Toward night we returned to our steamer, which resumed her journey the next day.

CHAPTER XXIX.

CEYLON'S ISLE.

EVERY revolution of the steamer's wheel now brought us nearer our home, though it was still more than twelve thousand miles away. All the afternoon our thoughts naturally wandered to our far-distant native land; every kind of conversation in which we engaged invariably merged in this same topic; and when night came on, it was the subject of our dreams.

The next morning all the pleasant scenes which had visited our pillows while we slumbered were quickly dispelled by the sad intelligence that during the night one of our fellow-passengers had slept his last sleep, and was now about to be buried in the bosom of the ocean. With serious faces we hastened on deck, and found that one of the missionaries before referred to, had already begun a brief service for the dead. The corpse, wrapped in a winding-sheet, was lying upon the deck, one end of which projected over the side of the vessel; and the missionary was repeating those sacred words "I am the resurrection and the life." At that moment the other end of the plank, which was supported by two sturdy sailors, was slowly raised, and the body of the sleeper sank to its last resting-place, in the depths of the sea. Heavy leaden weights had been attached to it, in order to ensure its sinking to the bottom, and thus escaping the jaws of voracious sharks which were prowling about the vessel.

We were now sailing up the strait, between Malaya and the Island of Sumatra, with a range of mountains on either hand. That extending along the coast of Sumatra rose up in grand proportions, seeming at both extremities to merge into the infinite, but owing to its distance we could see but little of the active volcanoes that heaved and exploded along its sides and from its peaks. Two days later we were sailing out

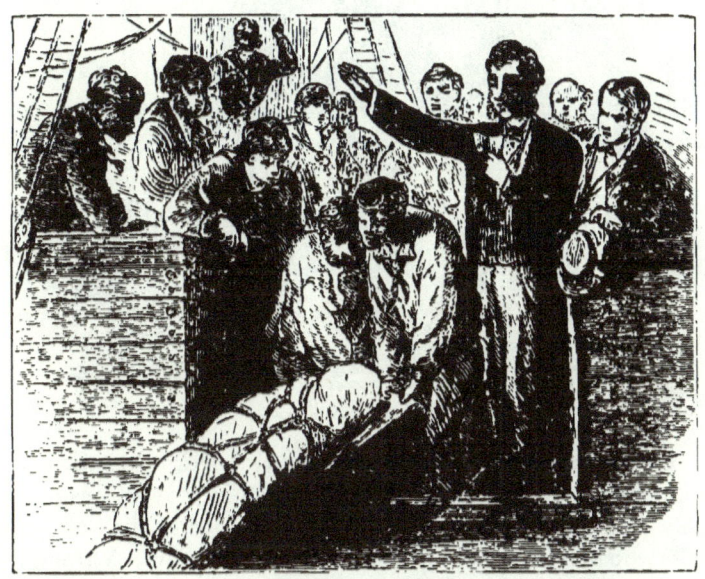

A BURIAL AT SEA.

of the strait close to the beautiful Nicobar Islands in the Bay of Bengal. These soon disappeared, and our noble vessel, bound for Ceylon, ploughed its way through the broad wilds of the Indian Ocean.

A large number of Dutch people joined us at Singapore, to return to their native land for a few months during the unhealthy season. Many of the richest islands of the East Indies belong to Holland; and among them are Java, Banca, and the Spice Islands. Sumatra, Celebes, Borneo, Timor, and New Guinea are in partial possession of the Dutch. Java is the chief commercial and political island of the East Indies; its capital is Batavia. These Dutch passengers were quite jolly and sociable, and told us about vast quantities of coffee, sugar, spices, pepper, indigo, India-rubber, and edible birds' nests, which were exported from Batavia; and of camphor, nutmegs, cloves and gutta-percha, from Sumatra.

THE SICK FRENCHMAN.

There was also on board our vessel a sick Frenchman, returning to Europe for his health which improved considerably during the voyage. He was accompanied by his Chinese wife who bestowed on him much care and attention. Through the livelong day she sat by his bedside to attend to his wants, and when he was able to walk about a little, she supported him as best she could. Her affection seemed all the more striking, since she was brought along merely to wait upon the sick man.

These Oriental wives are nearly always left behind, but semi-oriental children, especially boys, often accompany their fathers to Europe. Is it that men care more for their children than their wives? There were many such children on board our vessel, some from China and Japan, some from Farther India, and some from the East India Islands; their droll games afforded me a great deal of amusement.

Taken altogether the passengers on our steamer at this

time were a varied and interesting set, representing not only many nations and countries, but the different classes thereof. Conspicious among them were a party of aristocratic Malays, one of whom was said to be a genuine princess. In her appearance and behaviour she seemed worthy of the high honor.

A PRINCESS OF MALAY.

When we were yet a hundred miles from Ceylon, the odors of cinnamon and spices came floating upon the breeze; and in due time this green and beautiful isle came within our view off to the northwest. A little later, and the city of Point De Galle smiled upon us as it sat, with its citadel and light-house, upon a point of land extending into the sea. Before us the great waves from the ocean were rolling into the indented bay, dashing high upon the rocky beach, and tossing the anchored vessels from side to side, while their tall masts swayed to and fro like forest trees during a storm.

This port was rocky and dangerous, and when a mile away

we saw a pilot, in a little boat rowed by a couple of natives, coming to guide us into the harbor. His boat was quite narrow and very high above the water, and was kept from being capsized by the waves, by fastening the ends of two long poles to one side of the boat while the other ends were fastened to a log which floated alongside.

THE PILOT AND HIS BOAT.

We were soon anchored safely in the middle of the bay, and scores of the natives, with boats similar to those just described, came rowing towards us. Some sought to carry the passengers ashore; while others came on board to sell articles of native manufacture, consisting of boxes, baskets, canes, inkstands, etc., made of porcupine-quills or ebony-wood, or inlaid with tortoise-shell. Many of the articles were beautifully carved and studded with ivory. There were also tortoise-shell chains, pearls, jewels, and, as we supposed, precious stones of many kinds such as topaz, carbuncle, ruby, the blue and the red sapphire, and diamonds. Altogether, the display of articles was a dazzling one.

Of course they asked good round sums for such costly goods, but as all who purchased wished to buy cheap, the prices were reduced to meet the views of customers; and in some cases buyers got them at as low rates as their consciences would allow them to offer. But all is not gold that glitters. It was found out subsequently that the jewelry was plated brass, and that the precious stones were nothing but colored glass cut up into small bits.

When Caleb and I went ashore we were met at the waters' edge by a crowd of natives who seemed almost crazy to sell their trinkets and other commodities, or to serve us in any way we saw fit, provided they could make a little money honestly or by cheating, it did not appear to matter which. Some offered themselves as guides, to pilot us through the city; others proposed vociferously to take us for a drive; others screamed out that they could show us to the best shops; in fact, there was nothing that one or another did not shout his willingness to perform in our service.

As soon as we could make ourselves heard, we stated that all we wanted was a cab and driver; a guide we did not particularly care for. This was soon arranged, and we set out to inspect the city. As we started, a brazen-faced fellow jumped on to the rear of our vehicle. We looked very hard at him to let him know that we considered his presence an intrusion, but as our honest cabman paid no attention to him, we presumed it might be one of the customs of the country for guides to force themselves unasked upon visitors, and so we submitted with as good grace as we could. We had not gone far when our unwelcome friend, to our great astonishment, began to address us in English—at least his language was a sort of *patois*, part English, and part something else, which we could very easily understand. It was not long before we learned that this obliging gentleman was not a guide, but simply a "runner" for the shops. His business was to find out newly-arrived strangers, introduce himself into their company, and then persuade them to visit the shops by which he was employed; and for said services he received a certain percentage on all their purchases.

It was not long before we came to a gay-looking shop filled with curiosities, jewelry, and gems of various kinds. Into this our friend persuaded us to enter, and if we had taken his advice we should have emptied half the shelves of their glittering baubles. We were, however, deaf to all his seductive arts, and after making a general survey, entered our cab once again. As we drove on, our would-be guide freely offered his advice. Sometimes we came to stores which, to us, had all the appearance of being really first-class, but the guide shouted loudly "No good! no good!"—at the same time pointing to some other establishment beyond, into which he proposed we should immediately enter.

We knew his tricks by this time, and would not be put off; but even then he was sharp enough to take advantage of us. More than once when we insisted upon going into some handsome-looking store or other, with which our friend had no connection, after endeavoring all he could to persuade us not to enter, he placed himself in front of us, and bowing with profound reverence to the proprietor of the establishment, pointed to us, intimating that *he* had brought some customers, and as a matter of course would expect a suitable gratuity if we purchased anything.

We expected that when we dismissed the cab, our friend would look for some small gratuity in return for his valuable (?) advice and assistance. This we were prepared to give him, but were perfectly astonished when he coolly demanded a fee of five rupees.

"What!" we both exclaimed, "five rupees for playing 'guide!' Why, you are nothing but a shop-runner. We engaged this cab for ourselves alone, and here you have been riding in it all the afternoon. It is *you* who must give *us* five rupees." Saying which, I held out my hand for the money, to his utter amazement.

The honest driver then thought that he was called on to say something, expecting, of course, a percentage of what the runner would receive. Pointing to the latter, he shouted:—

"He guide! he guide!"

We now turned round and walked off, as if we did not intend to pay either of them. This startled the cabman, who began to change his note, crying:—

"He *no* guide! he *no* guide!"

The runner was insulted, and immediately a fierce war of words began between the two; each, in a way that was utterly ludicrous to the by-standers, hurling at the other the very ugliest and most defamatory words that their vocabulary contained. Such abuse I never heard before; and about such a trifle, too!

A WAR OF WORDS.

There they stood, jabbering like lunatics, cursing and swearing, and uttering the most horrible threats that they had not the slightest idea of putting into execution. It reminded me of a quarrel which I had at school when the "other boy" and myself were equally valiant in wordy defiance, and equally afraid of each other at heart. But we grew tired of the noisy confab at last; so we paid the driver according to agreement, threw the "guide" a rupee, and then left them to make it up or fight it out, just as they pleased.

We now wandered down the street toward the vessel. Scores of natives, with their trinkets, followed in our track, and swarmed about us. One of them had three parrots in a small bamboo cage, for which, cage and all, he asked six shillings. Although this heathen could talk English about as well as a monkey can eat sauer-kraut without grinning, yet he knew the names of the principal coins, and could make a couple of Christians understand a few things by signs. We did not want his parrots, but he followed along showing us how nicely they ate sugar-cane. Presently he took one from the cage, letting it walk up his arm, on to his shoulder; but as we didn't buy, he reduced his price by degrees until it was only a shilling! At last, fearful lest he might give them to us unless we purchased, we handed him the money, and took the birds.

On arriving aboard the vessel we opened the door of the cage to play with our pets, whereupon two of them immediately flew away, showing that they were not very tame after all. We gave the remaining bird to a queer-looking fellow whose brain was slightly unbalanced, and who naturally enough had taken a liking to parrots.

ONE OF OUR PASSENGERS.

CHAPTER XXX.

RAMBLES IN AND AROUND CEYLON.

I FANCIED when a boy that Ceylon was the very next place to heaven. Its spicy breezes and gorgeous scenery had become familiar to me through the beautiful hymn by Reginald Heber, and as we approached its shores I almost imagined that we were drawing near to the abodes of the blest. I was, however, destined soon to be undeceived.

The day after we landed, Dot showed us the forts built by the Portuguese, Dutch, and English, who each in turn have possessed the island. At present it is under English rule, and the armed fortifications and the presence of the huge guns, the piles of cannon-balls, and the sentinels pacing to and fro, give it anything but a poetical or celestial aspect. It began to dawn upon us that we should be greatly disappointed in our visit to this famous island.

In the streets of the city we met with some jugglers, and to drive away the feeling of *ennui* which began to oppress us, we requested them to give us a short performance. Immediately one of them fell upon his knees in the street and opened a red bundle, out of which rolled a number of balls covered with red leather; while a boy, who I presumed was his son, blew vigorously on a large horn. In unison with the music, the father struck the balls with his stick, jabbering to them the movements they were to take in the dance, just as if they could understand what he said; and they really seemed to do so from the way they obeyed orders.

After that he scolded at the balls and they all mysteriously disappeared, as if hiding themselves; but when he spoke again they seemed to come from his mouth like words rolling from his tongue. Then he swallowed them all, and they shortly appeared on his breast, one after another, and were extracted like huge bullets lodged just under the skin.

THE MYSTERIOUS BALLS.

Another juggler pointed out a particular spot on the ground and then covered it for a few moments with his mantle; then he snatched the garment up, and a shrub was seen just peering through the ground. He then alternately covered and uncovered the shrub several times, and before it had been above ground ten minutes it had grown into a little tree thirty inches high.

We turned from such vain delusions as these to watch a traveling menagerie, for such things are sometimes met with even in Ceylon. The procession, consisting of one man carrying a cage containing two small birds and a white mouse, moved grandly along till it reached us, and then halted to give an exhibition. The doors of the cage were thrown back, and one of the birds was taken out and placed in a chariot, on its back, with its feet upwards. The other bird walked out of the cage, put its breast against a cross-piece in the shafts of the chariot, and pulled it toward their little home. Then a cannon was fired; the recumbent bird jumped to his feet, and both beat a hasty retreat into the cage.

The second scene now opened. A flag-pole was erected, and a flag attached to its summit was unfurled to the breeze. The mouse marched out, and ascended up, and up, until at the very top! The audience watched with breathless attention. The flag-staff was lifted from its socket and carried gently but safely to the ground; and a murmur of applause ran through the audience as the flag was borne triumphantly to the cage by the patriotic cheese-eater.

After witnessing the show, we hired two carriages, lest one of them should break down. I think the Dutch must have brought those carriages to the island about a century ago. As we passed along the shore, the foam of the breakers splashed over the cocoanut trees which grew down to the edge of the sea. Rolling out under their dense foliage we passed many a hut which did not appear larger than a hen-coop, the roof and sides being covered with palm leaves. The inmates were happy, unambitious, and contented as the tropical birds which revelled in the forest, making it vocal with their notes, as they basked in the light of their own gaudy plumage.

The tropical growth soon became so delightfully monotonous and heavy that we would have given almost anything to have seen the groves and meadows of our own native land, which change with the seasons. But here no changes come. Here an eternal summer reigns, while the lazy ox and sleepy elephant graze quietly on through a never-ending spring.

Finally we arrived at the Cinnamon Gardens and Waukwalle. Here lived a couple of Portuguese descended through three centuries from the old rulers of the island. At the houses of both, cheap drinks could be bought at enormous prices. There were pointed out to us gangs of deformed natives, for whom the proprietors of the establishments made piteous appeals, begging us to give them a few pennies. Having already through sympathy contributed to some with eyes turned wrong side out, and some with shrivelled legs, we reasoned the case with the proprietors of this suffering

"MANY OF THEM IMPROVED SURPRISINGLY."

throng, telling them that these natives had no use for money; that they could live on the natural products of the soil; and as for clothes, they could go to the wharf and beg some more old sacks and mats to throw round them; or if they desired something better, they could sell some fruit to the vessels or some cocoanuts to the oil-mills. But one of the

Portuguese gentlemen quietly remarked that their present mode of life evidently pleased these poor creatures best, and that they were unfitted for any other—as we could see.

With that we walked out under the trees; and were surprised to see the poor cripples recover sufficiently to follow. Many of them improved surprisingly in a very short time, and were able to climb the trees, throw us down breadfruit, pumpkins, and nutmegs; and to cut branches of cinnamon and camphor, which they brought down for us to smell, taste, and buy for walking-sticks. To show us that the branches would not loose their odors, they were continually scraping their own old walking-sticks—cut from the same trees—and sticking them under our noses that we might judge for ourselves.

We passed on to the summit of a neighboring hill where we obtained a fine view of the surrounding country. An occasional opening revealed a rice field, but beyond were the dense forests where both foreigners and natives went to hunt the wild elephant for the sake of his tusks. In the distance rose up Adam's Peak, which was alike sacred to the Buddhists and Mohammedans. They say, that when Adam left Paradise he used this peak and the boulders lying here and there in the channel as stepping stones to the mainland. As a proof they show the visitor, near the summit of the peak, the rude imprints of a foot as long as a man's. It is carefully guarded and protected from the weather by priests, who spend their lives in this place, and are always willing to show the miraculous footprint to strangers.

Just as we were leaving this interesting place, a native presented himself with a printed card indicating that it was customary to give a certain sum for the privilege of visiting the gardens. This eternal begging in one form or other was becoming a nuisance; so we gravely shook our heads, and told the driver to go on. Upon this a number of impudent rascals caught the bridle of our ponies, saying that we should not depart till they were satisfied.

At this demonstration Dot exclaimed "It is a d——d fraud!" and thereupon we all jumped to the ground and started on afoot, leaving our driver to get off as he could. He soon overtook us, however, and we resumed our seats and returned to the city.

CEYLON A FRAUD.

Dot's emphatic expression that the thing was "a fraud," brought vividly to my mind an incident of my younger days, which I will here relate.

While I was attending college a young gentleman made his appearance, and at once attracted the attention of the students. He wished to be looked upon as a fast young man, and considered himself the smartest fellow in the world. He had a great ambition to join a secret society to which many of the students belonged, and having scraped acquaintance with some of us he wanted to be proposed for membership. We held a consultation, told him we would make it all right for him, and he went straight away and told all his friends that he was going to be initiated. Of course we only intended to get some fun out of him.

Next day the time was appointed; he was to meet us at

an old deserted foundry, a little distance outside the city—time, half past nine at night. At that hour ten or fifteen of us groped our way down the dark hollow in which the foundry stood. It was about as dreary a spot as could well be imagined. We found our victim sitting on a stone waiting for us. We whispered in a mysterious manner that it was necessary to blindfold him. This done, we began to

INITIATING A CANDIDATE.

march him up and down, giving him the idea that we were going an immense distance. We led him into all the unearthly places we could think of, dragged him through mud and mire, pulled him over fences, marched him into cellars of unoccupied houses, dumped him down upon a sleeping cow or two, and finally landed him among the inmates of a pig-sty, causing a great excitement and noise therein.

Then we hurried him forward again, and took him a mile or two up the ravine. By this time we were pretty well tired out; so we made him sit down under a big tree, and began the questioning part of the performance, and as he judged it his duty to be very frank and truthful in answering our questions, his replies gave us great amusement. After the confession was ended, we bade him remain perfectly motionless while we went a little distance to arrange the "second degree." How long he sat there shivering I don't know, but it was subsequently reported that he was not seen at home till past midnight.

We saw nothing of him the next day, but late at night as I was on my way home from a "meeting" of the society when going by a lonesome place I heard a rustle in the direction of a hedge, and soon a dim form emerged therefrom. It drew nearer—a monstrous club was in its hand. The terrible words—"It's a d——d fraud!" fell upon my ear, and the next instant I was running for life, for I knew what those words meant. The form followed; nearer and nearer it came, its huge club uplifted, and fearful denunciations proceeding from its mouth. I was near home now; but a neighbor's yard was nearer, and I jumped over the fence just in time to escape the descending blow. Into the woodhouse I ran, and closed the door after me. There was a terrific pounding outside for a few moments; then a pause; then the ominous words, "It's a d——d fraud" again fell on my ears, followed by retreating footsteps.

I concluded, however, that it would be better for my health to remain where I was, and so I made a night of it.

CHAPTER XXXI.

EASTERN CIVILIZATION—THE BRAHMINS.

WHILE in Ceylon we met with a great many persons, of various nationalities, whose conversation very much interested us. Among others was an American gentleman who seemed anxious to gather all the information he could respecting China and Japan.

"To what extent," he asked, "does the present intercourse between America and Japan influence the national life of the Japanese?"

"To a very great extent, as far as we could judge during our short visit," replied Caleb; "Western ways are becoming quite the rage among the people."

"And they will be their curse," replied our friend. "It has been so with every nation which modern civilization has reached. What has it done for the tribes of North America?. What has it done for the natives of Mexico and South America? They were farther advanced at the time when the continent was discovered than they are to-day. Then again, look at the Sandwich Islanders. Before the coming of the Europeans they were a happy and innocent people; and what has our boasted "civilization" done for them? It has brought civilized sins and civilized diseases among them, and has demoralized and degraded them until from one hundred and sixty thousand their numbers have decreased to sixty thousand—and that too has been the work of but forty years."

"But," questioned Caleb, "are you sure that the diseases you mention were previously altogether unknown among the natives?"

"Certainly," was the reply; "it is a well-established fact. Why, when the small-pox, as well as certain other infectious diseases which I will not specify, began their ravages in China, the people thought that sick persons were afflicted with a curse from the gods. At the same time they had intelligence enough to see that the Europeans were the instruments of propagating that curse, wherever it might come from originally; so they actually sent their sick to the European settlements.

"But I will give you another instance," he continued. "Before the western trade was opened, the Chinese never dreamed of adulterating their teas; but they saw what foreigners did, and realizing how profitable it was they imitated and even excelled them. I assure you, the advance of crime is parallel with the advance of what we call "civilization." Every new invention or improvement enlarges the sphere of the criminal and puts fresh power to do evil into his hands; and the natives of countries with which we have hitherto had no intercourse, as soon as they come in contact with us adopt the criminal part of our civilization long before they are able to comprehend that which is good in it. The Chinese, for instance, soon found a use for all the opium that English ships could bring them, but other and useful drugs, or a more rational pharmacopœia than their own, they failed to comprehend. The American Indians, too, quickly learned the use of the white man's whiskey and the white man's deadly fire-arms; but the advantages of a settled life, labor, agriculture, education, and so forth, seemed quite beyond their grasp."

"Excuse me," said another gentleman, "I think you are hardly just to western nations or western governments when you make such broad and indiscriminating statements as these. Consider the noble efforts which the missionaries have made. Besides which the various governments have certainly tried of late to Christianize the heathen nations with which they have held intercourse, and to raise them to a higher social position."

"I admit," returned our friend, "that recently a very great improvement has taken place in this respect, but still it may very well be questioned whether the amount of good attained is in any degree proportionate to the amount of means expended. As for former times, why, men did not even pretend to be actuated by moral or religious motives when they explored or took possession of heathen countries. What but the thirst of gold actuated the Spaniards when they took possession of Mexico and Peru, and reduced its inhabitants,—then in a far-advanced state of civilization—to a condition of slavery and degradation? What but the same motive, and the lust of conquest, led the English to subjugate the great Indian Empire? Is it out of love to the natives that France has taken possession of Algeria? And is it because we Americans love the Redskins that we have seized their lands, driven them further and further from their own domains, and in exchange have given them powder and poison?"

"What you say is true to some extent," replied Caleb, "but still I believe that the missionaries exert a great influence for good when they are not bound down by government patronage, nor forced upon a country by its conquerors. Though the morality of the heathen is very low, there is much that is good mingled even with their superstitions. What we really want is for the heathen to retain all that is good in his own system and to add to it the higher teachings of Christianity. Everyone must deplore the evils which have accompanied our intercourse with heathen nations, but no one in his senses would wish to restore India to the barbarism of two centuries ago, or to give back the North American Continent to the Redskins. The means adopted may have been bad, but Providence has shaped the end and brought forth good.

"It is the advanced civilization of the West that gives her the power of both wronging and benefiting the Oriental nations. The world is moving; and barbarous tribes, innocent in their ignorance and powerless in their inferiority,

AN INDIAN MOSQUE.

must either be swept from the track or be carried forward."

The American gentleman was about to reply to this long speech of Caleb's, but I thought we had had enough of philosophy and moralizing, for that day at least, so I proposed that we should visit a neighboring temple and witness some of the religious ceremonies of the native religion therein. To this they agreed. I had been much interested in the opinions which our American friend had expressed, but I suspected that his sympathies with native wrongs would become stronger when he left Ceylon, for I had observed that resident foreigners never were very pathetic about the poor harmless heathen until they were safely on board the steamer and on their way home. It is so everywhere. In the States we talk of the "poor Indian," but in the territories the same gentleman is styled a "treacherous savage."

As we stood in the temple we were strangely reminded of the ancient ceremonies among the Jews, for the priests brought in a number of little boys belonging to the sacerdotal caste and invested them with the privileges to which their birth entitled them. These children were but eight years of age; to each was given the sacred string; over each were pronounced the regenerating words; and they were then declared "twice-born." Their initiation into the mysteries of the priesthood began from that day. When they arrived at maturity it was expected that their lives would then be moulded into the proper form, and their passions all subdued; their hair and beard would be cut off, they would assume the white mantle, the staff of Venu would be placed in their hands, golden ear-rings would be given them, and a copy of the Vedas, or sacred writings set before them. Those writings it would henceforth be their duty to expound; besides which, as holy men, they would be expected to give the counsel of heaven, and to administer justice, upon occasion, between man and man.

Years after when these boys became old grey-haired men another scene of their lives would open—they would become hermits or devotees. If a priest becomes a hermit he betakes himself to the woods, and there lives a life of rigid abstinence, mortifying all the passions and desires of the flesh. If he becomes a devotee he leads a life of religious contemplation, with the view of attaining to a state of final beatitude; he attempts to free himself from the slightest taint of sin and error; he reflects with all the powers of his mind upon the

A BRAHMIN DEVOTEE.

mysterious essence and existence of the Supreme; he contemplates the time when his own soul shall become incorporated in the being of the Deity; in fact his whole mind and soul is abstracted from earth and fixed on heaven.

We saw one of these devotees: he was in a sitting posture and appeared to be wrapped in silent meditation. If familiarity with dirt and rags tend to extinguish pride and self-conceit, he seemed likely to attain his end. We went near him, but he neither stirred nor lifted up his eyes: he was indifferent to all external objects, and an utter stranger to curiosity. The people held him in high veneration, and brought him daily all that he needed—to them it was a sacred duty.

Some of the teachings of this religion—Brahminism—are full of pathos and sublimity, similar to the doctrines of the Bible, but they are seldom practiced in their entirety. One of its worst features, the system of caste, is the most prominent. The Brahmin stands at the head of the several classes. He is supposed to have sprung from the mouth of Brahma.

The Kshatriya, or warrior is to defend the people, and is enjoined to give alms, offer sacrifices, read the vedas, and guard against sensuality. He is invested with the sacred cord at the age of eleven—three years later than the little Brahmin—but his cord is made of hemp while the Brahmin's is of cotton.

The Varsya or agriculturist is supposed to be chiefly engaged in the pursuit of riches, either from tilling the soil or from commerce. He also is invested with the sacred string, but at the age of twelve, and his string is of wool.

The Soodra, or man of the lowest caste, is doomed to wait upon those above him. He receives no investiture, can never change his condition, and is treated with the vilest contumely and contempt. He has neither sacrifice nor religion; there is no hope for him in this life or the life to come.

Strange to say, this class, together with those who for some atrocious crime or some unpardonable sin against religion have been ostracized from the other castes, form the great mass of the people, and with them are included all unmarried women—for unmarried women have no place in the religion of Brahma. In this respect it is a religion of degradation far beyond any human slavery, and utterly repugnant to Christianity which teaches the universal brotherhood of mankind and the equality of all.

CHAPTER XXXII.

OVER THE ARABIAN AND RED SEAS.

HAVING remained at Ceylon upwards of two weeks, we sailed out from its port on a September evening, while the light-house sent its twinkling rays after us until we were miles away. For several days our course was south-west, as by sailing pretty well toward the equator we hoped to escape the worst of the monsoon which we should be likely to encounter further to the north. On the fifth day out our course was changed to the north-west, and we were then within four degrees of the equator. During the first day or two of our voyage the sea was not boisterous, and the time passed pleasantly as we promenaded the deck, lounged upon the long sedan chairs, or chatted with passengers whose acquaintance we made. We talked with one of the chief officers of a British company extensively engaged in laying ocean cables, who was returning home on a short visit. At that time his company was laying a cable from Singapore to connect England with her possessions in Australia by a line already extending from Europe down the Red Sea, across to India, and from there to Singapore. In a little upwards of a year afterwards, this line was completed so that several of the East India Islands, and even the southern part of Australia, beyond her burning sands, were connected by the magic telegraph, with the civilized world. The line to Singapore had already been extended up the eastern coast of Asia, and across to Nagasaki in Japan, so that messages sent from there in the morning might be received at San Francisco on the same day.

On our vessel were some Englishmen who had been hunting in India for sport, and were returning home by way of Ceylon. They had much to say of their experiences in the wilds of India; and one day a powerful fellow, whom they called Doctor, told us the following yarn:—

"On one occasion as we were out hunting among the jungles in the central part of India, we were suddenly startled by a terrible noise which seemed to come from a spot a few hundred paces in front of us. It was a growling and a roaring noise, as though the muttering thunders were rising from the earth! We climbed a small eminence close by, and as our eyes turned toward a circular plateau not far away, we

A FIGHT IN THE JUNGLE.

saw that a tiger and a lion were grappled in deadly contest, and rolling and tumbling on the ground. We hurried on through the brush till we came to the edge of the plateau, where we were so close upon them, that we could see their great glaring eyes and wide spread mouths, as each shook and tore the other, while blood ran freely on both sides. After a fight, seemingly of an hour, the tiger fell backward, the lion instantly grasped him by the throat, and the conflict was soon ended by the death of the tiger. The lion loosed his hold, and stood gazing upon his prey as if in meditation; but it was only a moment, for we poured a full volley into him, and he too fell dead upon the ground."

Some of the party then told us of a combat they had seen between a wild boar and a lion, which resulted in the latter being ripped open by the great tusks of the former. They declared that the boar was fully a match for either the lion or the tiger, and that upon being approached by the hunter on horseback, this animal frequently turned upon his enemies, cutting the horse's legs to the bone, and sometimes despatching him in an instant; or should the horse wheel in time to get out of his way, it was a very close race for a few minutes, although the boar would seem to be incapable of fleetness. They further remarked that during the day-time the lion and the tiger were rather timid, and generally remained concealed; but at night they came from their hiding places and prowled around with great boldness. They would spring upon cattle and horses, and toward morning the tiger, if his appetite remained unsatiated, would attack the elephant. This animal would sometimes use his trunk with such force that only a few blows were required to drub the life out of his assailant, or to bring him to the ground, where he would pin him with his tusks.

These parties had also been bear-hunting at the foot of the Himalayas. As they commenced to speak of their bear hunts, one stout-looking man who was all scarred up, began to speak more freely than usual; said he:—

"One day as we were out hunting, I became separated some little distance from the rest of the party and pretty soon I espied a large bear in the adjoining brush. As I was ambitious to kill him myself, I fired upon him, but I only inflicted a slight wound, and he at once "came for me." In my haste to reload I made no headway; everything went wrong, and he was upon me before I was ready. I called for help, and contrived to run the gun-barrel down his throat, but he gave his head a twist, and it slipped out. Then his great claws seized my breast and shoulders, tearing deep into the flesh, and just as his mouth was opening upon my face, I jerked the dagger from my belt, plunged it into his stomach, and with a nerve unknown before, ripped him open! We tumbled upon the ground together, and there we lay struggling as the boys came up, but they quickly put a bullet into him which finished him."

These remarks brought to mind a night's experience while Caleb and I were in the mountains of Colorado, and I related it as follows, as an offset to the bear story.

"The mountains were infested with wild animals and Indians and were thinly settled, so that frequently we were obliged to camp out. On one occasion after riding till late at night without coming to a house, we built a fire among the fallen pines, collected some leaves for a bed, and lay down to sleep. Towards morning I was startled from my slumbers by a noise as of approaching feet, and immediately awoke Caleb. Neither of us spoke; but in an instant we were on our knees and elbows with cocked revolvers in our hands. The tread was among the leaves under some trees not far up the hill. What caused it? man or beast? The fire had almost died out, sending a flickering light only a few feet into the surrounding darkness. The thought flitted through my mind:—If it be an animal we had better stir the fire to keep it at bay, but if it is a man the light would only give him a better aim.

"The tread appeared to be that of a four-footed beast, but still we were not certain. It seemed to walk from side to side, but all the while coming nearer and nearer. Then it halted, and thinking I caught a glimpse of its form, I whispered:—

"'I'm going to fire!'

"'No, no!' said Caleb, 'wait for closer contact.'

"Just then I ventured to reach out my trembling foot and stir a brand of the fire; a blaze instantly shot high into the air, lighting up the scene and giving us a good view of the intruder. We shrank back to rest crest-fallen, though greatly relieved, for it was only an innocent squirrel turning over the leaves in search of an early breakfast."

When we were a few days out from Ceylon the ocean grew rough so that the vessel plunged and rolled at a fearful rate. The oncoming gale rapidly increased, and all night long the timbers groaned and creaked under the storm. Next morning a few of the women managed to get on deck by holding to this and that, but when once there did not attempt to move; while the men were seen staggering about as they tried to go from one place to another. When the vessel rolled to one side, the men who were moving about balanced themselves upon one foot, while the other sometimes presented the appearance of attempting to kick sideways at the person who stood nearest. Again they grabbed at a bench or mast, or at the railing on the upper side, but when too slow, went skimming down to the opposite side; or occasionally two ran into each other and fell upon the deck, to slide, and tumble, and roll together till they reached the protecting railing on the lower side.

By noon all of the fair sex on deck were driven below. In the afternoon the storm was still increasing, and we sat with our sedan chairs crosswise of the vessel to prevent their upsetting. Every now and then came a larger wave than usual, and then, as the deck was wet and slippery, away we went abreast, like a score of sleighs down the steep side of an iceberg, increasing our speed till the lower railing was reached. We finally adopted a new plan, and that was to tie our chairs to something permanent; when they were thus fastened we sat down again, and all went happy till by-and-by came a large wave and swept away one chair and its occupant to the other side of the deck. The crowd enjoyed it, but the fellow looked rather sheepish as he brought his chair back, and tied it over again.

The Doctor, the hero of the tiger story, was up to all kinds of pranks, and he now slyly slipped his hand around, untied the same chair, as he had before done, and away his victim went a second time, at which the crowd again applauded. The chair was again fastened, but just as our hunter was attempting the trick for the third time, some one untied *him* and away he shot, coming with a crash to the deck, where he sprawled among the broken pieces of a demoralized chair! The crowd again roared and shouted, but just as the Doctor had picked himself up and was holding on to a post, a gigantic wave came pouring over the side of the vessel, breaking loose many a chair, and washing them and their inmates in a torrent against the lower railing, where they all tumbled ingloriously upon the watery deck. When half way down the inclined plane, the chair of one passenger upset and left him sprawling on his back whence he was washed to the foot of the hill and completely saturated by the oncoming tide. I never could make Caleb believe that this passenger wasn't Wildair, although I tried hard to do so.

EFFECTS OF COMING ON TIED.

As soon as the wave had passed on through the railing, the drenched crowd scrambled up, some with a hearty laugh, others, whose hats were overboard, with a put-on grin, while the Doctor, who had almost entirely escaped by jumping onto a bench and clinging to his post, swung his hat ecstatically as we all beat a dripping retreat to the cabin below. During the night the storm somewhat abated.

On the seventh day of our voyage we were leaving the monsoon-tossed waters of the Indian Ocean and Arabian Sea, and steaming up between Asia and Africa. The waters became smoother and smoother, so that in the evening not a ripple was to be seen on their surface. Our vessel, which during the previous days had tossed and worried so constantly, seemed now to be calmly sleeping as upon the bosom of a smooth lake; while with bright lights upon deck, the passengers danced and sang to music as merrily as if at home. Araby the blest was on our right hand, and on our left was the desolate looking coast of Africa.

Two days after this we arrived at Aden, Arabia, the ancient port near the foot of the Red Sea. This place was captured by the British in 1839, and since that time has been to them a second Gibraltar. It is thrown open as a free port, and as it is situated about half way between Bombay and Suez, nearly all passing vessels stop there to coal. As we approached, high towering rocks rose up almost perpendicular from the water's edge to the height of 1700 feet, presenting a very imposing appearance. We soon discovered that this was a volcanic promontory or peninsula projecting into the waters, and only connected with the mainland by a low narrow neck of sandy earth. A few European houses and shops were collected toward the extreme point where we anchored; while Aden itself was situated about three miles further on in the direction of the mainland.

We did not go ashore till the next morning, at which time we were met by scores of Arabs who desired to take us into the city. Some of the passengers concluded to ride in cabs, others on donkeys. As it was very hot, Caleb and I preferred the cabs; and after getting into one away we went helter skelter, for the horses attached to the vehicles were real Arabian horses, said to be the swiftest in the world, with fiery eyes and broad spreading nostrils.

As we wound up the gradually ascending but broad and winding road toward the summit of the promontory, the cabmen were continually running past each other; while the donkey-boys who ran behind to scare up their long-eared animals, whipped and punched away, yelling at the top of their voices, each one trying his best to outstrip the rest. Occasionally we passed a string of loaded camels, one behind another, to the number of fifteen or twenty. The first one

HEADS AND TAILS.

was led by an Arab, and its tail was fastened by means of a strap, to a ring in the nose of the second; the tail of the second one was fastened in the same way to the nose of the third, and so on till the tails came to an end.

As we ascended higher we had a fine view in one direction of the country inland; it was desert-like in appearance, with here and there a village, or a drove of cattle or horses herded by the nomadic Arabs. We could perceive at once that the inhabitants were divided into two classes—one class partially civilized, occupying towns and villages, and the other class roving about with their herds, and living in rude tents.

When toward the summit, we passed through a great gateway in the side of the extinct volcano, and on emerging on the inside, found ourselves overlooking Aden, nestled from the world, far down in the lap of the crater. From the elevation which we now occupied, we had a fine view of the walls and fortifications which in many places, capped the encircling rim or summit.

Our motley caravan now made its way down at break-neck speed into the very heart of the city. Excepting a few European dwellings, there was nothing here inviting; native huts low rock houses, narrow filthy streets, and swarms of dirty men, women and children, interspersed, for variety's sake, with swarms of equally dirty camels, are the characteristics of a place which was in the seventeenth century the home of science, industry and wealth. Only a few years since it contained but a thousand inhabitants, but now according to geographers it has about fifty thousand.

To the south of the city is a great reservoir of solid masonry, built centuries ago by the natives, but recently improved by the English. It lies in a deep ravine in the side of the crater and was constructed with various compartments, one above the other, running up the ravine, each compartment holding many thousands of hogsheads. When the rainy season comes, these are filled with the water which runs down the sides of the crater. During the dry season the water is used from the lowest compartment; then that in the next above, by means of a gate, is let into the emptied one and used, and so on till the water from the highest has passed down through the intervening ones to the lowest.

We patronized the cabmen and donkey-boys a good deal while we were in Aden, and of course had no trouble in settling with them for their services; they were satisfied with whatever we happened to give them. The other natives were equally agreeable in their behavior toward us. They would not have robbed us had they had a chance; no, nor would they have taken anything as a gift had we offered it to them. They gathered round to try to sell us eggs, some of which were as large as a two quart cup, which led us to suppose that their hens were a monstrous breed. Not being able to sell us any, they afterwards came round with ostrich feathers of many varieties; and then we no longer wondered at the size of their eggs.

The prices which they first asked for their feathers appeared to us to be high, especially as their eggs were warranted to be

"EGGS-TRAORDINARY!"

fresh; but when they reduced them from several dollars to a few cents, we concluded it was a favorable time to buy.

Not long did our ship tarry at Aden; we bade the place and its people adieu one fine evening, and next morning found ourselves steaming up the Red Sea, the waters of which, by the way, were not of the color which their name might indicate. We were sorry for this, for we had seen enough of the ocean, and longed for a change. The sea-gulls too, which I had hoped would disappear forever, were flying thick over the water, and were just as keen-sighted and keen-scented as before. Some of the boys gulled one of them into swallowing a baited hook which was dragged behind the vessel, and then pulled on deck. It was a pretty bird, and as its eyes watered, and its body quivered from fright and pain, I was sorry that we had indulged in the sport.

As we continued our voyage northward the shores of Arabia and Africa were visible, and we frequently saw, on either hand, sandy mountains, and long ranges whose serrated or saw-tooth summits stood out clearly against the sky. In many places beautiful corals lined the shores of the mainland and island.

On the second day out from Aden we passed Mecca, the great city of the Mohammedan world, to which thousands make a yearly pilgrimage. It is an inland city, but only a few miles from the sea. Two days later we passed Mount Sinai, which Moses ascended to receive the Ten Commandments. It is northwesterly from Mecca, and appears to be about the same distance from the coast.

On the evening of the fifth day after leaving Aden, we arrived at Suez, the southern terminus of the famous canal which unites the waters of the Mediterranean and Red Seas.

CHAPTER XXXIII.

GETTING ACQUAINTED WITH EGYPT.

AS we dropped anchor in the harbor of Suez, I looked with curiosity toward the shore, and called to mind that through the mountain-pass leading down to the water's edge once came the terror-stricken hosts of Israel. Then I pictured to myself the tender feet of infants, and the sandaled feet of mothers, and the march of that mighty multitude treading the sands beneath our vessel until they issued from the deep and stood upon the opposite shore, where their joy found vent in lofty acclamations and shouts of triumphant song.

Far out we looked over the sea of sand out of which rose the bold and jagged mountains of Sinai, and noticed with interest what a desolate region it was. No wonder the joy of the wandering Israelites was soon turned to sorrow, as they were seized by hunger and thirst on those scorching deserts where not even a shrub or tree was to be seen. That the bones of the entire hosts did not bleach in the sun, was nothing less than a miracle. In all the waste fields of parched sands which met our gaze, we could only discern one well, round which were a few wandering Arabs watering their herd. The natives pointed towards it and muttered, "Moze! Moze!" meaning thereby that it was Moses' Well.

These Arabs we found to be abominably lazy fellows to say the least. A Chinaman will row you ashore without thinking of hoisting a sail, but these fellows will raise a sail in a dead calm, and never dream of moving an oar until you pay them a double price. The wind—what there was of it—happened to be directly against us, so that sailing was a very slow process; but there they lounged, happy and contented, until we were becoming doubtful about ever reaching the shore. Our uneasiness however only seemed to do these beggars good; they evidently relished it. Finally we found that only a rupee or two would prove an effective argument to bring us to our destination, at which we arrived an hour or two after dark. Here we found one of our old comrades who had outstripped us, although he left the ship long after we did; but as he had often been here before I suppose he knew who he was dealing with.

We felt joyous as we again trod our mother earth, although in a far-off land and among strangers. Our companion led the way, and we were soon wandering through the dark and dusty streets of Suez. After stumbling over a donkey or two we came to the European part of the town, when our friend asked us to accompany him to a musical entertainment and we gladly consented.

Entering a wide, open door we were charmed by the sweetest Italian strains, and to and fro within moved the graceful forms of French and Italian girls, who, after bidding us welcome, brought round sparkling wine and offered it with hands flashing with diamonds.

Shortly afterwards many others of our fellow passengers arrived from the ship, all eager to enjoy themselves. There were fat laughing Dutchmen whose sides shook from their cheeks downwards; politely scraping Frenchmen; John Bull and his varied descendants; but no one more attracted our attention than a young Portuguese,—a third class passenger on the ship, though he was all the time trying to force his way among the first class. He was now dressed up as smart as any coxcomb could be, and his wasp-like legs flew over the floor as he whirled his fair partner in the dance, which became promiscuous. Wildair and I had not at first the least idea of the character of the house we were entering, the politeness of our companion having deceived us; and now when we desired to depart in peace he urged us to remain, saying that since we were traveling to see the world the best way to become acquainted with the people of these countries was through the ladies, as the men were reserved. When he finally consented to accompany us, the rest of the passengers collected round with their arguments, while the fair angels of the establishment, departing far from the pretence of either modesty or decency, vied in their attempts to retain us—but in vain.

Young men contemplating traveling know little of the temptations they will encounter. Those who drink a little and carouse a little to be in fashion, and just because others do the same, may tremble to leave the moorings of home and drift out into the currents of foreign travel and society.

From Suez we went to Cairo by rail; but how strange it seemed to be rolling across the sands of Africa in a train of cars, while the caravans, as in times of old, were still seen winding their slow but steady way as if the rolling ages had brought no change. Some of them perhaps were returning from a pilgrimage to Mecca or other venerated localities, which railroads will soon render so familiar as to break up the feelings of awe and superstition with which many mortals now regard them. Then unconsciously my thoughts reverted to the past, and I imagined one caravan to be that which Abraham sent with his servants to find a wife for his son Isaac; or the one that carried away Joseph as a slave. As we passed the natives journeying alone on those long-eared animals so frequently mentioned in the Bible, I called this one Moses, that one Aaron, another Abraham, and another David.

In still another personage we met, I fancied we had run across Balaam; not that he looked like that heathen prophet, or even resembled the priestly natives with their long gowns; he was a queerer specimen of humanity than any of these. But notwithstanding this, he reminded me of Balaam from the energetic manner in which he applied his guiding club to the sides of his donkey's neck and head. This ass however had not heard the voice of an angel, but simply the shrill braying of the "Iron Horse" accompanied by the endless din of the railroad train. It was perhaps his first introduction to them; at any rate he acted badly, and caused his rider, with his flying turban and dangling sword, to cut considerable of a figure.

A MEETING IN THE DESERT.

When Joseph and Mary with their precious charge, fleeing from the wrath of Herod, journeyed into Egypt, there was no Suez Canal to be crossed, but it is said the Red Sea then extended farther north than it now does; I can well believe it; for the brackish lagoons, and bitter lakes which we passed indicated that there, formerly, was the bottom of the sea. At Ismalia there was sufficient depression for a great lake, which formed a link in the canal. This place witnessed the ceremonies at the opening of Egypt's new river; it was the scene of stirring events then, but like some of our railroad towns, its day was short and evil. Its growth now bids fair to be sober and steady; and it may perhaps some day become a great city.

We now rolled over high sands toward the Delta, occasionally passing spots having some appearance of fertility, where the miserable looking inhabitants, living in huts of sun-dried-bricks, were trying to eke out a livelihood. At a station, well tanned boys, with skins of water shaped like geese strung on their backs, halted beneath our window to gaze longingly into our faces, and mutter," Wader, wader;" at the same time they proposed by signs to pour some out into their cups that we might drink and be refreshed. Men and women sat in long rows on either side of the track, beside baskets of tropical

FRUITS OF COMPETITION.

fruits. We motioned for one of the lasses to come to our window. She took up her basket, placed it on her head and was approaching, when a brakeman with a fez cap on his head viciously threw her basket down the embankment and shoved her sprawling after it. We took pity on her and gathered up a portion of the fruit, but noticed that the official took care to help himself liberally. We threw the poor girl a franc, and she went off crying; gladly would we also have bestowed
19

on her oppressor his due, but it would not have been good policy in Egypt. The fellow had been hired by the proprietor of an eating-house to keep off these fruit-selling peasants, who were really little better than serfs.

From these desert sands we now rolled into the wonderful "Garden of the Desert," where the golden fruit of the orange and lemon tree, ripe figs, and pomegranates large and rosy as apples, hung from bending boughs; while from the tufted tops of palm-trees drooped dates and bananas in clusters so large that a man would not want to carry more than three or four as a load. Here reigned in great perfection the poetic idea of eternal sunshine; while cotton pods just bursting their casing, and scattering here and there, whitening all the fields, gave the natives the best idea of snow that they could have at home.

The Delta was as level as the surface of a smooth lake; and when it is covered with water, as we saw it afterwards, no land is in sight save the artificial mounds on which the villages are built. In some places dams are built across the Nile so as to flood the banks as often as needed, and thus increase the certainty and quantity of the crops. On the borders of the Delta and the Nile Valley where the water does not overflow, we saw them elevating it by oxen or donkeys moving in circles at the end of a sweep, and doubtless these higher lands will soon be irrigated by ditches.

Continuing on above the head of the Delta, the high outlines of the desert, through which the broad valley of the Nile takes its winding way, rose up before us; and soon the minarets and domes of Cairo's three hundred mosques pierced the softly-tinged atmosphere, presenting a most enchanting scene. Ten miles beyond, in the sleepy distance, were the forms of three pyramids keeping guard over the Nile just as they did in the days of the Pharaohs, thousands of years ago.

As soon as our train entered the depôt, the Arabs thronged outside and even inside the cars, ready and anxious to do anything for anybody. We pointed out to one of them our luggage, consisting of a couple of valises and two small boxes;

and after carrying them out of the cars he stacked them upon his head and started off for our hotel, with us after him.

Of course we had a hundred offers to ride, but we declined all, as we wanted to see how far the fellow could go before our baggage caught a fall. We were frequently startled by the shooting across our path of a donkey almost hidden by his rider and followed by a swift impetuous runner.

A STIFF-NECKED EGYPTIAN.

We pressed on after our baggage-carrier with increasing astonishment at his powers of endurance, and concluded that he was a lineal descendant of some "stiff necked" Egyptian of ancient times. He took us up a broad street that was being cut through the heart of the city, not sparing even the old mosques that had stood for centuries; then through the narrow streets of old Cairo, among whose labyrinths we wound our way between high walls where even the little donkey was crowded out. At length all branching passages came to an end, and only a narrow arched opening led through a dark wall, looking so forbidding that we did not care to enter it. But just then our guide muttered, "Hotel, hotel," and on taking a closer look we saw the glimmer of a light beyond.

Venturing on, we passed through the dark passage, and at once found ourselves in a spacious Oriental court, surrounded on every side by long shady porticoes. In the centre were bowers, and walks, tropical trees and plants, playing fountains and snowy statues.

We involuntarily exclaimed, "How delightful!" It seemed to us like a little paradise on earth: in fact, it is from the beauty of courts like these that the Orientals gather their ideas of the original Eden as well as the state of the faithful after death.

LOST IN CAIRO.

I have referred to the donkeys of Cairo in a preceding paragraph. At a subsequent period we had leisure to contemplate in a calmer mood some of these long-eared animals. Tremendous bundles, seemingly in mourning, were mounted thereon, and Wildair, by instinct probably, declared that each bundle contained a woman. I was incredulous for a while; but presently the outside covering of one package caught on a nail in a post, and lo! it unveiled to our view a pale but pretty feminine face. Involuntarily I started toward her hoping to render assistance; but she shrieked and shuddered so much at my presence that I left her to her fate.

Our guide told us that the prettiest girls covered their face the closest. This one made fuss enough to be extremely handsome—which she was not. Perhaps he was not a judge of beauty, but he claimed to be; and he frankly confessed that when he first saw the face of his wife he did not like her and that he intended to let her go, and buy another one.

HARD ON THE DONKEYS.

CHAPTER XXXIV.

A VISIT TO THE PYRAMIDS.

ONE morning, not long after midnight, we were riding through the dark and narrow streets of Cairo, bound for the wonderful Pyramids.

"Oh Wildair" I cried, "we forgot to put those sardines in our lunch-basket."

"So we did."

"Say, son of Pharaoh," said I turning to the guide, "can you possibly get us a couple of cans of sardines? We don't want to starve on the desert like the Children of Israel."

He gave us an answer in the affirmative, and soon afterwards, jumping from his seat, he commenced thumping at a door, kicking and banging as if he meant to burst it open. Presently we could hear a man grumbling within. I translate the conversation as we then imagined it.

"Say! say! halloo! I want a couple of cans of sardines for two American gentlemen visiting the Pyramids."

"Let those Americans go to ———;" and the speaker was gone to the land of Nod.

Again the guide hallooed and thumped, but the sleepy response was:—

"What do you wa—a—a—nt?"

He renewed the attack, but with less success than before, for although he redoubled the force of the assault, yet as soon as he ceased, the man within replied with a snore. Finally however, the "Son of Pharaoh" was too much for the sleeper; he arose from his couch, threw open his shutters, and handed out from his dusky cell—or rather, his niche in the wall—the articles we desired.

We had not proceeded far upon our way when our guide began to halloo, and we came to a halt. Back from dark streets or crevices came a murmuring answer, while across our minds flashed the thought that we were fools to start out in this strange dark city with a guide whom we had never seen before. We remembered all we had ever read of the treachery of the Arabs, and we felt anything but comfortable.

Presently up from the rear came the sounds of approaching men, and we felt for our arms only to find we had left them in our room. So we grasped our canes; but fortunately we didn't need them, for we presently discovered that the guide had only been arousing the gate-keeper, and that three other men had also come, bringing extra donkeys for our use when those we were riding should give out.

It struck me that these people were not so enlightened as some of our countrymen or they would have robbed us. Only think of treacherous Arabs, bloody Mohammedans, being so much behind the times as to permit "Christian dogs," whom they suspect of having money, to pass through their narrow unlighted streets in safety. Oh, these stupid people, we should elevate them at once!

On we went, passing by women and even children sleeping far out along the roadside awaiting the time for the morning market. I admired the innocence of one youth who pillowed his head upon his donkey. Not a care troubled his mind; his dusky form required only half a covering, and with open mouth he still slept on and snored, utterly regardless of our approach.

Further along we met other parties driving their loaded donkeys and camels toward the city gates, which closed and opened with the sun.

The Arabs of the Pyramids were not too proud to sleep on the ground, and our arrival in their vicinity awakened them. They approached swiftly, and though quite humble at first we soon found that they were up to all sorts of mischief.

They laid hold of us unceremoniously, and at once commenced boosting our bodies up the high stone steps, which led up the sides of a pyramid. We imagined that those below were playing foot-ball with us on their heads, while those above were catching us; but, anyway, there was no helping it. Our faithful guide now deserted us and turned back, probably to make up for loss of sleep from starting so early in the morning. His parting words to us were:—

"Beware of your pockets."

It was soon after the sun rose upon that desert world, and over the sleeping Nile, that we reached the summit, set our feet upon the uppermost step, and felt the inward satisfaction of having gained the eminence of our loftiest aspirations. The point of this pyramid had stood in our boyhood's fancies as some prominent object stands out in a dream—something mythical that might be thought of but never handled—something too remote in space and origin to have any tangible existence; and therefore it was not strange that as we now stood upon these stones,—stones as real as those we saw in childhood—we should feel as though we had awakened in the new sphere or been lifted to a pinnacle above the changing scenes of time, that we might look out over the wrecks of bygone ages.

To one standing here, the rise, progress, and fall of empires seemed as but ripples upon the ocean shore. The histories of Germany, France, England, America, and the various nations of modern days, seemed but as things of yesterday. The glory of Rome, Greece, Persia, and Babylon seemed also to be nigh at hand, while far beyond, fading away in the dim mists which overhang the boundless sea of time, we could discern faint outlines of the histories and traditions of Egypt and the Pyramids.

But these mischievous Arabs evidently didn't want to see us reflecting. The rascals, by repeated nudges or pulls at our coat-tails, soon brought our minds back to meditate upon the present—and especially upon the fallen state of modern Egyptians. But we could not even think of that long; they would not even permit us to look at the miserable mud-colored villages so poetically perched—or rather squatted, upon mounds rising from the water. In fact, we soon forgot entirely that we were on the Pyramid so incessant were these beggars in their importunities. They were rubbing our limbs to keep them from becoming stiff, touching thimbles of water to our lips, and then kneeling all round with out-held hats, calling us "good Americans" and a variety of other equally pretty names.

We told them we had paid our guide double price with the express understanding that his fee should cover all possible expenses; but they only commiserated us for employing a "cheating guide," "no-pay rascal," "deceptive wolf."

We informed them that the guide had told us that they would compliment him in this manner but that we were not to mind them. Then they swore by Mohammed that he was an impostor and would not donate them a cent. As evidence of their truthfulness they bowed down before us with their faces toward Mecca, and repeated their sunrise prayers, accompanied by crossings, bowings, and repeated rising from and again falling prostrate upon the ground.

When they found that all was of no avail, they proposed that one of them should run down the Pyramid, across the intervening sand, and up Cephron, the second great Pyramid, all in ten minutes, for two rupees, or one dollar. They showed us by pantomime how he would go down our Pyramid and up the other one, and did it so well that we could almost see him doing it. They accompanied their motions with much clamor and hurrah, and seemed to think as a matter of course that we would accept their offer. But we declined it, and told them in a deprecating manner, that they couldn't impose on us after that kind of style; for they had run not only to the top of the other Pyramid, but there and back again for one of our countrymen all in the space of nine minutes. Was not our money as good as his? To this they replied indignantly:—

"Tell him he lied!"

Wildair replied that it could not be so; for the countryman referred to was never known to joke or to exaggerate in the least.

As this seemed to excite them still more, we told them that we presumed the native who had made the quick time, was getting rather old and stiff now, but that his name was "*Traditional.*" At this they laughed and said:—

"Oh, he has been 'dead' a thousand years."

Nothing piqued by our refusal to pay for a race down the Pyramids, they now renewed their polite attentions, expecting of course pay for all they bestowed. Whenever we approached the edge of the Pyramid they hovered near to prevent our falling off; and once when Wildair got within a yard thereof, they seized him by the coat-tails and pulled him energetically back. This was too much for Wildair to stand; so jerking loose from their grasp he went wildly bounding down from step to step, with nearly the whole flock, who looked like tattered kangaroos, after him, yelping at every jump:—

"He crazy! he crazy!"

Others caught hold of me, afraid lest I should follow suit. Wildair tried to tell them that they were lunatics, but not understanding their language, his efforts were a decided failure.

In the eyes of the Arabs this Pyramid, barely five hundred feet in height, was loftier than the highest mountain in the world; and without exaggeration it certainly was immense for a work piled up by human hands. Even now, after the lapse of so many ages, and notwithstanding that the neighboring inhabitants have made of it a free quarry for building the mosques of Cairo, it covers an area of thirteen acres, and must originally have been much more extensive.

Descending the northern face of the Pyramid, we met our slandered guide but a few steps from the only entrance to the interior. While he was engaged in lighting the torches, we proposed engraving our names above the dark opening, that straggling visitors, two or three thousand years hence might look at the inscription with awe, and perhaps hand us down to the end of time as the openers and explorers of the

ENTRANCE TO THE GREAT PYRAMID.

Pyramids! But the guide snatched the garland of fame from our brows, by declaring that the lights were ready.

With heads bent almost to our feet, and in single file, we now entered the little square opening leading to the dark recesses therein. The pathway was exceedingly steep, and the roof or ceiling very low, but we found no relief until far beneath the base of the mighty monument above, away down in the eternal rock. Then turning round we looked upward and could see only a square bit of sky. The shaft leading to this aperture was boxed or lined with immense slabs of polished granite. I suspect that it was Pharaoh's telescope through which he used to observe the North Star

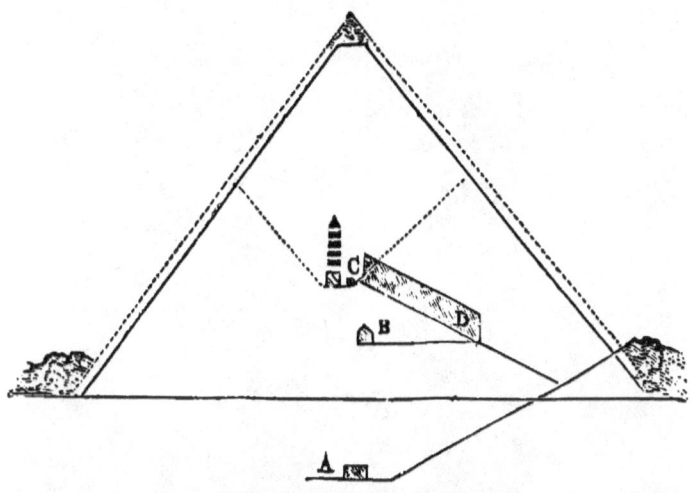

PLAN OF THE GREAT PYRAMID.

A. Subterranean Chamber.
B. Queen's Chamber.
C. King's Chamber.
D. Grand Gallery.

in the daytime. It was about twenty rods long, but did not magnify any, or point towards the stars that it used to, for although we called them "fixed" they have been moving during the last forty or fifty centuries.

A few steps more and we were standing in the Subterranean Chamber excavated in the limestone beneath the desert, for the final abode of a king. But the monarch for whom this tomb was prepared was so high-minded that he could not be content with his lowly resting-place, but constructed for himself a new tomb, up in the centre of the Pyramid.

To this newer tomb we now proceeded; first along the shaft which we had descended until it seemed we should have reached the entrance; then back, and up, and up, until finally we stood erect in the Grand Gallery, the floor of which still ascended at the same steep angle as the shaft which we had been wearily climbing. What length! what height! what emptiness! what vast stones crowding closer

THE GRAND GALLERY.

and closer together toward the lofty ceiling! An Arab now climbed a ladder to show us a shaft cut through to the outside for purposes of ventilation.

From the upper end of the Gallery a short creep more

brought us into the King's Chamber, and before us was the sarcophagus or stone coffin of the monarch who had erected the Pyramid. As we halted a moment all seemed silent as death. Should he awake! what account could we give for entering his tomb! Just then we noticed by the dancing light that the lid was lifted! We shuddered for a moment and then approached, but the dead body once there was gone.

Many weary centuries before Christ, the King of Persia came into Egypt and plundered the tomb, cutting out the granite blocks that stopped the entrances. How many mortals from every nation, in the different ages since then, have gazed for a moment with wonder upon this open coffin, as we now gazed, and then passed the way of all the earth!

But how far back in the dreamy past came hither the sable procession bearing the mighty king who built this pyramid, and, under priestly blessings, laid him in the great granite coffin which he had placed here to receive his mortal remains —who can say? He probably supposed that his tomb would remain closed until the Archangel rent the rocks and called him into the presence of the greater Monarch who rules the universe. He left no name upon his coffin, but it was discovered a few years since in one of the little cells made above his "Chamber" to break the weight from the ceiling. The hieroglyphics were extremely rude, having been cut on one of the stones by a workman during an idle moment; but when deciphered it proved to be the name of Cheops, who, according to Greek historians, built this massive pile.

We were now standing where the king had stood when in the height of his glory. Here he contemplated human power and earthly grandeur, and surely if any mortal ever dreamed of rendering his name immortal he was that one. He had erected for himself a monument and resting-place, which he supposed would defy the hand of Time and remain forever a visible witness of his greatness. But vain was his ambition! Mortals with sacrilegious hands have invaded his retreat and carried him hence, no one knows whither; while the Arab as he stands with smoking torch within this dreary and empty abode, drops no tear nor even breathes a sigh. The kingly name has long since passed from among men, except as it is preserved by Herodotus, and even at his hands, it finds but little honor. The "Two Mites" dropped by an obscure woman into the treasury of the Lord, will in the light of the judgment become a nobler monument to her memory, than are these massive Pyramids, to that of Egypt's King.

Leaving the empty sarcophagus we visited the Queen's Chamber, but as it was entirely empty we concluded it had been misnamed by modern explorers, or that she too had been carried off by some of them.

Then we crept out into the light of day and gazed upon the world-renowned Sphinx, the wrinkles of whose sublime cheeks mark the layers of rock that underlie the sand. Then we walked round Cephron, a smaller Pyramid, and were told that its builder was the brother of Cheops. He tried to erect as large and imposing a structure, but he failed and died unhappy. Near by was a still smaller structure built by their successor—perhaps a second cousin. It was not opened until within the last few years, when a coffin was found, but it dropped into the ocean on the way to the British Museum. Around these three were a number of diminutive pyramids built in memory of relatives; and interspersed among these were the vaults of the more distant friends and relatives who could not afford monuments. We went down into some of them, but the great bats blew out our lights, and flapped their hideous wings in our faces, and as they are somewhat disagreeable on account of their claws, we exchanged their society for that of our donkeys, and mounted them to return to Cairo.

As we started off, the donkey-boys gave a whoop, and each one struck his animal a smart blow which put them at once into full speed. In a moment more another whack and shout almost sent them running from under us, and ourselves from under our hats. After pitying the donkeys and their masters awhile, we concluded that if they could stand it we could.

They continued at a very fast "lope," or run, for nearly six miles. These Arabs of the desert are as wiry as steel.

We were now coming to deeper sands which had been drifted by the wind, filling up a space between a low ridge of rock and the main desert. Here we passed men by the dozens, digging into the sand for bones, which when found they sold to sugar-refiners. In one place where the rock was cracked open we approached as near as we could conveniently; and what should we discern in the crevice but mummies; while beneath us were the Catacombs of Memphis, the ancient capital of Lower Egypt.

We were now passing Aboo Seer, a group of three large pyramids making the burial-place of another dynasty—perhaps the one that overturned that of Cheops. A couple of miles further on we came to a third group, the principal one of which was the Lakkarah. To climb the steps of this pyramid would have required several gigantic strides of one hundred feet each, and so we did not ascend. Still beyond were the two majestic Pyramids of Dashoor. We looked at them longingly and meditatively and then turned slowly back into the desert.

Through the flooded valley we wound our way through dikes, thinking of the paved streets that lay silent beneath the sands and mud of the Nile. Two or three thousand Sphinxes guarding the approaches to fallen temples, had been discovered, but we could not see them now.

Finally we came to a large island covered with the ruins of Memphis—consisting chiefly of immense heaps of sun-dried bricks, made, we supposed, by the Children of Israel. What a hard time they had under those task-masters! Every day was splendid for making brick. A rainy hour never interferred, else all these mud bricks had crumbled; but they remain to this day. A few wretched-looking inhabitants, contented and happy, were thriving on the fruit of the date-palms growing out of the ruins.

A short distance beyond this point we came to a little railroad station, where a group of squatting Arabs were waiting to take the cars. As the train came along just in the nick of time, we tumbled the donkeys into one car, jumped into another ourselves, and rolled away toward Cairo, through groves of date-palms where the inhabitants were wading or paddling from tree to tree, then climbing and gathering the clusters of fruit, while our cars stirred up an awful cloud of dust that ran an even race with us.

At the station opposite Cairo we got into the awaiting carriage and rolled away for the city, past one of the palaces of the viceroy, where two or three thousand cavalry were stationed, while cavaliers on fine horses rode up and down along the walls. As we passed the gates, guarded on either side by Turkish soldiers, we obtained a few glimpses of the grounds, gardens, and parks within, which seemed like a fairy world. On we rolled, along the finest drive in Egypt, as level as a floor, and embowered by acacia-trees, and then we crossed the Nile, full of strange, leaning masts, over a long bridge built for the pleasure of the ex-empress of France, that she might indulge in a drive to the Pyramids during her visit at the opening of the Suez Canal.

In the evening we tendered our guide a napoleon to visit the market and bring us a fine melon and a basket of grapes. Upon his return he threw down a lot of Egyptian coins of whose value we knew nothing, and when we proceeded to make inquiries were told by this Mohammedan, that we ought not to suspect our servant; that God would take care of us. Before leaving he took care to ask us for a donation in behalf of the donkey-boys and himself.

CHAPTER XXXV.

SIGHT-SEEING UNDER GROUND.

EVERYBODY said that we must see the Catacombs before we left Egypt; so we suffered our unclean guide to convey us thither. We found them to be immense excavations in the hard rock underlying the desert; quarries, in fact, from which the ancient Egyptians cut the stone to build their temples, palaces, and national works; with now and then an odd block for a god. They had gods in vast numbers, and when they wanted a new one they joined two of those already at hand, and got up a compound of lions with men's faces, and men with birds' faces, fishes with legs, and all sorts of variations on the usual order of things, the object seeming always to be to make something more hideous than before. The excavations being made, the next thing to do was to utilize them; and when the idea of using them as human sepulchres was decided on, they prepared the thing in a proper manner, cutting galleries at right angles to each other, with here and there a chamber, as a relief to the labyrinth of windings, upon the walls of which they carved the various scenes of life, here and hereafter.

The most successful digger seems to have been one Ben Hassan,—short for Benjamin, I suppose. He appears to have been one of those old "governors" who would sit round the tavern stove, and discuss every subject, from the proper manner to trap a musk-rat to the details of a patent churn. The guide books say he was a king, and so of course he must have been one; but he was a democratic old fellow for all that, and the people knew it or they never would have taken such liberties as to write down a royal personage as Ben!

The tomb of another, whose name is, alas! forgotten, indicates that he was an enterprising poulterer, and did not feel above his business. There he sits, plucking flinty feathers from a granite goose, and there too sits his chief clerk, ready to give the finishing touch to the bird before

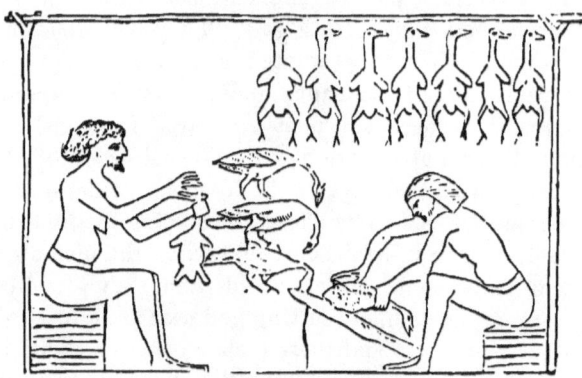

A HARD GOOSE TO PICK.

hanging it among the stock-in-trade, which already makes a respectable show in quantity at least. We thought the dress of this group a little scanty, but said nothing about it, as near by were four festive damsels engaged in a combination of leap-frog and base-ball. One of our party said he would like to see some young ladies of the present day play ball in this manner. Probably he did not remember that the dresses now worn are not so well adapted to the games as were those of these ancient maidens.

There was also another party of four young ladies, who were engaged in throwing balls in the air and catching them as they came down. This exercise of the balls was, I presume, taken just before going to bed, or just after getting up, as they all had their night-dresses on. I noticed that their feet were large, and that their lines of beauty were poorly developed.

We passed by a whole raft of serious-looking personages, whom we took to be religious functionaries. They were

MORNING RECREATIONS.

presenting bowls of soup and variously shaped dishes to the gods—that is what our guide called them, although some had bills long enough to drink buttermilk out of a churn. What a liberal old fellow that Ben was. He used to patronize all

BED-TIME EXERCISES.

kinds of things, even to dancing on the tombs; and you can imagine how the young ladies danced and tumbled from the way they played ball. The young ladies loved jewelry; but that was a natural weakness which they have not outgrown to this day. We saw how the finger-rings, necklaces, and bracelets were made from the weighing of the gold to the giving of the finishing touch.

Passing on, we recognized at a glance the good old Egyptian husbandmen of forty centuries ago, with their wooden hoes and equally rude plows and sickles. Some of their oxen had half-a-dozen marks of the branding-iron on one side, and perhaps as many more on the other side; I could not see it. It seemed as if he had changed hands rather too often; and what was worse, a new owner had tied the four feet of the helpless animal and was about applying another hot iron.

Some of the Theban kings were great aristocrats, living by themselves in spacious mansions, and cutting out for their last resting-places vast apartments, on the walls of which they carved the scenes of time and the imaginary scenes of eternity. They delighted particularly to thus record their numerous battles, from the conquering of an army to the despatching of a mosquito.

A TOUCHING SCENE.

A certain kingly warrior, renowned in his time, went out hunting one day, and when he came home he had his exploits all carved out upon the walls of his lonely mausoleum, as an eternal witness of his achievements. We know that he was a great king, for none but such a personage could accomplish such feats. It was touching to see the consideration of the wild bull which stood still with something like a drum-stick in his mouth, while this expert hunter is making up his mind what to do with him. A book on this subject says that "the hunter is supposed to have been hiding behind the tree near his right foot." We could not suppose such a thing, however, as the tree is not as high as his knee, and would make only a mouthful for the bull.

RETURN OF THE HUNTERS.

A group in another place represents a doe suckling a young fawn. This scene so touched the hunter's heart that instead of killing them he had them brought home and put in his park. Like everything else, the execution is a trifle exaggerated, but still it possesses affecting simplicity. A representation of a servant carrying a slain deer on his shoulders, and leading two greyhounds, is very faithful at least as far as the dogs go.

There was one slab representing a man out shooting with bow and arrow. He had succeeded in beguiling a cow and bull within short range and was sending his missiles so fast that the fourth arrow was ready for a start while yet the second and third were on the fly—thus showing the superiority of ancient weapons in the hands of ancient hunters over modern fire-arms. It is worthy of notice too, that had the cow been hit by a ball instead of an arrow, the noise of the explosion would have startled the bull from his serene meditations, and he would have had a better chance to dodge the second ball. That this archer was also a great hunter there can be little doubt, for other game is lying about which he had previously secured. Among the lot is a bird without any tail, another without a head, and several specimens of races now extinct. An accordion and a fish-hook near by are suggestive of a person of meditative and musical tastes.

Near by the stone which pictured forth the exploits of the mighty Nimrod, we stumbled over a skull, and thinking from its proximity that it might have once belonged to the hunter, we tied it up in a handkerchief and carried it along as a memento of our visit to the Catacombs. We were subsequently tempted to leave it behind in our room at some hotel as a joke on the chambermaid; but it clung to us, and with us arrived safely at our home. Our friends, to our surprise, did not take kindly to it, and it was soon wrapped up in a newspaper and deposited in an upper chamber of our wood-house. In the course of time it was discovered by mice and appropriated to the uses of a large family thereof; and when the intruders, in turn were discovered, they and their castle were demolished by blows rained on them by a sturdy "giant-killer" armed with a huge club.

For a long time we wandered about among the ancient relics of humanity, laying up material for moralizing and meditation in after years. Kings and warriors had here endeavored to leave behind them names which would be forever remembered; but already ruthless explorers had dragged the last relics of departed greatness from their sepulchres, and trampled them in one indistinguishable mass of bandages and bones, through which the traveler wades knee-deep, stirring up clouds of dust at every step. When we finally left the Catacombs, it was with a consciousness that we had been guilty of little less than sacrilege.

One day as we were riding over the sands near where once stood ancient Memphis, we chanced to meet an antique-looking excavator who took us a short distance from the road and showed us where a hole had been dug in the sand, to the underlying stratum of rock. Thence we followed him through a passage which led into an immense underground hall, whose dimensions were only revealed as we proceeded with our torches. On either hand were smaller apartments, to the number of forty-two, each of which contained a beautiful rose-colored sarcophagus made of polished granite.

As we wandered from one stone coffin to another, a feeling of respectful awe filled my mind; they were so fine in finish, and so immense in size and weight, that I could not doubt that great and renowned men, worthy of my sincerest reverence, rested within them. But I felt ashamed of my emotions when we were told that each chest only contained an embalmed bull. These bulls were the venerated gods for which the old Egyptians had poured out their lives and treasures; to which they bowed with veneration while living; and for which, when one died, all Egypt mourned, until the priests had searched the land and found a suitable successor.

SUBTERRANEAN HALL OF THE BULLS.

When a new bull had been thus secured it was borne in more than kingly pomp to On, the city of temples; where, during forty days, the people rejoiced, and men and women cohabited publicly in his presence. It was the image of this Egyptian bull that Aaron reproduced with the earrings of the Israelites at Horeb; and when Moses returned from the mount he found the people enjoying their forty days of feasting and wantonness around the golden beast.

The followers of Mohammed who showed us the sights and wonders of the country seem to have lost all respect for the gods and images of their forefathers. They not only refuse to worship them, but even imagine that the devil and other evil spirits lurk about the dark ruins. After our experience with the bulls we, like them, no longer reverenced any mementoes of departed greatness.

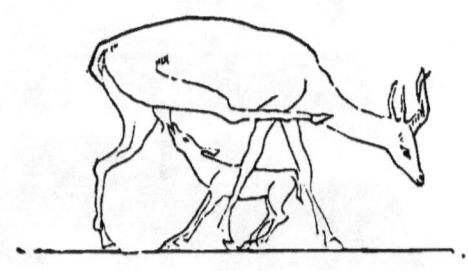

CHAPTER XXXVI.

THE LANGUAGE OF THE MONUMENTS.

WHEN I stood in the presence of the Great Pyramid, I felt that when it was built brute force must have ruled the world. In its erection no genius was displayed, as when at the touch of Grecian sculptors blocks of snowy marble sprang into ideal life, full of grace and beauty. There was no display of art and skill such as is seen in the temples of Italy, among whose aisles the visitor wanders enchanted. The gigantic pile was merely a collection of coarse stones brought together by thousands and tens of thousands of men who drudged out their slavish existence in accomplishing their task.

Learned men have concluded that the largest stones of the Pyramids were brought hundreds of miles on rude sledges drawn by multitudes of men. For what great end was all this toil and hardship? Was it for the good of the public, or to celebrate some great event, or to honor the memory of some renowned character or benefactor of his race? No! It was built by a race of slaves to gratify the unreasonable ambition of a tyrant who had just invaded and subdued their country.

Yet some persons are found who are ready to laud this ancient despot and to magnify the work of his crouching menials. Often do we hear men who have never visited the pyramids say that in these days it would be impossible to erect such structures. But I have not the least doubt that plenty of Yankees can be found who would contract to build a dozen pyramids within a specified space of time; and who

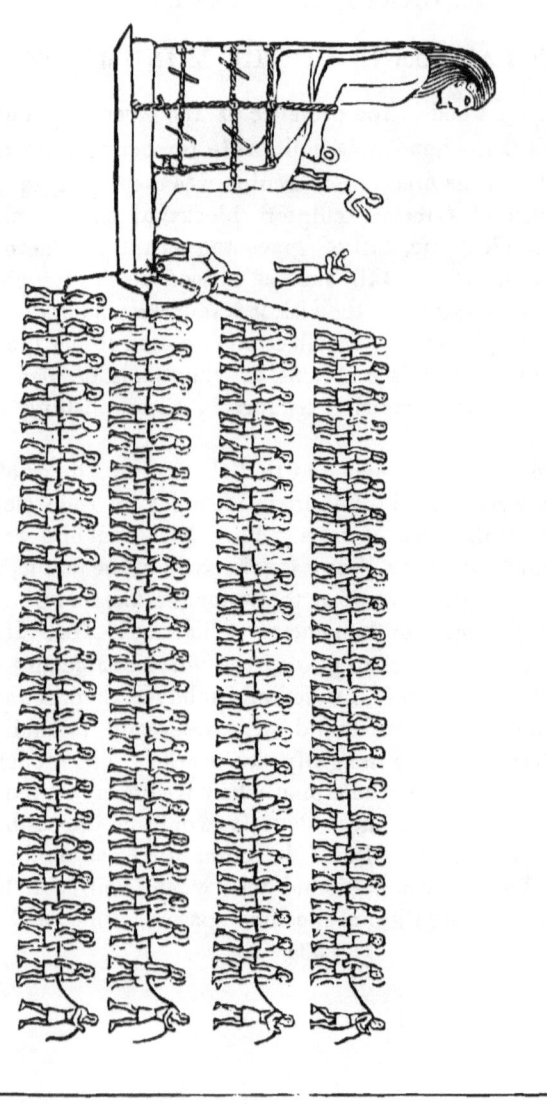

A TRANSPORTED GOD.

would do it too at a rate never dreamed of by the original builders. Instead of dragging the stones thither by hand, and laboriously raising them in the same manner, the few workmen required to do the job would have a comparatively easy time of it, while the "iron horse" and stationery engine did the work.

The Obelisks impressed us more favorably than the Pyramids. They evidently were erected at a later period when art was more developed. But still the single idea of power and solitary superority was prominent in these imposing shafts of hard unornamented granite. It is said that they used to be erected at the entrances of temples to inspire in mortals an awe for the gods.

YANKEE PYRAMID BUILDERS.

The obelisk in which we were most interested carried us back forty centuries to the days of Ben Hassan—"Old Ben"—whose name it bears. It stood at the apex of the Delta, lone and solitary, in a field of growing corn. From fragments of history, hieroglyphics, and tradition, it appears that here was built the most ancient city of Egypt—if not of the world. It was a city of schools and colleges, and in it Joseph is supposed to have received the hand of Asenath, the daughter of the high priest of Egypt, who was next in influence to Pharaoh himself. Here the learned men of Greece pursued their studies; and here Plato spent thirteen years of his life in poring over the old Egyptian philosophy and mythology. The world may rejoice that those old papyrus manuscripts to which he had access were afterwards burned at Alexandria;

for the Greeks have transmitted to us through their mythology all that ought to be known respecting them.

RUINS ON THE NILE.

While amid the monuments of the Egyptians we made a study of their picture-writings, and attained such proficency, that when we saw a line of hieroglyphics in which there was a cow, a pig, a knife, and a pair of scales, we read it thus:—"Cows, sheep, and pigs are butchered here, and weighed out to customers." When we observed in another line, a man, a lion, a bow, and an arrow, we understood that a gentleman went out hunting the king of beasts with his bow and arrows. Such groups as these were specimens of the earliest picture-writing of the Egyptians.

But these ancients made new discoveries in the course of time. As a stock-dealer was corresponding with various parties about the number of donkeys, geese, and camels he had for sale, his son said:—

"Now father, I don't fancy making a donkey every time I have to write that animal. Why would not two long ears do as well?"

INGENIOUS LEXICOGRAPHERS. 339

"And the neck of the goose and the hump of the camel would surely suggest their owners," remarked the second son. The father assented.

Thus they and their descendants continued to shorten and render easy the writing of each word, until finally they bore little or no resemblance to the objects or thoughts they were intended to suggest to the mind. There came into use a writing in which few or no hieroglyphics were seen, like the Chinese symbols of to-day,—a curve representing one word, a straight mark another, a cross a third, and a dot a fourth.

But as ladies began to wear various kinds of jewelry, and different textures of laces, and to adopt a perplexing number of styles, terms so multiplied that it became impossible to find symbols to represent all the words; so the lexicographers fell to joining old symbols together to represent new words. Finally, this combination suggested to some ingenious fellow the idea of letting a symbol stand for a sound, and as the same sound was found in thousands of different words, it cut down the symbols to a score or more and gave us our alphabet.

But the priests clung tenaciously to the original hieroglyphics, and hence on the sides of temples, tombs, and mummy-cases, one sees all kinds of animals, plants, and other objects.

EGYPTIAN HIGH ART.

Out of this picture-writing sprang painting. Instead of placing a cow, a girl, and a whip in a line, to be read: "A girl drove home a cow," they put the whip in the maiden's hand and represented her in the attitude of urging homeward the milk dispensary.

Later artists made slight improvements upon this picture, by putting a little flesh upon the arms of their figures and bearing in mind that a hawk's nose did not adorn the countenance of a cow. One can trace upon the monuments how each wielder of the brush benefited by the experience of his predecessor; but the most clever in his profession never attained to more than a stiff and imperfect representation of the human form divine.

On Grecian vases and monuments which we subsequently saw, we could trace the development of painting, from its rude infancy to the perfect delineation of human forms in all their graceful attitudes. Life-like color was also given to the figures—a thing which the Egyptians never attempted—and to a certain degree light and shade were represented. But it was left to more modern painters to deceive the eye with perspective, throwing upon the canvas the appearance of receding landscape filled with thousands of familiar objects.

If our artists wish to give prominence to a general he is put life-size in the foreground, while staff officers and soldiers gradually grow smaller in the background. If the Egyptians wished to give prominence to their king, they made him many times larger than the other men around him. In their battle-pieces, one file of soldiers is above another, with a horizontal line running between the feet of the upper row and the heads of the next lower one. I know that antiquarians love to praise the art of the Nile, but this was its perfection.

Sculpturing too, like painting, sprang from picture-writing. The ancients scratched the outlines of their hieroglyphics, and then covered them with a coat of paint. Here was writing, painting and sculpturing in embryo. Succeeding generations learned to cut the outlines deeper and to round the figures, producing bas-reliefs. At a later period they carved still deeper, and figures assumed the high relief; and finally the form of statues in niches in the wall. Their finest images show a line along the back of each figure where it was broken from the main block. Though some of these images are of overpowering dimensions, yet like the paintings they all are painfully stiff. Greece carried this development in statuary, as it did in painting, to all its perfection in grace and beauty, but as sculpturing is a much simpler art than painting, little room was left for modern improvements in that line.

CHAPTER XXXVII.

THE VESTIBULE OF THE OLD WORLD.

AT last, leaving the truly Oriental city of Cairo, we took the railroad train for Egypt's celebrated seaport Alexandria.

"Hotel de Europe, patronized by the Prince of Wales" was the inscription which met our eyes on the door of a carriage as we stepped from the cars at Alexandria; and although we had never been able to trace our ancestors back further than Adam, it occurred to us that we ought to keep up the reputation of this caravansary by patronizing it—especially as the prestige of Albert Edward's visit might be wearing away.

After becoming duly ensconced in "our inn," which, by the way, was worthy of all its renowned guests, we set out to inspect the city on foot. We soon found that in this vestibule of the old world were mixed and mingled all the oddities of the earth; while the walls that surrounded it appeared as if they had been patched, mended and remodeled by every architect from the days of Noah down.

Thronging the streets were all kinds of people, from all countries under heaven, and of all shades of color. They wore all kinds of dresses—from a stove-pipe to a turban tied round the head—from the dandy-fitting suit of Broadway or Paris to the long, loose petticoat-pants of the Arabs, and the gowns of the priests. There were tall men and short men; rich men and poor men, and beggar men, and women ragged, crouching, shriveled, and haggard.

There were men of all kinds of beliefs—Christians, Mohammedans, and Pagans, and men of every kind of occupation. Upon the streets were passing various kinds of vehicles and conveyances, omnibusses, stages, wagons, drays like two long poles on two wheels, donkeys innumerable driven by donkey-

STREET SCENE IN ALEXANDRIA.

boys, upon which were seated Europeans, Arabs or anyone else; interspersed with people afoot, and people like the Chinese carrying burdens on poles.

Here was a store airy with Chinese or Japanese ornaments, carvings, and curious trinkets; there was another with large graceful vases and richly varnished boxes profusely ornamented with oriental figures. There were Turkish, Arabic, French, and English stores, filled with outfits for India, and other hot climates, grass-plaited slippers, hats like great turtle-shells but light as cork and hung with a white curtain to protect the neck and shoulders from the sun; suits of morning gowns, as loose as those worn by the men of

21

Japan, and thin as paper; and warm European outfits in all the national varieties. Some of the narrow winding streets were almost blockaded by the stands of street merchants selling many varieties of merchandise and fruits from every clime.

From this city one may take a donkey-ride into the country, a camel-ride over the desert, a canal-ride into the valley of the Nile, a railroad-ride past the pyramids or to the Suez Canal, or a steamboat-ride to almost any place in the world.

CLEOPATRA'S BATHS.

There has been but one Alexander in the world, and there is but one Alexandria. This city has never depended upon a single nation or empire, but upon the shifting fortunes of the world. Here has been the eddy or whirlpool around which human events have swept ever since Alexander set the world in commotion, by entering the field of universal conquest. Situated almost at the very entrance to those three old continents, Asia, Europe, and Africa, it has naturally been overswept by the pent-up forces that had accumulated in their interiors, yet when the equilibrium has been restored here, this has still been found to be the eddy point.

We of course visited the objects of interest connected with

the name of Egypt's beautiful and passionate queen, Cleopatra. Taking a carriage we drove first to "Cleopatra's Baths" on the sea-shore, and saw the very stone where her fair feet had trod, but tread no more, though the briny waves roll through a subterranean passage just the same as when her graceful form quivered before each incoming billow. I asked these surges which had demolished one corner of the apartment, and in another century would roll in unobstructed through the whole side, where she was whose charms had conquered great Cæsar and Pompey—men who moved the world at their pleasure; but they foamed on as before, and offered no reply.

I love to think of her passionate nature, and how, when summoned by the victorious Antony to appear at Tarsus, she willingly went hither at the behests of a master whom she was about to make her slave. Of her pomp as she approached, and "was rowed up the Cydnus with silver oars in time to silvery harmonies, reclining unrobed as Aphrodite, on her golden galley, with Nereids and Cupids grouped around her, and sails of purple silk fluttering in the wanton air, among clouds of incense that concealed the river's banks";—of the charms that fettered him, while his triumphs fell to pieces, and the golden opportunity passed for making himself victor of the world;—how in a fit of anger, she shut herself within a tomb, and caused it to be given out that she was dead;—how he threw himself upon his sword while his

CLEOPATRA'S NEEDLES.

dying command was:—"Bury me by the side of Cleopatra"; how she had his body brought, and bathed his temples with her tears, and then after ordering a splendid feast and robing herself as a queen, applied an asp to her bosom, the sting of which soon caused her death;—and how she passed away, tired of the world, after having drank at every fountain of pleasure which it could offer.

But neither these rocks, nor the billows, nor even the breezes that used to fan her cheeks, now whispered her name. So we drove to Cleopatra's Needles—the identical shafts on which she used to look in her melancholy moods and think of Egypt's departed glory. They were a pair of real Egyptian Obelisks brought from a temple of the ancient On which we had visited, and re-erected h e r e in the youth of the Roman Empire. One, however, was now toppled o v e r a n d broken.

POMPEY'S PILLAR.

At a distance, as if guarding the ruins, stood Pompey's Pillar, poetically named after one of Cleopatra's renowned and ardent lovers, although it was erected nearly three centuries a f t e r he was dead. Can either Pompey's name or this Pillar,—to-day standing bright and strong like a solitary granite column of a mighty temple—can either crumble into oblivion? Time answers "Yes; the ocean is limited, but boundless is the sea of time."

While reading the Greek inscription stating when and why this column was erected, we observed some ragged urchins pecking away at its pedestal. Knowing they could make no impression on this stone, we naturally kept one eye on the little rascals to see what they were up to. Soon, off flew three pieces of stone, which they eagerly scuffled for and brought to us importuning us to buy with such earnestness that we concluded to call them relics, purchase them, and bring them home; they looked like fragments of the Pillar, and who could ask stones to do more.

After visiting the ruins of Pompey's Palace we descended into the imperial tombs of that period. I am not aware whether we saw the identical tomb in which Cleopatra shut herself to break the heart of Antony, but I know we came across a very fine one which had been turned into a church in the early days of Christianity. Some of the pictures of the walls had been cut away and the slabs removed to modern museums.

When Joseph brought the babe Jesus into Egypt, had he gone into the Library of Alexandria, he would there have found a Greek manuscript in which it was written:—"But thou, Beth-lehem Ephratah, *though* thou be little among the thousands of Judah, *yet* out of thee shall he come forth unto me that is to be ruler in Israel; whose goings forth *have been* from of old, from everlasting." And when the apostles came here spreading the news of how a certain man had lived, died, and rose again, they read out of this same Greek manuscript, over three hundred years old, and from copies of it how "How he was wounded for our transgressions," and "With his stripes we are healed;" how "He was numbered with the transgressors;" and all those other prophecies of the Old Testament. Although that manuscript was finally burned, yet copies of it have come down to us. It is called the Septuagint because it was translated by seventy wise men chosen for that purpose, through the desire—if I remember correctly—of Alexander to read the Book.

Our most unpleasant experience in Alexandria occurred just as we were about to leave for Naples. We had employed a cab to take us and our baggage down to the wharf. There we were besieged by a party of Arabs, who under the pretence of seeing that we had nothing contraband about us, seized our trunks and valises, and began to overhaul them. They laid hands upon everything; opened every parcel,

WILDAIR EXPRESSES HIS OPINION.

peeped into our card-cases, and tumbled about our little Oriental curiosities, tearing off the soft paper in which we had so carefully wrapped them. Then they coolly demanded a tribute of two rupees for their trouble. This was too much for our equanimity. We looked at our open fans, beads, and strings, all twisted and tangled—many of them scattered over the dirty wharf—and without making any attempt to ventilate our ideas in Arabic, we gave expression to our opinions in downright English of the most personal description.

At this, however, the pirates were not in the least dismayed. They persisted in their demand, with a perseverance worthy of a better cause, threatening us with "Custom-house! custom-house!" if we did not comply. We had no desire for any more official inspection, and, while we hesitated, a bystander (who was also an Ishmaelite), stepped up and quietly suggested:—

"Just pay them a rupee and let them go."

We were far too angry to listen to this sage advice; so the Arabs gathered up the tangled heap in their arms and carried it off to the custom-house. The officer there bestowed a single glance upon us, and then passed by, without a word. There-

A STRIKE ON THE HIGH SEAS.

upon we laid forcible hands upon our own property, stowed it away as well as we could, and boarded a skiff, telling the boatmen to row as quickly as possible to the steamer, for we were late. The Arabs, however, still held on to us and attempted to prevent our departure. They actually seized hold of the boat. I never saw Wildair in such a rage as at that moment. He brandished his huge elephant cane over the rascals and threatened to demolish them if they would not let go. It was with difficulty that I appeased his wrath; and finally by loudly threatening to call in the assistance of the police, we frightened our half-savage intruders away.

We had not gone very far from the shore when we met with another difficulty—the boatmen declared for double fare. Wildair told them the proper charge, saying that he would pay no more. The boatmen stopped rowing. Wildair ordered them to proceed at once or else return to the shore. Their leader threw himself back in the boat and coolly pointed to the steamer, intimating that we should be too late. We threatened them with arrest when we *did* get to land again; and at last, somewhat intimidated, they reluctantly began to paddle on again. In a few minutes we were on board the steamer, rejoicing at our escape from enemies on sea and land.

"I hope you will be sunk in the bottom of the sea," was the tender prayer uttered by one of the disappointed boatmen, as he rowed away. I was almost tempted to toss a coin after him, for it was not pleasant to be cursed even by an extortionate Arab; but the vessel was moving on, and my opportunity of turning the curse into a blessing was lost.

CHAPTER XXXVIII.

FROM EGYPT TO SICILY AND ITALY.

OUR steamer was one of a French line running to and from Marsailles, France, and I judged at first glance that we should have a comfortable time while we were on board.

We were soon sailing out from the beautiful port of Alexandria; the city disappeared first, and then its lofty lighthouse slowly receded from view, until the coast of Africa was lost in the distance. The motion of the gently-rolling waves of the Mediterranean was scarcely noticeable in comparison with the troubled waters of the Indian Ocean; and to us the voyage seemed to be across a smooth and beautiful lake, while now and then the white sails of a ship appeared in the distance, or the smoke of a steamer on its way to the East.

The passengers consisted of English, French, Italians, three Turks, and a couple of long-gowned priests. On the afternoon of the third day we came in sight of the southern coast of Italy, and soon obtained a glimpse of the country near the shore. It was rough and mountainous, but green with vineyards; the mountains almost to their summits being thickly dotted with houses, which formed long straggling villages, while, lower down, the population was evidently much more numerous. The soil, although apparently sterile, is adapted to vineyards and fruit-trees, and the grapes, figs, oranges, olives, and other fruits, form a large part of the food of the native Italians.

Scarcely had we sighted the coast to our right, when a smoky mountain to the left came into view;—it was Mount

Ætna, the celebrated volcano in the island of Sicily. We approached nearer, until it was only about twenty or thirty miles distant, appearing to be nearer still. The smoke from the crater poured down the sides of the mountain, almost concealing it. At length the breeze sprang up, uncovering first one rough corner and then another, until nearly the whole peak was disclosed to view. Then again the thick sulphurous smoke gathered more densely, and a low rumbling noise was heard, like the sound of distant thunder. No eruption, however, took place.

THE SHORES OF ITALY.

There is a feeling of insecurity ever hovering round the base of this mountain; yet such is the richness of the soil, and so strong is the temptation it presents to an idle population, that many villages have sprung up there, as it were in the very face of death. During the past 2500 years the loss of life and property has been very great, and all efforts to avoid the force of the eruptions have been altogether futile. The walls of the city of Catania were raised to a height of sixty feet; but all in vain. When the evil day arrived the tide of lava came sweeping down against this wall, until at length it poured over the top, carrying death and destruction with it; and then flowed on, a distance of fifteen miles, to the Mediterranean, into which it rushed with a sound like thunder, while the vapor that arose completely darkened the sun.

We now sailed up the beautiful strait of Messina, between mountains covered with vines and rustic dwellings; and toward evening we anchored in front of the charming city, bearing the same name as the strait. It appeared like a vast amphitheatre rising with its white houses and dazzling spires and domes, bench after bench, up the mountain slope.

We decided to leave the steamer at this place, and going on shore were soon wandering over a broad beautiful pavement fronting the strait, and made of quarried slabs of lava. We ascended a narrow opening between the buildings, and stepped out upon a second street, paved in the same manner as the first, but broader and decorated with fountains and statues, while on either side were magnificent buildings. As twilight began to come on, the bells from the churches and cathedrals chimed out in harmony, swelling, and then floating off on the evening breeze; then dying away far out upon the waters. I have heard the chiming of bells at Naples, Venice, and other cities of Europe, but none seemed so beautiful as those of Messina.

When the Apostle Paul sailed through these straits as a prisoner, heathen temples occupied the sites where the churches now stand. The city was then old, wealthy, and renowned. It was the station for part of Cæsar's fleet, and it was here he brought into vogue the Messinian wine. After he drank of it, it of course became fashionable.

Less than a century ago quaking Ætna, fifty miles south, shook the city to the ground, burying many of its inhabitants; but before long it was rebuilt grander than ever and a population of a hundred thousand souls now resides within its walls. Each of these persons on an average sends to our country annually six dollars' worth of fruits and other articles. Whenever I taste a nice orange or drink lemonade I think of Sicily, just as when I attack what I think is a pumpkin and find it to be a pear, my mind reverts to California. Never before did I see such fine peaches as were here, large as a large apple, and as rosy as the cheeks of a bride.

After remaining a short time on the island of Sicily, we went on board of an Italian steamer bound for Naples, and were soon under way. At the eastern end of the strait, we passed through the narrow channel where

—"Scylla guards the right hand coast,
The left is fell Charybdis' post."

This Scylla, said in heathen mythologies to have been a beautiful nymph transformed into a sea-monster by the jealousy of Circe, is in reality a common rock on the Italian coast; and opposite is the boiling whirlpool of Charybdis. The pass, so famous in Latin song and Grecian story, is, although somewhat perilous, by no means such a hell-gate as the old poets would have us believe it to be. It was formerly more dangerous than now; for in 1793 a large portion of the rock was broken off, enlarging the channel and stilling forever the barking of Scylla's fabled hounds.

The falling of this rock proved fatal to the prince of Scylla and many of his people who, to escape from the frightful earthquake shocks on shore, had taken refuge on the fishing boats. About midnight, while they lay asleep in their boats the rock fell; the sea instantly rose twenty feet high and rushed with overwhelming power upon the beach. All the boats were sunk or wrecked, and 1430 Calabrese perished.

Shortly after midnight, Stromboli, the eternal lighthouse of the Mediterranean, like the torch of Jehovah, lighted up the sea grandly, sending its rays far and near over the waters.

The morning found us anchored at a small town on the coast of Italy, and during the day we stopped at other places to receive and discharge freight and passengers. We had a smooth sea all the way, but on account of the peculiar shape of the vessel or an insufficiency of ballast, we rolled from side to side not a little. In twenty or thirty minutes after passengers came on board, they almost invariably became sea-sick, and a very unpleasant scene ensued on deck. Two Italian lovers who, even amidst all the pains of *mal-de-mer* would not separate for a moment, amused us not a little.

In many places along the coast the mountains rose up nearly perpendicularly from the very water's edge. The houses were scattered over these mountains even to their summits; some of them looking like mere white specks on their lofty eyries; and some, beneath which the clouds hovered, looked as if they were resting in the midst of the sky. In the evening we enjoyed a still more beautiful sight as we watched the rows of light from those elevated abodes, shooting out upon the water, like guiding stars to the wandering mariner.

When we arose early the next morning we were anchored in the Bay of Naples, justly renowned as being the most beautiful in the world. From its semicircular margin, gradually at first, but finally more abruptly, rose the mountains, forming a vast amphitheatre. A little to our left the white marble buildings, grand cathedral, the columns and spires, all glittering in the morning sun, seemed to smile across the bay toward the eastern shore, still blushing in the shadow of the mountains, while Vesuvius raised its smoky head into the sunlight, standing forth prominently in the gorgeous scene. A feeling of profound interest attracted our minds towards the foot of Vesuvius, although it had not the glitter which filled the world around it.

Shortly after sunrise Caleb and I went ashore, and were at once conveyed to the "New-York Hotel." Upon our arrival there a dozen or more street-boys collected round to help us with our baggage. We expected European boys would have had some manners, but those of Naples disabused us of such ideas. There was no one at the door to receive us, so we thumped and rang, and pounded away. It was a long time before we heard anyone stirring, but in a moment more the landlord came to the door. He was bare-footed and in his night-dress and looked as though he had just had an attack of nightmare. It took him some time to get wide awake enough to comprehend why he had been disturbed. He then confusedly called a servant to show us to our room, and excused himself for leaving us.

Our cabman, a street-boy or two, and the servant, carried our baggage up stairs; but as we did not like the appearance of things in general, either in the room or about the hotel, we ordered a retreat to the street. At the foot of the stairs we again met the landlord, now metamorphosed into a well-dressed man. He appeared more surprised than at our first interview, and stared at us as we went out, but said not a word to his departing guests.

At a French hotel not far away we found things more inviting, and were soon ensconced in a pleasant room.

The comical figure which the American hotel-keeper cut when he appeared before us called to memory a night visit which we once made in the mountains of Colorado. Belated and very hungry we stopped at a log house to ask for something to eat. All within was silent, and there was no light; so we supposed they had gone to bed. Caleb alighted and knocked. No one opened. Caleb knocked again, hallooing at the same time. He waited a moment, and then by the way the chairs rattled we concluded some one was coming. We almost dreaded to see the door open, for we feared that instead of a polite welcome we might meet the muzzle of a shot-gun.

At length the door was partially opened, and a ghostly-looking man very scantily attired cautiously stuck his head through the opening. It was plainly to be seen that he was more frightened than we were; so by way of reassuring him we said:—

"Good evening."

"How are you," was the trembling response.

"We have been riding all the afternoon without anything

to eat, and we expect to ride on to the next village to night; can you let us have a little something?"

"I'll see the old woman," said the ghost; and then he drew in his head.

A COLORADO GHOST.

In a moment we heard a harsh voice, which we guessed belonged to the "old woman," shouting:—

"Who are them fellers, anyhow? What are they wantin' to eat this time of night for?"

The ghost explained.

"Well," growled the unseen lady, "here's a parcel of bread; that c'll do 'em."

The bread was accordingly brought. It wasn't larger than one's fist, yet woe to the toes upon which it might drop, for it was as hard as a stone. I asked him if we could not have some butter and meat.

The man of the house stepped back again to ask his wife; and she responded:—

"What *don't* them fellers want? I guess they hain't had nothin' for a week. Here, take 'em this. We'll pick 'em up dead-foundered in the morning somewhere along the road—see if we don't!" Then the ghost brought us some butter.

'You can get us a little meat, can't you?" said Caleb. The ghost again withdrew; then from within we heard his wife saying:—

"Ze swizzards, that's enough for 'em to die on without wastin' any more on 'em! I want you to understand they sha'n't have nothin' more about these diggins'. Keep a woman a cookin' and a sweatin' to 'com'date some of your long yeard friends! Do you hear? they shan't have nothin' more."

Without waiting to hear the man's report, we settled with him as soon as possible for our bread and butter, and then went on our way rejoicing.

CHAPTER XXXIX.

NAPLES.

THE first thing on the docket after arriving at Naples was to procure the services of a guide to show us around. A stately-looking individual was accordingly introduced to us as a candidate for the position, and we proceeded to investigate his ability to speak the English language correctly.

We found that he was able to say a few cut-and-dried words prepared for such occasions, in good style, but after that they were so intermixed with languages foreign to us that we failed to understand them. Wishing to give him a fair chance, we asked him to explain what was meant by the expression "Everything is lovely, and the goose hangs high," and other equally simple questions. A perfect torrent of unconnected semi-English words was his response. In short, we did not know what he was talking about; neither did he seem to understand us any better when we told him he would not answer our purpose, and tried to send him away. His jargon threatened to be interminable, and neither words or motions would induce him to leave us. So we were forced to be impolite, and to appeal to an *attaché* of the hotel who, in response to our earnest ejaculation, "Take him out," led him away by the coat-collar. A second guide now presented himself, and although he was an improvement on the first as far as talking English was concerned, yet as he could not run well out of his accustomed rut, we sent him away also. In a third individual we met a man whose education had not been neglected, and speedily engaged him.

It was Sunday, and we visited the Church of San Martino. We were conducted down a marble stairway to the basement of the church, where we were shown a sculpture representing the "Descent from the cross." Our guide told us that the English had offered to purchase it for its weight in gold, but had been refused. The couch upon which the Saviour lay, the crown of thorns, the thin white covering thrown over him, were all sculptured from one piece of marble; yet they looked as distinct and as natural as though real. One could scarcely believe that this delicate covering as it floated in graceful ridges and curves over the form of the Saviour was actually part of the same marble that composed that form. Add to this, that heavenly look that shone from the eyes and features under that covering, and surely this sculpture deserved its place among the finest works of art.

"TAKE HIM OUT!"

Then we visited the Cathedral—of course the principal ecclesiastical structure of the city. The services within attracted our attention at once, as they were of peculiar interest that day.

Saint Januarius was born in Naples, and at the time of his martyrdom was Bishop of Benevento. During the reign of Diocletian this saint visited some Christian friends who had been cast into prison on account of their religion. For this he was carried in chains with other prisoners to Pozzuoli, a few miles south-west of Naples, where, as the people of Naples believe, he and six others were cast into a den of wild beasts, but as they remained there unharmed, they were taken out and beheaded.

Afterward, it is supposed, the remains of the martyr were brought to this cathedral, and interred in one of its chapels. Two vials containing a hard-looking substance supposed to be his blood, and a glass vessel containing his head, are kept in another chapel. At three seasons of the year, in May, September, and December, these vials and the vessel containing the head are brought near each other, and miracles are said to result; for on such occasions the hard substance in the vials softens and turns into a liquid.

The exhibition of these miracles is made on eight consecutive days. It requires a longer time to perform it on the first day than on the following days, while toward the last it can be done in a very short time. While it is in progress the priests pass round collecting money from the audience.

Our visit chanced to be on one of these miracle days. As we stepped in, the bishop, in his robes and accompanied by a couple of priests holding up his train, with a stately solemnity marched down from his throne and passed to and fro behind a balustrade, holding these vials in his hands for the people to kiss. They crowded round him with eager enthusiasm, and as they stretched their necks to touch their lips to the sacred relics, their countenances shone with ecstasy; then, completely happy, they stepped back to let others enjoy the same boon.

All over the cathedral were confessionals, round which the women were collected, to pour the secrets of their lives into the ears of the priests within; after which, they received a few words of advice or consolation in a low tone from their spiritual guides, and then through an opening in the side of the confessional, moved away to make room for others.

In this cathedral all that was beautiful and to be admired in fresco, painting, sculpture, statuary, and other ornamentation of every description seemed to be scattered everywhere in the greatest profusion. The first great feature that we noticed was, that a nave much higher than the two side aisles ran parallel with them from end to end. On either side of this nave, and separating it from the two aisles, ran a row of granite columns so highly polished as to shine like a looking-glass, wavy in places like marble. They were square, yet fluted at the corners, finely based and capped, very large, high, and imposing to the greatest degree. The paintings and frescoes on the ceiling were most exquisite. The high altar, choir, and balustrades of this nave, with their various costly ornaments and gilding, dazzled the eye; while the two candelabra on jasper columns, and the chapels with their frescoes and bas-reliefs, were ideals of beauty.

This cathedral is built in the form of a Greek cross, and has various crypts beneath the ends of the transverse portions and under the side aisles, for chapels and altars. Of the various chapels, that of St. Januarius is the finest. On the great bronze gate leading to it were statues of St. Peter and St. Paul. Inside and around the chapel were forty-two Corinthian brocatello columns cut with niches containing, besides those of bronze, thirty-seven silver statues of different saints. The marble of the high altar was composed of porphyry set off in the most costly style by ornaments, while the bust of Januarius was covered with rich embroidery. A large jeweled collar was about the neck, attached to which were gifts which this saint has received from different kings. The mitre upon his head was studded with nearly four thousand precious stones, not a few of which were diamonds. The six common altars of this chapel, three on each side, were beautifully frescoed at the angles and lunettes, and were, upon the whole, extremely beautiful.

In the sacristy of this same chapel, were a chalice, dishes carved with representations of our Lord's passion, a pyx surmounted by a cross studded with jewels, vases, and various other objects, all in massive gold. There was a large sphere of silver, studded and inlaid with precious stones, and circled with a row of diamonds, above which were two golden ears of corn which were presented by Maria

Teresa of Austria. But why attempt a description of such treasures? Hundreds of objects caught the eye, that could not be noticed by the pen.

Leaving the cathedral, we visited the Museo Borbonico, or Bourbon Museum—named after the late royal family. It is situated in the northern part of the city and is the chief object of interest in Naples. As we rolled along, we observed vegetable and fish-stalls, wherever there was room for them on the sidewalks. Children, ragged and dirty, thronged the streets; yet they appeared gay and active and apparently in no danger of starving; for many stores

AN AFFLICTED NEAPOLITAN.

were full of macaroni, for sale so cheap that ten centissimi, or two cents, would buy enough to supply a child with food for a day. We passed a crowd collected round a man who was recounting the miracles performed by a waxwork image, and met several uncarthly-looking beings—ragged, maimed, and apparently suffering every possible affliction. One, in particular, was pointed out to us as "from America"; but we judged our guide was mistaken.

On arriving at the museum we entered, and at once, from the indication of the number of halls, and the numberless objects of interest from different nations and of different epochs, perceived that we had a grand treat before us; but before we were half through all the windings of the building, or had seen a quarter of the objects—numbering a great many thousands—we found that our first idea of its vastness and variety fell far short of the reality.

On the ground-floor, most of the ancient paintings were from Pompeii and Herculaneum; but many of them though beautifully executed were now considerably faded. Venus weeping over the death of Adonis; the thirteen female dancers, very graceful in appearance; the Trojan horse; Hercules slaying the Nemean lion, and Charity, or Perronea suckling her own father Simon, were among the number.

The collection of ancient marble statues and bas-reliefs was mostly from Pompeii, Herculaneum, and other ruined cities not only of Italy, but of Greece. Here was a dying gladiator, a victorious athlete, and a group in which two men were skinning a hog to offer as a sacrifice. There, in bas-reliefs, were figures that stood out boldly from the slabs; and again, those that only slightly projected. Here were delineated, on different slabs, the sports of the circus; a faun striking a child, and a cupid riding a dolphin; and an antique Grecian work representing a hunter resting; also Bacchus, followed by bacchanites and fauns, just sitting down to the banquet.

BACCHANALIAN DANCE—POMPEII.

In the gallery of Adonis was the celebrated hermaphrodite faun, covered by a transparent garment, allowing only a glimpse of its curious shape. This divinity was found in the ruins of Pompeii.

In another gallery was the renowned group of the Toro

Farnese, or the Farnese bull. This represented the two sons of Antiope avenging their mother by tying to the horns of a bull, Dirces, the wife of Lycus, king of Thebes. This king, having ascended the throne, slew the husband of Antiope, and carried her to Thebes, where she was cruelly treated by Dirces; upon which her sons rose up, took the city, and put to death her persecutors.

The gallery of bronze statues contained the finest collections of their kind in existence. Most of these were from Pompeii and Herculaneum. The dancing faun was very graceful; the wrestlers, the huntress Diana, and an equestrian statue of Nero, we very much admired; while the statue found in Herculaneum, representing Mercury in repose, is considered to be the finest bronze statue in the world.

Passing from the ground-floor to the one above, we immediately entered the halls, six in number, of the small bronzes. These halls contained a collection of upwards of fifteen thousand objects, consisting of various articles representing the domestic life of the inhabitants of Pompeii and Herculaneum. There were lamp-stands, lamps, chandeliers, balances, weights, steelyards, instruments of husbandry, kitchen and bathing utensils, tools, horse-trappings, armor, pieces of carts, objects of religious and public worship, theatrical tickets, surgical and musical instruments, and various other objects.

The cabinets of gems and precious objects were especially interesting. Here were upwards of forty thousand coins of various periods, from Magna Græcia, Sicily, and other countries. The jewelry, cameos, intaglio ornaments, and precious and peculiar objects from Pompeii and Herculaneum were numerous. Here were loaves of bread and biscuits, considerably charred, but of the same shape as when put in the oven to bake, having been left behind in that terrible flight before the torrents of ashes, cinders, and lava, which overwhelmed those cities nearly two thousand years ago. Fruits in glass dishes, just as they were placed in the safe or upon the table, bottles of wine, vegetables, and nuts, were among the collections in this part of the museum. Also finger-rings, still on the skeletons fingers of those who once owned them; and other jewelry which had been removed from skeletons which now looked grimly out from their glass cases.

We now came to the other halls of painting. These halls are eight in number. The paintings were collections from different schools, from the eleventh century down to the present time. They were almost entirely representations of Christ, the Virgin Mary, the disciples and martyrs, and of the struggles and battles between Christians and their persecutors. The hall of the master-pieces was the finest. Here we saw Cupid slumbering while the Zephyrs shook his wings; Christ seated in heaven crowning the Virgin Mary with the clouds; the Last Judgment, copied from Michael Angelo's picture at Rome; "The Holy Family" by Raphael; Titian's celebrated Magdalen in Prayer, and many others.

This ended the museum, and we returned to our hotel feeling that our day's work had exhausted us more than mauling rails would have done; yet we felt fully repaid for the time and fatigue.

Soon after reaching our hotel we saw a procession coming down the street. In the van were fifteen or twenty priests in their proper robes. Behind was the bishop in full ecclesiastical vestments; while on either side were two priests carrying a canopy over his head. On either side and behind were soldiers bearing muskets. As they passed along, the people in the street and on the side-walks fell upon their knees, and crouched upon the ground; and even our French landlord—a very intelligent man—did the same. We had heard of some instances when foreigners who did not bow down to the processions, had been struck on the knees by parties bearing clubs to enforce the necessary amount of reverence.

After taking some refreshments, Caleb and I took a stroll on foot. I had often heard that in Italy, and especially in Naples, the greatest contrasts in social life were to be seen; and we were soon convinced of the truth of this statement. Here came a carriage and horses, finer than any we had ever seen before. The horses were large fiery blacks with feathers in their heads. Two stylish gentlemen wearing white kid gloves, one of whom acted as driver, sat in front on a lofty seat, while their long coat-tails hung down behind, sparkling with bright buttons. In the carriage proper sat four laughing belles, with hats well feathered and richly trimmed, to say nothing of the shiny ribbons floating from their necks and arms. As they passed they bestowed a smile on Caleb and myself. Scarcely had they disappeared when there came a donkey drawing a sort of go-cart, containing an old woman and her numerous family of daughters, all ragged and dirty, piled in among old rags, bags, baskets, and trash.

Then we heard most enchanting singing and instrumental music floating from the parlor of some Italian mansion. It

MUTUAL RECOGNITION.

was a lady's voice; and we listened delighted; but in the midst of the song we were suddenly startled by a horrible braying close to our heads.

"He-haw! he-haw!"

"Get out you jackass, or I'll be the death of you," was my polite reply.

We passed on a short distance, and then across the street

came three young ladies with flowers in their hands, as if to intercept us. They drew near, smiled, and then began to place a flower or two in our button-holes; at the same time making significant gestures. Caleb's virtuous indignation luckily came to our relief, and before it they quailed and shrunk abashed away.

At sundown we wandered back to the hotel, and after dark amused ourselves in looking across the waters of the bay to Vesuvius, as it poured down its fiery stream of lava. We retired to rest with the pleasing thought that we were soon to see the volcano face to face.

CHAPTER XL.

WONDERS OF THE COAST WEST OF NAPLES.

AT early morn we were in our cab, and wheeling through the streets in the western suburbs of Naples. We halted at the Villa Reale, a magnificent promenade for the fashionable world, or rather a place for mutual admiration and self-exhibition. It was too early for Caleb and myself to show ourselves off on the promenade, so we gave our attention to the attractions of the place. Its natural beauties could hardly be excelled, for the Villa Reale runs lengthwise along the bay, with pleasant alleys and winding paths, shaded with evergreens and acacias, and adorned with some remarkable grottoes, gardens, fountains, and statues, and two small temples dedicated to Virgil and Tasso.

In one place was an elliptical fountain, from the centre of which rose up in large proportions two marble statues representing Hercules strangling the giant Anteus. In the centre of another fountain was a group of three figures representing the rape of Egina, the girl turning her eyes toward her defender, in whose arms she was held, while her despoiler was trampled under his feet. In another part of this promenade we noticed a fighting gladiator whose muscles and nerves were finely executed; and, again, Hercules killing the Nemean lion—the hero has his knee upon the lion's back and is rending apart his jaws.

A short distance beyond the Villa Reale, the shore curves round a hill or promontory. Through this elevation the ancients cut a tunnel, as a means of easier communication between Naples and the country round the bay. It was called the grotto of Porilipo. Immediately before entering, we noticed, a few steps to the left, the supposed tomb of Virgil. Naples was the poet's favorite resort, and it is said that after his death Augustus had his remains conveyed to the place he so much admired. However this may be, the

TUNNEL AT NAPLES.

people of Naples should be ashamed of themselves, since they believe this is his tomb, to have allowed it to be so sadly neglected.

We passed through the tunnel and found it a delightful place for a drive. It is nearly half a mile in length, twenty-two feet wide, and in some parts sixty-five feet high, and arched at the top.

Passing out from the tunnel, we observed that the ground near its entrance was of volcanic origin; in fact, such was the case for miles along this shore. Old craters, and the *débris* which they had thrown up were frequently to be met with. At different places we stopped at mineral springs of various degrees of warmth, each having a peculiar quality of its own. The ancients made them a constant resort, as they were supposed to effect wonderful cures, but for some reason, in modern times, they have fallen into disuse.

In one of the smaller hills, facing the lake of Agnano, was that peculiar phenomenon, the renowned "Grotto del Cane," a dark-looking place four feet wide and nine or ten deep. At the bottom of this grotto is a deposit of carbonic acid gas which rises to the height of about a foot and a half. A man, may safely enter; but dogs, who do so, except the larger species, inhale the poisonous gas, which immediately proves fatal to them. The ancients were acquainted with this phenomenon, which to them was a mystery, and on that account they gave it its present name, which signifies the Dogs' Grotto.

The young rascals in the neighboring villages used to drive quite a profitable trade in animals of the canine and feline races. On auspicious nights they used to lie in wait, at back doors and corners which their four-footed victims were likely

ENTICING A VICTIM.

to frequent. If not frightened away by the sudden appearance of the ragged urchin and his bag, the animal's fate was sealed. The tempting bait allured him nearer and nearer, until within the clutches of the enemy. The next day he would be sold to inquisitive travelers, and for their edification let down into the poisonous gas of the grotto.

Leaving this interesting grotto, we drove westward along the bay, and soon came to the city of Pozzuoli. Ruins everywhere met the eye, and the place presented a very dilapidated appearance. When Pozzuoli was founded, no one can tell. Its origin dates back to the obscurity of long-past ages; some historians believing that it was founded many years antecedent to the Trojan war. It was a flourishing city during the days of the Roman republic, for Cicero called it "Little Rome." In those days, this city, together with the villages farther along the shores of the bay, were resorted to by the wealthy and powerful citizens of Rome during the summer months, and here they had their magnificent baths and villas.

After the fall of the Roman empire Pozzuoli was taken at various times, and was almost reduced to a heap of ruins. The incursions of the Goths, Vandals, Lombards, Saracens, Normans and Turks, together with the earthquakes and volcanic eruptions by which this city has been visited, helped to reduce it to its present condition. During the earthquake and eruption in the year 1538, it was so greatly injured that it was almost entirely deserted. So fearful was the shock that the sea retired from the shore upwards of two hundred yards; and in the short space of two days the Monte Nuovo, which we saw soon after leaving Pozzuoli, rose to the height of four hundred feet.

As we gazed upon this place it presented to view a collection of old foundations, old walls of brick and stone, partially crumbled houses, temples, and theatres, all scattered here and there upon the rough hills among a few new, and, of course, inhabited, buildings. By the word new, I mean comparatively so; for many of them were more than a century old.

We visited the temple of Serapis, and noticed, several feet above its pavement, holes in the columns, eaten by mollusks; in fact, many of their shells remained partly embedded, adhering as firmly as though they were a portion of the original stone—thus indicating that the sea at one time flooded the lower part of this temple. Again, from pavements of former years being found below the present sea-level, it seems that at one time the sea was much lower than at present, and about thirty feet lower than at the time when those mollusks were at work upon these columns. Other edifices, also along the shore of the bay, not far from this point, which were on dry land at the time of Augustus, are now partly under water.

In the centre of Pozzuoli was the amphitheatre; well preserved, and stupendous in structure. Thirty thousand people could easily be accommodated with seats within its walls. The great arena was three hundred and sixteen feet in length, and one hundred and thirty feet in breadth. This was the scene of combats between men and men, men and wild beasts, and between wild beasts themselves. Surrounding this arena was a wall ten or twelve feet high, surmounted by a railing to prevent the furious wild beasts from springing over, while from behind the railing rose the seats, one behind another, like a huge flight of steps, reaching back to the outer wall and rising to its summit. Here were iron bolts running down into the wall, by means of which a canvas was stretched over the vast concourse of people. The gladiators entered from doors at each end, while the wild beasts were suddenly sent up from their dens below through trap-doors in the platform of the arena. Then the combat commenced, which was to end in the death of man or beast, or probably both; while the shouts of the spectators rose louder and louder, as the danger of the combatants became more imminent, till the fatal climax was reached.

We went below and visited some of the dens for the wild beasts. They were generally dug into the side of the earth, walled round, and closed in front by an iron gate. Our guide conducted us to one of these, into which Saint Januarius (spoken of in a previous chapter) was said to have been thrown unharmed.

The boat-fights between gladiators were held in this amphitheatre. Part of the platform of the arena was removed, and then heavy sliding doors closed in a rectangular space, into which the water flowed through an aqueduct connected with the bay. The boats of the gladiators were then introduced, and the deadly combat began.

It is recorded in the twenty-eighth chapter of the Acts of the Apostles, that,—"After one day the south wind blew, and we came the next day to Puteoli." We found that the ancient Puteoli is the same as our modern Pozzuoli. Our guide showed us some marble steps running down into the water, which the people held in great veneration. They considered them to be the same that St. Paul first set foot upon when he landed at Pozzuoli. What a contrast!—we alighted at these same steps from a cab.

As we were about to proceed, a score of little boys collected round us, and brushed the dust from our carriage seats. Notwithstanding their number, nearly every one contrived to give the cushions a rub, or at least a touch; and some of them volunteered to brush the dust from our boots. As we stepped into our vehicle, two score of little paws were

RESULT OF PAYING OFF THE BOYS.

thrust towards us. As we could not undertake to reward them all, Caleb thought it would be the fair thing to give every one an equal chance; so he threw a handful of coins towards them. The result was a big scramble, a pile of legs and necks, heads and feet, arms, hands, and bodies, scraping and rooting in the dust, while from beneath came mingled cries of pain and disappointment. We hurried away, for we were fearful that we might be called upon to pay a surgeon's bill.

Our attention was drawn to the extensive ruins of the villa of Cicero. These ruins were partly submerged in the bay, yet the walls looked as if they would stand the washing of the waves for long years to come. Here Cicero composed his "Quæstiones Academicæ." Continuing our journey, we scarcely ever lacked entertainment from some ruin or other, while the baths especially attracted our attention, their size and numbers being almost beyond belief.

We passed the Lucrine Lake, only a short distance from the bay. Unfortunately this beautiful lake was, by the eruption in 1538, partially filled, and much of its beauty spoiled. It was celebrated among the ancients for the pleasure parties that visited its waters at night; and as I looked out upon its surface I almost realized the gay scene which it must have presented in that far-off time.

Lake Avernus to the west of Monte Nuovo, appeared to be situated in an extinct volcano; extinct probably ages before Homer's time. At least he sang of the thick and wild forests once surrounding this lake, and the grottoes into which the light of the sun never penetrated, which were the homes of the Cimmerians—a people who took the greatest interest in hearing or relating stories of the marvelous eruptions of the volcano. From the peculiar vapors arising from these waters, the ancients supposed that every bird that winged its flight across them dropped lifeless; and tradition said that this was the place where Ulysses made his descent into the lower regions.

A short ride to the west of this lake terminated our excursion in that direction. This was at a point ten miles west of Naples. Here were to be found the ruins of Baiæ, situated on a bay of the same name, extending into the land, from the larger bay of Naples. This city was never equal to Pozzuoli in commercial importance, but if possible was more lovely in appearance, on account of its position on this beautiful little bay, and also because of its thermal springs and delightful climate; the north winds being warded off by the hills in the rear, while the delicate breezes from the waters of the bay came fanning the city into repose. According to Horace, it was the most delightful place on earth. Magnificent villas once existed here belonging to Cæsar, Augustus, Pompey, Tiberius, Nero, Domitian, Adrian, Crassus, Caligula, Caracalla, Piso, Hortensius, and other wealthy and ambitious Romans.

At the fall of the Roman empire the splendors of this place decayed, and now the warm springs, from long disuse, have become stagnant pools, and from the innumerable decaying ruins scattered here and there, miasmatic vapors arise, spreading sickness and disease over this once fair and salubrious resort. An old castle, near which now and then a vessel anchors, together with six or eight houses built out of the surrounding ruins, are the only signs of habitation.

The ruins consist mostly of bricks, mosaics, and broken walls, scattered over the soil, with here and there the foundation of some palace or bath, extending now far down into the water, thus indicating a change of surface in the ground. There are, however, three structures pretty well preserved. These were once thought to be temples of Diana, Mercury, and Venus; but subsequent research has proved that the two first at least, were baths; the last probably was what it was first supposed to be—a temple of Venus. These structures stand at the foot of a hill. Before each is built a house, fenced round, with a gate which is opened by the inmates when visitors wish to enter. Within the enclosure are small gardens containing grapes and other fruits. We made a trifling purchase as it was, of course, expected that we would.

When visiting one of the baths, three or four women and girls, with turbans round their heads, and some rude musical instruments in their hands, followed us. They danced, sang, and played. Although they had not the lightest feet or the most delicate steps, their performance was comical in its rudeness. When the dance was over they passed a basket round for donations. We contributed a few small coins, but from their dissatisfied looks and actions they evidently expected more.

DISSATISFIED DAMSELS.

The appearance of the two baths was very singular. Without and within they were circular, and appeared like vast domes resting upon the ground. An immense basin was scooped out of the ground in each; the bottom of which was inlaid with mosaics. The temple of Venus had also the appearance of a dome, and was of beautiful proportions, octagonal on the outside but circular within.

At a rude hotel close by, we took a late dinner. Our meal consisted of bread, cheese, and eggs boiled very hard. Our guide ate in the kitchen; I do not know whether it was on account of his not wanting to impose his presence upon us while at the table, or because he wanted something better than was set before us.

As the sun was sinking in the west, we were again rolling along the streets of Naples toward our hotel, forgetful of the ruins, for all around us were objects more attractive to young men—ladies taking their evening rides. "Beautiful" is too weak a term to apply to the "sweet sixteens" of Naples. I never saw ladies that more completely took my eye—with the exception of one. Even Caleb was captivated; his countenance never shone so pleasantly as when these laughing belles rode past us. I could not blame him. The black flowing hair, the black sparkling eyes, the rosy complexion, and the almost perfect Grecian features of these Neapolitan ladies, would surely captivate any gentleman who admired the fair sex. They are scarcely ever seen in the company of young gentlemen, as that is not allowable, unless one of their parents is present. Consequently, time spent in courting is very limited, and lovers labor under difficulties unknown in America. The Americans possibly have too much courtship; yet, on the other hand, the Italians perhaps have too little, and their customs in this respect may account for the fact that so many of the women of Naples follow the most degraded lives.

Nor do the great majority of the virtuous ladies of the higher class of Naples society live very happily. The chief recreation of those who can afford it is carriage driving; those who cannot ride, stay at home, as it is thought degrading for a lady of any pretensions to walk, while many think it would never do to be seen at work. How can such ladies, without anything to do, without the enjoyment of gentlemen's society, and sitting all day pining away in their dark parlors, be other than idle, useless, unhappy women—the fairest of their sex while in the bloom of youth, but anything but beautiful when they grow old?

CHAPTER XLI.

HERCULANEUM AND VESUVIUS.

THE following morning we resolved to visit Herculaneum, and conducted by a guide in due time approached that celebrated ruin.

We descended slowly, lower and lower still, the flickering lights only revealing the fringes of the dark chasm below. The layers of soil could be distinctly traced between the numerous strata of lava; for after each eruption the earth accumulated over the red deposit, to be itself in turn covered by a fresh inundation of the fiery stream when the next outbreak of the mountain took place.

We had already descended about a hundred feet into the bowels of the earth, and had begun to wonder whither our grimy guide was taking us; so we asked him whether the road really led to Herculaneum, or whether it terminated in the bottomless pit or the ever-raging fires of Vesuvius. He grinned and motioned for us still to proceed, and as he was the presiding deity of the place, there was nothing left for us but to obey.

We followed him in silence, and before long were walking upon the pavement of a city which for eighteen centuries had been hidden from the light of day. Our foolish thoughts and idle words were hushed as we realized the lesson taught by the scene around us. Here were the deep ruts worn by ancient Roman carriages long before the coming of Christ. Here were houses and shops at which St. Paul might have gazed, or into which St. Peter or St. James might have entered. Here were old houses shattered by an earthquake eight years before the final catastrophe which overwhelmed the city. The hands which propped them up were still strong and muscular when the fiery torrent descended and the burning ashes fell, and every living soul perished. Wandering there, we seemed to live in that far-off time, and vividly as we might have pictured the habitations, men, and manners of by-gone ages, we realized now, as we trod the streets of the buried city, far more perfectly the every day life of the people of Italy two thousand years ago.

HERCULANEUM—THE THEATRE.

Our guide conducted us to the theatre, and as we followed him we could hear the rumbling of the carriage wheels in the street far above our heads, sounding like distant thunder; for over the buried cities of antiquity, modern abodes had been reared, the inhabitants of which, until the last few years, were all unconscious that beneath them lay such wondrous relics of the past. In fact, although Herculaneum and

Pompeii were both historically known, and the story of their destruction familiar, it was only recently that their exact sites were discovered.

The theatre particularly attracted us. It very much resembled that mentioned in the last chapter, the seats rising in tiers from the ground, reaching the summit of the outer wall at the top grade. We stood there on the floor or platform where the actors must have performed their part in that *very* "olden time;" and as we gazed on the vast steps rising one above the other, we thought how different must the scene have been when eight thousand persons were seated there, and eight thousand pairs of eyes were riveted on the spectacle below.

When we returned to the upper world the sun was descending toward the west, and we bespoke lively horses for our journey up Vesuvius; but in our hurry an uncouth guide was forced upon us. At the start he took the lead, but we soon overtook and passed him. Our horses were fiery animals, and we gave them the rein. Glancing backward, we saw our guide far in the rear, spurring, and whipping his lazy beast; but on we flew without paying any attention to his clamors for us to go slower. Our road wound up the side of the mountain along a graded road. At times it was almost level, and then again very steep, twisting here and there in order to avoid great chunks and masses of lava. Now we passed through a broken field or stream of this volcanic matter, the light color of which bespoke its age. Again we came upon some that was fresher, and of a darker color; or upon a new stream almost black-looking, as if it had cooled but yesterday, appearing in outward form—but without the motion—as it did when first it swept down the mountain-side. Not infrequently we saw a fresh stream coursing through an orchard, cooking the fruits and burning everything with which it came in contact.

When we were about two-thirds up we stopped to look back and rest our horses. We could see where the lava coursed its way down the mountain-side until lost in the luxuriant valley miles away; and we wondered how many a village and skeleton might speak from under those deposits had they but living tongues. We recalled to mind the eruption of 1779, during which hot stones, one of them measuring over one hundred feet in circumference, were hurled two thousand feet in the air; while sulphurous smoke in dense rolling clouds rose to the height of twelve thousand feet above the crater, and vivid streams of fire shot upwards

"OUR HORSES WERE FIERY, AND WE GAVE THEM THE REIN."

to the sky. We remembered also the eruption of 1861, when a great orifice opened, about one-fourth of the way up the mount, and others gaped at different points, from all of which red-hot streams of lava poured, and forked streams of electric fire shot out their livid tongues. From a combination of several of these was formed a stream of lava half a mile broad and twenty-five feet deep, threatening in its course the utter destruction of Torre del Greco, a city of twenty-two thousand inhabitants. All this we called to mind; but had our visit been a little later we might have had more to think of, for three or four months after our visit several villages were partly destroyed, many of the inhabitants fled, and some even lost their lives.

As before stated, we had left our guide a long way off, but he soon rode up, cursing and swearing. Caleb didn't believe in fighting; neither did I. So we put spurs to our horses, and again ran away from the fellow, at which slight he seemed to grow more angry than ever, and indulged in many

"OUR ASSAILANTS SOON LOST THEIR LEGS."

impolite expressions respecting us. At last we approached the foot of the steep cone, about four thousand feet above the level of the bay, and as we did so, out from a piratical-looking house issued five or six roguish-looking fellows armed with long sticks. They immediately grabbed our horses' tails, and pretended to urge them forward with their poles, while really they did their best to hold them back. Not caring for their assistance or company we spurred on our steeds, who seemed to feel the insult as much as we did, and sprang forward at such a rate that our assailants lost their legs, and were soon left in a demoralized condition far in the rear.

At the foot of the cone we singled out a boy to hold our horses and hired four robust men to assist us in our ascent. Our conductor had not yet arrived, but the rascals behind us, having picked themselves up, were approaching as fast as they could. We did not wait for anybody, but with a mountaineer attached to each arm, moved on at once, while a boy, unbidden, followed behind, carrying wine, and eggs to roast on the lava.

We ascended diagonally over gnarly chunks of all shapes and sizes, our attendants pulling and pushing, and staying us as best they could, sometimes being of service but more frequently in the way, until we found ourselves at a stream of red-hot lava, ten or twelve feet across, and three or four feet high. It was slowly winding down the side of the mountain, but was so small in volume that it was lost among the obstructions long before reaching the valley.

It is strange how long the lava holds its heat. Among the crevices it has been known to retain a considerable amount of warmth for eight years. As we stepped close to this stream it burned our faces, scorched our hands and clothes, and forced us to retreat. Our attendants dipped the ends of their green canes into it, when they blazed up and were quickly consumed. Presently, they drew out a couple of lumps, and pressed into them two Italian coins which we had handed to them. In an instant the coins were red-hot. Then our egg boy rubbed some spittle on his eggs, searched out an old streamlet of lava that looked as if it was about cold, put his eggs upon it, and in a moment handed them to us very nicely cooked.

We now pressed on for the crater, past other streams of lava. By the time we reached the summit it was growing dark, and the fiery abyss was revealed to us in a frightful manner, glaring, blubbering and swelling like the bottomless pit of perdition. The angry surges almost splashed upon us, and we retreated appalled and scampered down the side of the cone, slipping, and stumbling, and occasionally barking a limb and sliding on our backs, till at last we reached our horses. Here we found our guide who appeared to have recovered his temper and to be contented and happy; but the five other fellows looked angry, grinned sarcastically, and even menacingly. We grasped tightly our green wooden canes—not that we had any apprehensions, but to try our nerves. One

"I LET MY HORSE OUT A LITTLE."

of them vented his wrath by slapping the boy who had held our horses, but we made it up to the boy by giving him an extra franc.

In going down the mountains, at a place where the descent was gradual I let my horse out a little, and when going quite fast he came suddenly to a steep pitch where he stumbled badly and turned a complete somersault. Luckily for me I was thrown from the saddle at the outset, and regained my feet and horse without suffering serious damage.

As we continued on down the mountain we were delighted with the sight of the many hundred lights of the city, curving round the bay like necklaces studded with sparkling diamonds, and with the view out upon the smooth waters gemmed with many a green island reaching out one beyond another, even to the sea; for they formed a beautiful picture such as one seldom sees even in the course of a lifetime. At the bottom of the mountain we found the cabman and guide who had conducted us to Herculaneum, awaiting to take us back to Naples. On the way, we told the last named individual of our experiences with the mountain guide. He was considerably amused thereby, and laughingly replied:—

"Hiz horse not zo lazy—hiz swerin' an' cuzin' all putz on. You knowz hez paid by ze company; he no want to ascend ze cone."

This revelation caused a revulsion of our feelings. We had felt quite jolly at being able to leave the fellow in the rear, and had supposed that he felt very badly at being deprived of our company. But it turned out that we had been victimized after all, and he had doubtless chuckled over his ruse for the balance of the day. Had I known his game sooner, I would never returned till he had gone up to the crater or starved on the side of the cone.

Then we told our companion of our experiences with the assailants whom we had left in a demoralized state. The serious look which he put on and his reply made us feel better, for it proved that one genuine victory was inscribed on our banners. He said:—

"Zey runs for zemselves—zey dangerous fellows."

When we reached our hotel, we could see from the window a stream of lava appearing to cover the very spot where we had stood such a short time before.

CHAPTER XLII.

THE BURIED CITY OF POMPEII.

HARK!—men stand aghast! face is turned to face, pale as death! That shock, that rumbling as the mutterings of distant thunder —what can it mean? Louder and louder it grows, peal on peal, the ground trembles and rolls beneath the feet like the troubled ocean. Angry clouds of smoke from yonder mountain rise! They spread, they roll their black garments over the face of heaven! Through them the livid lightnings leap up to lick the sky. The hot elements come showering down. Terror seizes men! The wretches flee through the glowing cinders. Not all. Some are upon beds of sickness unable to flee. Darker grows the day, and more portentous the volcanic storm. They choke, they struggle and wail, while they are being shrouded with smoke and coffined by the hot cinders pressing closer and closer about their quivering flesh. The prisoners tug and wrench at their chains as the torrent comes on, but it is stronger than they. Some, terror-stricken, are overtaken in their flight while still in the city; others who escape beyond the wall are suffocated with the smoke, or struck and covered with the falling rock and cinders. Some thinking the day of judgment has come fall upon their knees, groaning and wailing their prayers toward the throne of heaven. Some curse the day on which they were born, and fling out their oaths defiantly. Children cry for parents, parents for children, husbands for wives, friends for friends, but all in vain.

For eight days this volcanic storm continues. By-and-by

the heavens began to clear, the sun takes off his mourning veil, but weeps as he looks down upon the wide-spread desolation without a landmark to tell where once were verdant villages and proud cities. The number of persons buried, no one knows, but it must have been very great, as the effects of the eruption extended as far as Stabiæ, some five or six miles beyond Pompeii, burying all those regions in one universal tomb of oblivion, until little more than a century ago, when by chance an unlettered peasant while sinking a well discovered a house far below the surface of the ground.

THE GREAT CATASTROPHE.

It was along the excavated road leading from buried Herculaneum that we approached the renowned Pompeii. We halted at an inn where the flying inhabitants, laden with their valuables, had taken refuge from the increasing fall of cinders. Here they lodged with their riches during the long and dreary night of centuries. Near by we entered a branch-road from the Appian Way, and here were summer resorts of renowned persons from the imperial city—Rome. We wandered about Cicero's villa where he used to entertain Augustus. But the most interesting dwelling was Diomedes.' Down a descending corridor we followed the footsteps of eighteen young men, two children and a woman, who never returned. Against the wall of the cellar was the form of the mother, with her two children by her side. There she stood until her darlings had been buried by the hot ashes which the wind and the floods of rain alternately carried in, and then she dropped her head and died. In the museum at Naples we saw the ring on the skeleton finger of the mother It was inscribed with the name "JULIA A. DIOMEDES." Round the walls of this long circular cellar yet stood the large wine vases from which the servants used to draw.

EXCAVATED STREET OF TOMBS.

Approaching the city gate, the road was lined with the monumental tombs of those who slept in peace during the awful terror that startled the living. Upon one tomb was a vessel lowering her sails, emblematical of the close of life. Here in the sacred decline of a summer's evening, friends had softly trodden, had dropped the silent tear, and had with flowers strewn the resting-places of those they loved. Pugilistic, hard-hearted relatives occasionally wandered out to the tomb of one Scarus, proudly looking at the raving beasts and gladiators carved upon the monument of him who had won the prize.

On the city gate was an advertisement of a gladiatorial combat that was to take place in the amphitheatre. Twenty years previous to the eruption, the beastly Nero became disgusted at a sanguinary fray in this same amphitheatre, and closed it for ten years, during which an earthquake almost shook the structure down. It opened for ten years more, and then the vengeance of Jehovah closed it forever!

We passed the gate through one of the side entrances, treading the pavement worn by sandaled feet, silent now. Two long steps took us over a street-crossing. In the centre lay a huge stone, astride of which ran the wheel-marks deeply guttered. Ladies and gentlemen promenading the streets leaped upon this stone to effect a crossing. We imagined ourselves following them to their homes. The façades were adorned with paintings and inscriptions suitable to their owner's rank in society. Presuming to enter, the inscription "Salva," welcome, greeted us; so we stepped from the vestibule into the principal chamber or drawing-room, round which were arranged the servants' apartments. But as no one stepped out to receive us, we passed on to the open court surrounded by a portico supported by columns, where once were sparkling fountains and fragrant flowers. Wandering through the various apartments we glided over fish, birds, animals, and fanciful figures painted with life-like fidelity upon the floor; while still finer mosaics and fresco paintings covered the stuccoed walls. We knew the taste of the occupants. In the rooms of the uncultivated were pictured highly-plumed cocks; in the home of a patriotic Athenian was the superb representation of a battle between the Greeks and Persians; in the studio of a young amateur were female forms receiving in their aprons bouquets of flowers; in the bacchanalian's house were carved figures in wild revelry; and in the home of the poet were scenes from Homer.

In each house entered we seemed to catch glimpses of its former inmates. Here were the deserted chairs and tables, uneaten loaves, dates, chestnuts and grapes. Round the festal board the father, mother, and dear ones had met for the last time, and for the last time the innocent babe had been dandled upon the mother's knee. About the room and now open to our view, were objects familiar to every member of the household, just as they left them forever. We glanced at their tutelary gods, and then followed their footsteps to the temples, which were about as numerous as the churches in a modern city of twenty thousand inhabitants. We fancied we saw them bowing before those beautiful bronze and marble statues, as do the inhabitants of the neighboring cities of to-day. They worshiped and gave their means in sincerity and truth, and then they went on their way rejoicing. The columns were the models of those in our most beautiful modern temples. Our guide, with a sacrilegious cane, broke off the marble flowers and leaves from the corinthian capitals which the chisel of some noble artist had carved, and generations of Pompeiians admired.

Down a street sufficiently broad for the easy passage of carriages, we came into the vast Forum, surrounded by rows of once beautiful but now broken columns, where beneath the soft sky those who enjoyed the right of franchise exercised their respective influences on occasions of public gatherings. Back of the judge's seat we descended into a dungeon, where during eighteen centuries two forms lay chained.

In the unexcavated half of the city we saw the grimy diggers bringing to light bronze lamps, scales, and various domestic utensils. On a table they had laid a petrified body, just exhumed. Our guide said it was supposed that this was the body of a man who had returned during a lull in the storm to pillage houses, and instanced another man who was found in the attitude of a burglar grasping the key and treasures. Surely if the culprit loved darkness he found sufficient there.

In another place we entered the room of a sick man. It

seems that he must have been a stranger just arrived from a distant city, for all had deserted him. Darkness came on, but he had heard no footsteps upon the floor. The fallen ashes shut out every ray of light, yet in his feverish visions he looked for day and called for friends, but none answered.

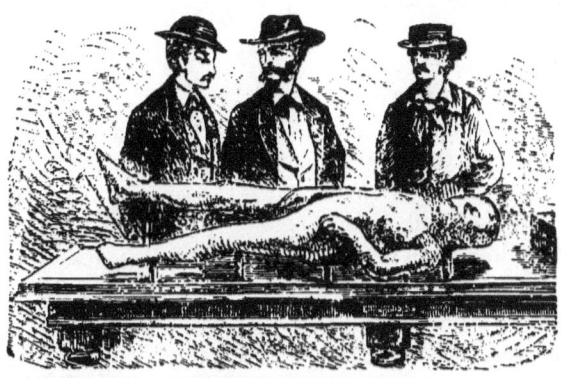

A WARNING TO BURGLARS.

After the storm had passed, his wife doubtless came and looked over the sea of ashes, but her husband was entombed on his dying couch.

We visited the public bath, with its pipes, double walls, and great vats for steaming (almost scalding) the bather, before plunging him into the great marble basin of cold water to temper him and quicken his blood. We saw the various fragrant ointments, combs, brushes, and mirrors, and thought how like a child in a bed of perfume the bather must have lain down and sweetly slept after the exhaustion of the bath.

We visited the Comic Theatre, then the Tragic, whose high walls were never sufficiently buried by the eruption to preserve them from crumbling on top. In fact the summits of the city towers were all exposed, and now projected from the plain of barren ashes, enabling us to trace the three mile circuit of the wall. These ramparts, in old and warlike times, kept the prowling enemy from the gates.

We glanced down into the labyrinth of streets winding among low buildings, into which the same sun shone as when up and down them hurried the clerk going to his office, or the father returning from business to his pratling ones, or the laughing girls tripping along from shop to shop. Around us was every evidence that for ages these happy scenes had transpired. When, a minute later, we ascended to the dress-circle, the thick steps of lava were worn almost away by many generations of hurrying feet as eager for amusement as the restless throng of to-day.

THE TRAGIC THEATRE.

Beneath us was the orchestra, silent for these eighteen weary centuries. The soft music that enervates the soul had not yet unnerved the arm of the dauntless Roman soldier. Between the theatre and the gate leading toward Stabiæ were the soldiers' barracks, where the rigid discipline which had led the Roman warriors to meet death and conquer the world now held them firm to their post, while frightened wretches were fleeing from the volcanic storm.

While we were wandering and musing amid such scenes as these, we were suddenly started from our reverie by the shrill whistle of a locomotive. At first thought it seemed almost sacrilege that such a noisy intruder should invade a place where silence and the repose of sleeping inhabitants was so long unbroken; but its presence drove away serious reflections and reminded us that it was time that passengers for Naples were "all aboard."

CHAPTER XLIII.

FROM NAPLES TO ROME.

WHEN we settled with our Neapolitan host, before taking the cars for Rome, we were greatly surprised to find that Caleb's bill was exactly seven times as large as Wildair's was. How it happened to be so we never found out.

On our arriving at the depot a boy grabbed our valises, and ran off with them to an official who weighed them and then made a demand upon us. Wildair pretended that he did not understand what he wanted, though anybody could have interpreted the man's gestures when he finally drew out his purse and displayed a five franc piece. But Wildair was bound not to understand, so he reached forth his hand as if to receive the money which the man held. At this a young lady with light complexion and hair, spoke to her brother in English and asked him to offer his services as interpreter. The result was that we paid over the amount demanded, but did not begrudge the money, for it was well worth five francs to again see a golden-haired, blue-eyed, English-speaking girl. We had almost forgotten there were any such pretty creatures in the world.

Our tickets admitted us to the first and second-class waiting-room, graced with carpets, cushioned seats, mirrors, and frescoed walls. A back door was finally unlocked through which we passed from this palace-prison to the cars. Before starting, the conductor ran along the platform, requiring every person to display his ticket or vacate his seat.

They don't believe in tempting any one to ride to the first station free.

At one of the country stations Wildair and I alighted to stretch our limbs. We were not particular whether we stood on the track or off; but we were soon frightened out of our wits by a man running toward us, hallooing and motioning as though he were driving sheep. By his voice

A SUDDEN STOP.

we took him for a beggar, but by his gestures an automatic painter who fancied the sky his canvas; we changed our mind, however, when he gave us a shove off the track.

At this station an old Italian lady got aboard the car, who we judged from her actions was having her first experience at traveling by rail. I was reminded of another lady traveler nearer home whom I had heard about. She had never seen a railroad, and having made up her mind to take a "tour," she was driven several miles to a country station, and took her seat on the platform. The train came in and departed, but she remained seated; and when the station-master asked her why she did not get on the cars if she wanted to go, she replied:—

"Git on?—why, I thought the whole consarn went."

Acting on the advice of the station-master she got safely on board the next train, and took a seat beside a benevolent old gentleman. She was very much alarmed when the train started, but gradually became serene, and interested in what she saw along the road. The old gentleman answered her

ARCHES OF ANCIENT ROME.

questions civilly. When he tried to explain the use of the telegraph wires, her reply was:—

"Wa'al, wa'al, you don't catch me ridin' on 'em, for this is as fast as I want to go, anyhow."

At length she had seen and heard about so many wonderful things that nothing could astonish her; and when, owing to a misplaced switch, their train ran into another one, thereby jolting all the passengers from their seats, she quietly remarked:—

"They fetch up rather sudden, don't they?"

At her journey's end she was surrounded by a crowd of hackmen, all clamoring for her patronage. Grasping her umbrella in one hand and her band-box in the other, she gazed into the face of the loudest driver, with the compassionate enquiry:—

"Are you in pain?"

Along the road we saw Italian peasants ploughing their impoverished grounds with sleepy, faded cattle of a dwarfed breed, yoked singly to a forked stick which they forced into the ground with one foot, while they hobbled beside the handle on the other. The ploughmen's wives or daughters, armed with goads, acted as drivers and occasionally woke up the oxen.

HACKMEN ABROAD.

Toward evening, just as the tints of an Italian sunset were painted on the sky, the dreamy arches of ancient Rome burst suddenly upon our view like a vision. For miles these arches stretched away, bridging the sky like closely-set piers spanning a river, though some of them had crumbled. Over those arches once flowed a stream of living water to the thirsty myriads who thronged the city in the days of her glory.

Finally, rolling through a real wall, the brakes brought the cars to a halt, and we awoke from our reverie. Passing through the depôt, we glanced at the long row of vehicles, and approached one with "Hotel de Amerique" in gilded letters over the door. The genteel attendant tipped his silk hat and bowed, as we asked if English was spoken at this hotel; and as he responded an English affirmative, we stepped into the carriage. Meantime not another person had offered his services to us or left his own carriage. It was a pleasing contrast to the way our hackmen at home treat foreigners as well as other people. I once saw a party of Italians astounded at the liberties taken with them by hotel runners on their arrival at New York. They did not understand our

HACKMEN AT HOME.

language any too well, and were speechless under the clamors of their assailants who seemed, as they looked at it, to be trying to pull them to pieces and steal their baggage. "Can this," they thought, "be the land of liberty of which we have heard so much!"

On the morning of our first day in Rome we chartered a carriage and told the driver, in not very intelligent Italian, to take us round where anything was to be seen. He did not seem to understand us exactly, and gazed back at us; but we motioned to him to go ahead, and he did so. We rolled up streets and down streets,—along fine streets and streets which were not so very fine; past open paved squares with playing fountains, where snorting horses with fish-like tails were rising from the water, and the sea chariots were driven by mythological beings, half men and half fish. Then we passed squares in which stood Egyptian obelisks, broken columns, churches, museums, and various other interesting objects too numerous to mention.

Our driver halted at times to enable us to alight and

A DRIVE THROUGH ROME.

inspect things more closely than we could in the carriage, and we finally gathered courage to enter the vestibule of one of the beautiful churches we came to. Just as we got there some priests passed near us, and we expected that they would attempt to kidnap us or order us out; but as they did neither and looked benevolently at us, we grew bolder and went inside where priests were ministering at the altar. Afterwards we visited other churches, and gazed on the beautiful paintings and statues everywhere displayed within them.

A LESSON IN POLITENESS.

Then we found ourselves venturing into buildings that were not churches. We went up long flights of marble steps, along winding corridors, and into rooms, which, from the statues, paintings, and other beautiful objects, we took to be galleries of art. At last, wearied out with our long morning ramble, we returned to our hotel, paid our driver, and received from him another lesson in Italian politeness.

CHAPTER XLIV.

AMID THE RUINS OF ROME.

WE now began to realize that at last we were amid the ruins of the "Eternal City" in which lived that galaxy of great men who shine in history as the stars in heaven, influencing even now the destiny of those modern nations which were formed from the wreck of Rome.

From the pavement of the present city we descended by a ladder of nineteen steps to the Forum, where the voices of Roman orators had so often resounded. The pavement was crossed by a foot-path partially worn by Cæsar, Cicero, Pompey, Antony, and a host of others whose daring deeds have been the admiration of succeeding ages.

It was here that Brutus ran from the Senate door holding above his head the bloody dagger, and crying, "Liberty! liberty! Cæsar is dead and Rome is free!" Through those triumphal arches, I fancied I could see the citizens rushing, and the august members of the Senate running out into the street, while the so-called "Liberator" gloried in having given—as he weakly imagined—freedom to his country by means of an atrocious crime.

Here, when quiet prevailed, Antony ascended the rostrum to praise the deeds of Brutus, and to defame Cæsar. But when the orator enumerated the fallen hero's generous acts and opened his will, which unexpectedly devoted his noble gardens to the use of the public, and bequeathed a sum of money to each citizen, and then lifted to their view the familiar robe of the murdered conqueror, stained with blood and rent with stabs: then it was that his achievements for the glory of Rome rushed upon the memories of the audience, and those who had torn the diadem from the brow of the warrior's statue, with a curse to the hand that had placed it there at night, now wept; and those who had remained silent until the conqueror had twice rejected the imperial insignia, and then joined with the throng to cheer, now breathed vengeance upon the fleeing conspirators who had murdered him.

THE ROMAN FORUM.

We saw the excavated fragments of statues and columns that once stood in beauty before temples and public buildings facing the Forum. During the last three centuries the antique has become almost as sacred as once it was profane, and now the temples not entirely wrecked are carefully patched over and converted into Christian churches, and then become doubly sacred. Even the prison behind the tribune of the Forum, where St. Paul was cruelly fettered, and confined, is now the crypt of a church, from whose altar daily ascends the prayers and chants of priests.

Our guide conducted us to what he called 'Trajan's Forum;" it looked a good deal like a cellar. There were in it four rows of upright marble columns broken off at various heights; and in their midst one mighty towering column, around which, like a vine clinging to a tree, wound the sculptured representation of the long procession of Trajan. Long and fierce was the struggle there depicted, for we saw the soldiers not only in combat, but also wintering in stone barracks. When the spiral procession had wound its way toward the top of the column, those who had not been slain by the northern barbarians were seen returning homeward with their trophies. But mothers came not out to welcome them, and many a lovely damsel had either pined away or found another lover during the fifteen years of their absence.

THE PROCESSION OF TRAJAN.

This was Rome's last conquest in Europe. But by-and-by the warlike hordes then conquered came down from the north and ascended that column also—but by the internal spiral stairway. They removed the statue of Trajan for coinage; and the pope, three centuries ago placed a bronze statue of St. Peter in its place.

Tired and weary we sat down to rest on the summit of the Coliseum, which was transfigured into a free quarry by the Roman people during the dark ages. In fancy, eighteen centuries rolled back the current of human events, and I seemed to see the long train of Titus returning across the campagna from the siege of Jerusalem. Over the way he erected a grand arch, upon which he caused to be carved the golden candlestick with its seven branches, the ark of the covenant, and the table of shew-bread, forever removed from the temple of the Lord. Immediately afterward the earth began to quake, the air turned black, and from the mouth of Vesuvius belched forth cinders and rolling fire which buried a number of Roman cities.

Ere the veil of heaven had been drawn aside, the topmost stones of the Coliseum had been tugged to their places, and the building was now to be dedicated. At an early hour the seats of the amphitheatre were filled. On the circling platform surrounding the arena was enthroned the emperor, with the senators, priests, and the vestal virgins. From receding seats above them, looked down the rich patricians; still higher the soldiers; and upon these vast upper rows, about one-third of a mile in circumference, sat the plebians.

But hush!—the murmuring of the vast crowd ceases, and a deathlike silence prevails. In the arena stands a graceful female form; she is a Christian, but as helpless as innocent. Then from a passage in the wall a ferocious beast appears, and all sit in breathless suspense at sight of the shuddering and shrinking girl crouching before them without one hope of escape. A thrill runs through the audience as the tiger springs upon her and bears her to the ground.

Then, one after another, other victims are brought up from the prisons below to suffer the same fate; and when a man is chased by a wild boar across the arena, and at last falls a victim to the beast's deadly tusks, the noise of the clapping of hands arises like the wings of a myriad birds.

Now two champions appear alone in the arena, eager for death or glory, and those who have no previous prejudice shrink or shout according as the one they favor is favored also by fortune. Of those who have nothing at stake most seem to sympathize with the smaller warrior, perhaps because he has already received a couple of wounds; and when with a skillful sweep of his sword he cleaves off his opponent's head, one hundred thousand infuriated people arise, and wave their hands and cheer.

Over such scenes as these, spectators gloated, till one hundred dreadful days expired, during which many thousand men and between five and ten thousand beasts, perished for the amusement of the Roman populace.

Here, along the miles of winding corridors leading to these horrible scenes, then stood graceful statues, the defaced fragments of which are now collected and valued at their weight in gold. Men learned in art and history almost worship the Coliseum, in whose structure are harmonized the various kinds of architecture, from the massive doric supports of the arched windows at the base, to the airy Corinthian column beneath the lofty entablature at the summit. In the crumbling arches of its corridors are now fourteen Christian churches, and in the centre of the arena stands the cross.

From the Coliseum we went to the baths of Titus, where he employed his slaves to fill up the wonderful Golden Palace of Nero with rubbish. This palace was so vast that Titus never hoped to equal it, so he thought to bury it. But the structure he reared above it crumbled away into a protecting cover.

From the fallen arch of Titus we descended by a ladder into the excavated rooms of Nero, in which were found many of the statues and works of art which this tyrant, who burned the city for his pleasure and lit tarred Christians for street lamps, used to enjoy. Our guide carried a bamboo pole about thirty feet long, fastened to the end of which was a lamp, which revealed the frescoed figures on the plastering as bright as if painted but yesterday.

From these lofty ceilings, high arched doors, and long halls we returned to our carriage and drove down into the lower part of the city, past ruins, and along lanes separated from vineyards by very high stone fences, built probably from the ruins of fallen palaces once standing near by.

We halted again before the arched and towering ruins of Caracalla's Baths, covering perhaps forty acres of land, and appearing like huge devastated mountains. Excavators were carting away the *debris* and bringing to light fragments of statues to crowd the Vatican and the museums of Rome. They came upon the mosaic floor worked into beautiful and brilliant designs, with here and there depressions for swimming-basins. Here, and to other baths, the enervated wealthy Romans of the third century came to bathe and enjoy themselves after the excitement and crimes of the Coliseum, while the poor groaned beneath the tyranny of the rich.

We visited, a day's drive from Rome, the tombs where the ashes of the aboriginal Etruscans were deposited in urns or vases covered with pictures. We descended into a lately opened vault, on the walls of which were delineated a breed of horses having green tails, blue manes, yellow bodies and pipe stem legs without joints. In another, evidently made at a later period when art had almost reached Grecian per-

MUSIC AND DANCING.

fection, flesh-colored figures with gracefully flowing robes were performing a lively dance to the music of the lyre and flute, which they themselves were playing as an expression of joy over the departure of a deceased friend to a better clime. Some of the ancient characters resembling Greek letters were interpreted to us by our guide as follows:— "While we departed to nought our essence ascends." "We ascend to our ancestors." "Raise the soul as fire." Upon the walls of others were winged angels with beautiful faces.

But perhaps the scene that interested us most was one representing the death of a father. The daughter was drawing

RUINS OF THE CARACALLA BATHS, ROME.

the hood over his eyes, which had just closed in death; a dutiful son was covering his feet with one hand, while the other was raised to hide his grief. At the head stood another youth in subdued sorrow, pressing his aching head and breast; while a professional mourner, having rent his garment, was smiting his breast and brow, accompanied with lamentations of woe suitable to the family grief. Although that daughter's

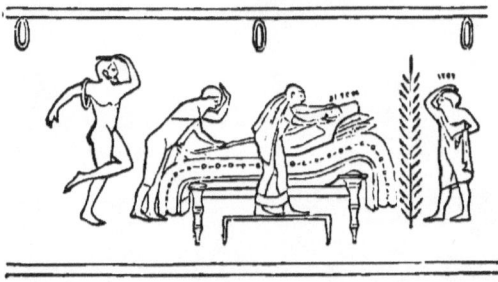

A SCENE OF WOE.

tender care ceased thousands of years ago yet her love was immortal, and it awoke in us feelings of sympathy and sorrow for her grief as if there were no separating chasm of time between us.

This home of the departed father had been fitted up by surviving friends in such a manner that his spirit might smile upon their kindness and meet them there. About the room were arranged his arms, memorial wine vases, sacrificial utensils, a couch, mirrors, candelabrum, jewelry, and other familiar objects. Here the living came to muse of the dead, expecting that as they did so his presence might be revealed to them.

Like the Egyptians, these ancients died to be remembered. But the dust of a hundred generations of plodding peasants enriched the soil above their peaceful resting-places, and it is but recently that they have been disturbed.

CHAPTER XLV.

THE SPIRIT OF THE ETERNAL CITY.

CLEMENT'S name, says St. Paul, is written in the "Book of Life." It seems that he distinguished himself as a preacher in Rome, and the oldest church of this venerable city bears his name. Of course we visited it.

We descended beneath the foundation, into a subterranean chapel, the walls of which once echoed the words of Jesus almost fresh from His lips; it still contains many early Christian pictures. Tradition says that St. Clement's church was built on the site of his house, and that when the foundations were excavated to a certain depth the workmen were astonished to find themselves in a church below the surface; while a passage connected with the church led to a dwelling of the Augustan Age—perhaps the parsonage of brother Clement.

The prison in which St. Paul was confined is near the Forum, and was pointed out to us. Then we drove toward the Three Taverns, along the anciently-paved Appian Way, still lined with the crumbling monuments of Rome's renowned dead. One, containing a great stone coffin, was like the Coliseum in shape, and, like it, served as a fort during the dark ages.

Four francs of depreciated Italian currency opened for us a gate in the high stone wall on our right, and we stood in a large vineyard hanging with clusters of grapes as plentiful as in the Promised Land. With torch in hand we then descended to the city whose inhabitants ever rest—unless up and down those narrow streets their spirits wander. We glanced at the rows of narrow niches, one above another, in the rocky walls on either side. On the tablets sealing them were recorded, in Latin or Greek, how "Adonis would ever weep for his own loved Helen;" or the name and age of a "Rosebud, plucked from a mother's bosom and a father's heart." We found that many of these vaults had been ruthlessly unsealed, and the tablets removed to European museums; the bones strewn about looked ghastly enough in the flickering light.

Beneath these almost endless corridors we descended to streets intersecting each other; and below these to an underlying labyrinth, where we shuddered as we went along lest

"WE SHUDDERED AS WE WENT ALONG."

we should loose sight of the grim keeper in whose hands was our return from the walks of death to the light of day.

Here we came upon chapels where the early Christians sought a quiet retreat from their relentless persecutors; a sanctuary hidden from the sight of the world in which they might worship their once suffering but now glorified Saviour. Here they committed to the tombs the remains of their loved ones, that they might rest until the glory of the awakening morn should raise them from the slumber of death, even as their Lord himself was raised. Upon their tombs were expressed the sentiments of hope and faith.

These retreats, as well as the other catacombs, and the perforated hills of Rome which served as vast quarries out of which her structures were reared, became after her fall, a subterranean city and the abode of robbers, against whom an army was finally sent to clear them out and block the passages with stone. Recent researches have removed these obstructions. Here, in these complicated retreats of the Christians, were found the bronze lamps which they used in their chapels, and on the walls were pictures of Christ the Good Shepherd, and other representations which, though simple, evinced the fervent holiness and spirituality of those who delineated them.

We went to St. Peter's,—the grandest and richest place on earth in which mortals pay homage to heaven. In it are deposited the ashes of St. Peter and St. Paul, and on its cloud-piercing dome is the cross for which they died. The steps, on which thousands of people can stand, lead to the portico whose columns rear their heads aloft one hundred feet. Above these steps stood the Pope of Rome just after he had been pronounced infallible, and there he raised his hands in blessing over the heads of myriads standing in awe beneath.

This vast cathedral, six hundred feet long, though without seats, did not seem empty. Art, beauty, grandeur, filled the place. The deeply-sunken coffers, one hundred and fifty feet above our heads, seemed intended to hide their treasures of glittering wealth. The columns dividing the aisles and the principal nave were each as large as the solitary obelisks of Egypt, or Pompey's Pillar, but their capitals bloomed into leaves and flowers that softened their vastness into beauty. The principle dome, supported upon four ornamented pillars, each sixty-nine feet in diameter, was the size and shape of the Pantheon at Rome which Pliny reckoned among the wonders of the world. The "Transfiguration of Christ," the "Creation of the World," the "Last Judgment," and the renowned paintings of the great masters, were copied in immortal mosaics upon the walls. Fifteen years were required to thus execute a single picture; fifteen thousand shades of colored glass were used, and fifteen thousand pieces of the same were set up in the space covered by one's hand. The surface was then polished, and the unfading figures of angels, sibyls, and prophets, looked down upon us "like beings to whom God had spoken, and who have never since ceased to meditate on the awful voice." The angels with snowy wings seemed to be descending from sublime heights, with trumpets to their mouths, while up the aisles rolled the thunder tones of the organ dying away in plaintive echoes.

Amid these towering columns, and beneath these lofty sublime arches, a thousand voices sound like a single harmony, melodious and grandly sweet. Here the people walk and worship. They lean against the column which it is said the dear Saviour rested against when weary; they cross themselves before the cross; they kiss the toe of St. Peter's statue in humility, and their children do the same. They bow at the tomb of a saint, and ask him to beseech the Queen of Heaven to influence her son Jesus to implore his Omnipotent Father to forgive their sins. They kneel before the pope or archbishop as he enters, with the bishops supporting his glittering robes. Priests reverently bear the trail of the bishops, and monks and little boys gracefully sustain the long appendages of the priests. The pope, when we were there, had shut himself up as prisoner within the Vatican, bewailing the breached gates and the capitulation of Rome — the last relic of his once world-wide empire. So an archbishop officiated in his place at one of the side chapels, instead of being seated upon the identical chair of St. Peter, **which is for the use of the pope alone.**

The officiating bishop repeated in a high tone one verse; the multitude of monks and priests responded another in a sweet spiritual voice; and the choir answered by chanting a

"THEY KISS THE TOE OF ST. PETER'S STATUE."

third, accompanied by the organ. When the singers bowed their heads or crossed themselves, the bystanders did the same, for they knew something sacred was being repeated, though in an unknown tongue. As the leader at the altar read, the other bishops supported his arms and his long jeweled robe in a becoming manner. They waited upon him as if he had come from heaven, because he bore the vessels of the Lord. They brought him a vessel, into which he dipped a fan-like leaf and sprinkled the two attending bishops; these then sprinkled the priests who supported their robes; and these, again, repeated the operation upon the various grades of priests and monks.

The leader waved before the altar, in complicated curves, the censer, from whose every crevice the smoking incense issued. Then the consecrated smoke from the silver censer like the fluid from the leaf, was shaken upon the heads of the bishops, and by them and their attendants passed on until it reached the remotest monks. Again, a consecrated touch was started from the leader to his immediate attendants, and by them to those next in rank, and so on from order to order till the farthest row of short gowns was reached. Then they formed in line according to their rank and varied uniform, and marched as the army of the Lord round the superb tomb of St. Peter, beneath the dome, armed with burning candles almost as long as spears, emblematical of their mission of light.

The monks of Rome cannot help being religious, for when they are not sleeping they are either saying the best prayers the pope can write, or chanting portions of the Bible, or walking over sacred ground on their knees and bare feet. Luther was once a monk, and the first thing he did when he came to Rome was to ascend the Scala Sancta. Like Luther, when I saw the people climbing those steps which, it is said,

THE SACRED STEPS.

our Saviour bathed with his blood, I felt inclined to ascend on my knees and press my lips to every stone.

How eagerly weary pilgrims climb those steps that once led to Pilate's judgment seat, and kiss them over and over, and look down through the cracks in the wooden frame covering the marble just beneath, which, if uncovered, their very lips long ago would have worn away. I no longer wondered at the power that Rome sways over her people; but unlike Luther I should have continued to venerate these stones.

We went to the palace of the pope, the great preserver and patron of art, where five thousand rooms are stored with the priceless relics of different ages. We climbed grand stairways, we strolled down long galleries whose mosaic floors vied with the ceilings, in pictures both modern and antique; we gazed with astonishment at what the skill and refined taste of man could effect.

We shuddered as we passed the Laocoön. It is a group consisting of a father and his two sons entangled in the tightening coils of two great serpents that were using their hooked fangs, producing excruciating pain! Perhaps never marble spoke such agony! And all that the father had done was to protest against bringing the Wooden Horse within the walls of Troy, proclaiming that it had not come down from heaven from Minerva but was placed there by the enemy; and so when they persistently brought it through the gate he hurled a javelin into its immense side. And he was correct; for that very night Ulysses and a company of Greeks issued from a trap-door in the flank of the horse, stepped out, opened the gates, and the Greeks rushing in fired the city, while the inhabitants, sleepy from the excitement of the previous day, at last awoke in terror.

But this poor father had gone to his long home and witnessed not the dreadful scene. After having given that faithful warning he returned to his temple to sacrifice to Apollo. But offended Minerva sent two monstrous serpents, which tarrying not, entered the sacred precincts as the priest stood by the altar. It happened that his two sons stood near, and upon these the vengeance fell. The father rushed to their rescue only to entangle himself. There he stands, while his sons look to him in terror and confidence for deliverance, and the strong muscles of the father's arms seem ready to remove the necks of the writhing snakes. I always sympathized with this priest and thought that he died a martyr. The Grecian artist who embodied this conception of his brain in marble, little thought that for so many centuries it would be buried beneath the rubbish of Rome to be again laid bare for the admiration of the world.

The popes have always been benefactors to learning by preserving tens of thousands of ancient manuscripts. Although most of the oldest ones have no dates, yet linguists, by carefully comparing them with others and with one another, can determine the time when they were written; for letters, punctuation, spelling, and language have been constantly undergoing change. Besides this, one author often quoted from another, which enables us to say which was antecedent. Few manuscripts in existence go back farther than the third century, for printing was not then invented, and the much used volumes soon wore out and their places were supplied by copies.

CHAPTER XLVI.

FLORENCE AND VENICE.

SEATED comfortably in the railroad-carriage we left Rome behind us, and began the first stage of our journey towards Florence. The dome of St. Peter's rose into view, grander and grander, for some time, and then became more and more shadowy, until it was entirely lost to sight. Then we began to regret that we had not made a longer stay in the Eternal City.

We passed near Lake Bolsena, with its low wooded shores. Here stood the ancient Etruscan cities, the remains of which are only to be found in a few granite pillars, not far from the deserted shores.

It was quite dark when we arrived in Florence, and we lost no time in seeking for a suitable hotel, but were somewhat disappointed, for we were directed to a very rough sort of place, where we passed an uncomfortable night. As soon as day broke, I left Wildair sleeping serenely, and made my way out into the streets to obtain a first view of the city called "The Beautiful."

The city was already astir, and some of its streets were thronged by early-rising shop-keepers, workmen, and people going to and from market. I followed their trail, and was led towards a beautiful stone bridge. Looking up and down, I saw other bridges supported on long arches spanning the same stream, whose waters gleamed below.

After crossing the bridge, I judged I was in a market-place, for the street was well lined with people selling vegetables, fruits, and various kinds of produce. A little further on I met other people of both sexes, and of every age, coming into market with their donkeys, ponies, and carts.

Still further on I came to an arched gateway, in front of which was a soldier standing on guard. Although I had some suspicions that he might turn me back, he took no notice of me and I went on unmolested. Then turning to the left, I passed along a lane or path, with scattered buildings on my right, and a high, old stone wall with a broad green-turfed ditch running beside it on my left hand. After going a mile or more down this lane, I came to another gateway guarded by a soldier, and again my fears rose; but he also slighted me.

My path now led me through a vast garden, and for nearly a mile I walked on admiring its beautiful walks, statues, and fountains. Then I saw in the distance a bridge which looked familiar, and started for it. On coming up to it I recognized it as the one I had previously crossed over. Hastening on, I was soon by the bedside where I had left Wildair sleeping. He was just waking up, and had no idea that I had been away from the room.

I afterward learned that the great garden I had explored was called Boboli Garden, and that it was one of the finest in all Italy.

Florence is full of rich, costly churches, with a very large number of priests and monks in attendance. I do not know which are the most numerous,—priests or beggars. One could not help noticing "The Duomo," for its cupola is very conspicuous. This church was begun about the time of the crusades, and is not yet finished. The square bell-tower, rising from the pavement near the church to the height of two hundred and seventy-six feet, was to have been surmounted by a pyramid ninety-two feet additional. Like the church, the tower is built of parti-colored marble arranged mosaically according to the taste of the middle ages, and it is so beautiful that Charles the Fifth used to say that it ought to be kept under a glass case.

The strangest structure in Florence is the Palazzo Vecchio. One is puzzled to know whether it looks more like the palace of a king, or an old fortress. It is beautiful, though odd in the extreme. From one side of it rises a beautiful square tower, to the height of more than three hundred feet. This building has no facade or portico to relieve its grandeur; it is a type of many similar palaces built during the middle ages, when defence was the only security, and every city was surrounded by a wall.

We found our way into the museum. Here we walked for two or three hours, until quite tired, and then we were satisfied to see no more. The hall we happened to be in was hung with cartoons and tapestry of the old masters, and seemed to be endless. So we looked out of the window to see if we could jump out, and were surprised to find that we were above the river. We might have jumped out into the water, but thought best not to do so. When at length we got out of the building, we found ourselves on the other side of the river from what we were when we entered it. We crossed back on a bridge, and found that the long gallery we had been in ran along side of it; as if this were not enough for one bridge, jewelry shops lined either side of the way.

The museum at Florence is considered superior to that at Naples. It contains the noted statue of Venus de Medici whose form stands unveiled before you, so graceful in attitude so beautiful in outline, so perfect in proportion, that one can hardly believe it to have been the work of man. On the plinth or foot-piece, is cut the name and country of the noted sculptor, Cleomenes the Athenian, who died B. C. 150. Although when found, during the seventeenth century, it was broken into a dozen fragments among the ruins of Hadrian's Villa, a few miles out of Rome, it was restored so nicely that one would hardly notice the fractures, or discover that the right arm and a part of the left arm are modern. It was carried to Paris by Napoleon in 1796, but returned after his overthrow.

When riding an hour in the cars in Italy one often passes

through ten times the number of tunnels that he does from New York to San Francisco. In Italy they run through the mountains: in America they wind about until they find their way over them. But the costly way is the cheapest in the long run, as it gives a near route and a level track.

But when on our way from Florence to Venice it was not very pleasant to ride through smoky tunnels by candlelight, or to pop into a mountain every time one became interested in a beautiful valley. Before evening however, we passed over a level expanse where not even a hill, however distant, met the eye, and the world seemed an Eden divided into garden spots by fences of tall, straight, slender trees. Sometimes, when going fast, the sunlight—afterwards the moonlight—seemed like one glimmering sheen of light and green.

Night came on, and hour after hour went by, but no Venice appeared. Finally, however, after we had passed over three or four miles of water, our train rolled into the city and stopped at the depôt. We alighted and walked through the building, but found no carriages waiting for passengers. In their stead were long dusky gondolas, in one of which we seated ourselves, and were soon gliding away over the water.

The streets were so narrow at first that there was just room between the lofty frowning walls on each side of us for the gondoliers to paddle, which they did in a standing posture, with their faces in the direction we were going. Just before turning a corner they shouted loudly to let others know of their proximity. Finally we came out into the principal street which was of good width. A mile along this street brought us to the marble steps of our hotel.

When Rome was in her splendor, where we now rested this evening amid marble palaces, was the wild ocean's home. During the fifth century, the barbarians from the far north invaded and overran all Italy, and buried the weak enervated Romans beneath the ruins of their former grandeur. Refugees from various ruined cities here found a safe retreat among the lagoons and little islands about the head of the sea. The storms which shattered the mighty empire produced not a ripple upon the peaceful water in which these islands slept.

Venice soon rose from the sea, like a magic city, and became not only the mistress of the waters, but also extended her influence far back upon the land. The distant islands of the sea dwelt beneath her protection; remote lands trembled at her arms; her ships helped to bear the armies of the Crusades; the oncoming hosts of Mohammedanism, threatening to flood Europe and destroy Christianity, received many a repulse at her hands; while far and wide her influence was felt. Her merchants were princes, her houses palaces, and here declining art and refinement found a home beyond the reach of barbarism.

Here, in the beginning of the seventeenth century, was issued the first newspaper that was ever published. Here was established the first bank of deposit and discount; and here appeared the first bill of exchange. Here, upon her forts, appear to have been used the first cannon which history speaks of.

During a great part of the thirteenth and fourteenth centuries, Venice was at war with her rival republic Genoa; but it was left for Columbus to inflict a more lasting blow on the prosperity of his country's foe than had been previously given. The discovery of America turned the attention of the world toward the vast wealth of the New World, and by exciting the spirit of adventure, led to the discovery, five years later, of a new route to India round the Cape of Good Hope. No wonder these changes shifted commerce into new channels. The decline of Venice was hastened by long and unsuccessful wars with Turkey. At the close of these wars in the year 1718, her spirit was broken and her aristocracy reduced to poverty. But now under the rule of Victor Emmanuel her spirit is beginning to revive.

Venice still retains all the public buildings, churches, palaces, and art collections she had in the day of her greatest prosperity, her stately structures of stone and marble remain anchored in the sea, though the vicissitudes of fortune have driven away her ships. Her railroad lines—one of which offers the shortest and quickest route across the continent by way of the Mount Cenis Tunnel—seem likely to bring back her scattered fleet.

Wishing to see Venice for ourselves, we dispensed with both guide and gondola and started out afoot and alone. The front door opened over a canal, so we went out by the back one into a very narrow passage or street, nicely paved with flag-stones. As the door we had just closed was its terminus, there was but one way for us to go. Soon, however, similar narrow streets from other doors joined ours, and we soon came into a broader street, fifteen feet wide and crowded with people. Into this thoroughfare we turned. On either side were shops with open fronts, under which were tables and baskets of fruits within reach of our hands as we passed along. Then we came to stores filled with hats, boots, and everything else that one could want in the way of clothing. Beyond these an arched foot-bridge spanned the narrow canal, running between perpendicular walls. This was but one of between four and five hundred bridges which span the twelve dozen and one streets along which the blue waters ebb and flow.

By-and-by we came to where the throng of people was very dense. We did not then know that we were in one of the nooks of the Grand Canal, which winds through the city like a pot-hook, crossed by only one or two bridges, and we made several attempts to proceed, but each street that we followed either ended at some door or before some unbridged canal, and we were obliged to retrace our steps. Finally we learned the secret which was simply to follow the street most crowded. In this way only can the Grand Canal be crossed. If a stranger is unable to decide which is the most popular thoroughfare he is liable to be led astray, but there is not much danger of getting beyond the limits of the city.

After about three hours wandering through Venice—where many of the children have never seen a foot of natural unpaved ground, and the earth to them is as mysterious as the ocean was to us in our childhood—we returned along the principal street past the narrow way leading to our hotel; and were soon in a richer part of the city where the stores were full of rich and costly articles.

On passing under an arch we were on the Piazza, in front of a building which we almost immediately recognized as the renowned St. Mark's Cathedral. The buildings surrounding it appeared different from any we had seen before, and we have seen nothing like them since.

Proceeding along the Piazza we came to the bell-tower standing in front of the Cathedral, and mounted to its summit by an interior spiral way without stairs. Napoleon once rode up the same spiral way on horseback, but it did not seem to us to be a very remarkable feat.

From the summit of the tower we obtained a good view of the city and distant islands. There was only one passage between them wide enough for ships to come in. This gateway was once entered by the fleet of Genoa, after it had vanquished the Venetian fleet; but it did not get out again so easily, for it was forced to surrender almost in the streets of Venice.

"No track of men, no footsteps to and fro
Lead to her gates. The path lies o'er the sea,
Invisible."

While we were on the tower, the chimes of the large bells just above our heads startled us. Looking out over the city we saw the pigeons coming from every direction. Then a man came out to feed these guardians of Venice—for so they are regarded—while they lighted around him in the piazza. Remembering that injuring them was punished as a crime, we did not wonder that they were very tame.

From the bell-tower we walked down the Piazza to where it opened over the sea, and had a beautiful view of a distant point of Venice. On one of the two granite columns overlooking the water stood a winged lion, the emblem of St. Mark, the patron saint of Venice. The building on our right was the Old Library, with its beautiful columns and arches; while overtopping all were

"The statues ranged along an azure sky."

On our left was the Doge's Palace, with "galleries so light that they might have been the work of fairy hands, so strong that centuries had battered them in vain."

After procuring a guide we passed through to the rear of the Doge's Palace, and stood high over a watery street, in a dark tunnel, with the beautiful palace which we had been admiring on one side, and the darkest of prisons on the other. We were

—" on the Bridge of Sighs,
A prison and a palace on each hand."

On our way to the bridge we passed up the Giant Stairway, in one wall of which we were shown two niches in which, before the French knocked them off, used to open the two dreadful Lions' Mouths, down whose throat, on dark nights, anonymous accusations against citizens were dropped into the letter box of the fearful "Three." In those dreadful days when men had lost confidence in men, no one knew when he was safe. While one was innocently sleeping, unconscious of danger, some one might be planning his death, some one might be dropping his name into the Lion's Mouth, thus charging him with being secretly a traitor and a plotter against the government.

We passed through the Great Council Hall—one of the finest rooms in Europe. The senators who assembled here numbered several hundred. The history of Venice might be read on the vast walls, in pictures of carnage and blood. Every victory, every great triumph of her arms was depicted here. Round the wall, in long rows, looked down the venerable old doges who had been elected to their office from the body of senators. A black blur covered the place of one doge's portrait, and upon the stain was written, "Beheaded for Crimes."

Further on was the hall of the Council of Ten, who were

chosen from the larger body, for the masses had lost all voice in the government. The senators were from the class of wealthy merchants who were called lords or patricians.

When the people began to struggle for their former liberty it only caused more strenuous measures on the part of the government, and the consolidation of power in the hands of the Ten. But the reins were not even then tight enough and the Ten chose the fearful Three, into whose council-room we next went.

In the Great Council Hall was a vast picture of paradise; another representing the Emperor of Germany kissing the ground beneath the feet of the pope; in still another we saw the pope presenting a sword to the doge. But the only painting in the room of the Three was a vivid portrayal of the infernal regions.

We now thought that we had seen enough of Venice; so we beat a hasty retreat to our hotel, thankful that our lot had been cast in a more enlightened age.

CHAPTER XLVII.

OVER THE ALPS.

FOR the last few weeks the world had seemed to us like an art gallery in which we had strolled through endless halls of paintings and statues. After leaving Venice we had gone to Milan, and when we left the latter city behind us, and saw her renowned cathedral with its thousand marble spires glittering in the morning sun disappear from our sight, it was with a sense of relief that we turned our eyes toward the snowy Alpine peaks, to view the wild scenes of Nature's chiseling.

Before long we found ourselves steaming up Lake Como, stopping to take in numerous passengers from the villages on either shore. This lake is twenty or twenty-five miles in length, but seldom over a mile in width, and frequently much less. Its bright clear waters are peacefully nestled between vine clad mountains, which rise abruptly to a height of between one and two thousand feet and seem to open and close as the traveler winds among them. Now a far-reaching view is had over the lake between them, and then it is again shut in from the outside world. Cosy houses, almost hid among vines and orange groves, or surrounded with beautiful gardens, were scattered here and there along the shore between the villages. Higher up the mountain side were castles and mansions gray and dreamy with age. Higher still the white faces of dwellings peeped out from the green verdure; and away up where the eagle soars aloft to perch upon the highest peaks or pinnacles, we could see objects which appeared like mere specks against the blue sky; but our spy-glasses revealed that they were the abodes of men. Clouds occasionally came sweeping along half way up the side of the mountains, at first merely obscuring the faces of the houses, but soon becoming an impenetrable veil, enveloping the base, but leaving the summit to smile upon the storm below. When the calmer evening came on we were seated in an ivy-hung portico, looking out over the lake, while the music of the guitar came floating to our ears from light canoes shooting across the waters. No wonder we thought that we were in one of the most enchanting places under heaven.

It was at Colico at the upper end of the lake that we exchanged our steamer for a coach. So level and green was the valley that it seemed like a continuation of the lake. This valley gradually became narrower as we pursued our way among the rugged mountains, and was dotted here and there with a garden or small patch of grain, though mostly covered with meadow in which roan-colored cattle roamed at pleasure, being tended by children who almost invariably fell asleep upon the grass.

The peasants in the mountains in the extreme north of Italy appeared to have no cares, and everything seemed to go easy with them. The women seemed to do most of the outdoor work, but there wasn't much to be done. Here was one raking up hay; there was another pitching it into the wagon drawn by oxen; there a third was digging potatoes while her husband and children lay sleeping in the meadow; and further on, a whole family were to be seen squatted upon the grass or stretched out in the sun.

At one place we saw an old gentleman sleeping with his head on a pillow of hay, while a fat, tame, and apparently pet stag approached him, and seeing the hay, seized a mouthful thereof, and with it, by mistake probably, some of the sleeper's hair. Thereupon the old man awoke in a fright, and started up so suddenly that he made matters worse, for the stag was in turn frightened and leaped back without remembering to relinquish his hold on his master's locks. The result was that the man was partially snatched bald-headed. As he scrambled up, seized his cane and made for the offender, one of our passengers called out to him :—

"Now, sonny, you'll help your wife dig the potatoes won't you?"

Toward evening we reached the little village of Cheaveuna at the foot of the Alps. Here we halted, as we were not to

THE OLD MAN'S PET.

make the ascent until early next morning. We were now on the Swiss borders, and there was more stir in the place than we had seen in coming from Lake Como. A band was playing, men, women and children were collected around, and young ladies smiled from the balconies above.

Some of the women and girls were distributing from a stand in the centre of the crowd, prizes to the successful competitors in a shooting match, held the preceding day. We watched the fair umpires as they awarded the prizes, and fancied we could guess from their countenances who were their sweethearts.

Later in the evening we wandered along the side of the little stream that went gliding and dashing in cataracts and falls through the village; and then we climbed up the side of the mountains, where the nimble-footed goats were springing from rock to rock. Occasionally we came upon a little cosy hut which had been concealed behind large mossy rocks; and further up we found groves of chestnut trees. Then, as we strolled along, we met singing girls returning home, their hands stained with grape-juice. We went on, and soon

"A WILD-LOOKING MAN WITH A CUDGEL IN HIS HAND."

found ourselves among the vineyards. Thinking that the grapes were wild, as they were growing so luxuriantly and apparently uncared for, we concluded that there would be no particular harm if we picked an occasional cluster. But we were soon undeceived. We suddenly came face to face with a wild-looking man with a stout cudgel in his hand. This individual showed signs of warlike intentions, and as we did not feel quite prepared to do battle with him, we begged him to accept a five-franc piece, saying at the same time that we should not have trespassed had we not supposed that the grapes were wild. Thereupon he took the money, and began to pick some of the fruit for us. We had already as much as we could eat and signified the same to him. He replied with a grin and a few words in an unknown tongue, evidently as much pleased as we were that matters had taken such a pleasant turn.

It was dark when we returned to our hotel, and shortly after we retired. At three o'clock the next morning we were awakened by a rap at our door, and heard a voice saying:—"It is now time to ascend the Alps." Those words shot through us like an electric thrill: in a few moments we were up, and seated in the hindmost of the three coaches that were to convey our party.

The morning was dark, and it was beginning to rain; but on we dragged up a deep black gorge, while the coach lanterns showed us occasional glimpses of the rugged sides of the chasm, and of a stream roaring and dashing far below to our left. In an hour or so, we came to where there was a large fall of water into this chasm, over the right wall along which we were passing. We went no further in that direction, till we had ascended higher than the falls by a number of short zigzag turns, one above another, on the almost perpendicular side of the mountain. Looking upwards during the ascent we could see the other coaches almost directly above us. As crack, crack, went the whips, and the horses' hoofs sounded against the rock, we shuddered, lest in the darkness some accident might cause them to come tumbling down upon us. When at a considerable height above the waterfall, the road continued on in tunnels through the rock, and sometimes, coming out to the edge of the chasm, ran along in defiance of the precipice, till we came to a bridge on which we crossed over the stream.

As daylight came on we had reached an altitude where

the storm changed from rain to snow. At a distance we espied through the gorge what we took to be a singular looking cloud, and as we ascended higher it seemed to grow larger and larger, and rise higher and higher above the surrounding mountains. We discovered before long that it was a rugged snow-capped peak resting in majestic sublimity among the clouds. As we continued to ascend, others rose up increasing in size. The storm became fiercer, the snow whirled in air, the heavens grew dark, and we were but just able to discern the dim forms of stately mountains and peaks, to which we were drawing near. We fancied we could see the avalanches forming on the sides. It was a snowy world of grandeur. The horses shook their heads in the storm, and there was some danger that the road might become impassable. But on we dragged up the side of the mountain till we approached the summit, and then the storm began to abate.

The upper strata of clouds were first dispelled, and we could look down upon those below. Through them many a peak, and occasionally the summit of a range, shot its frosty head or raised its icy back. The clouds continued to melt away, and scatter into fragments, between which we caught glimpses of the mountain sides below, and the deep gorges where the the cataract dashed and roared. It was a scene of chaos, as though the earth had been rent into ten thousand fragments, and the angry ocean rolled between. Finally, as the clouds became thinner, and began to roll down the gorges, allowing the rays of the sun to pierce through, the most beautiful colors appeared, as if the world had been flooded with rain bows.

When all was clear, and the snowy robes of the mountains sparkled in the sunshine, we began to descend the north side of the Alps through the Spluger Pass, one of the wildest and most fearful in Switzerland. We were now again in darkness; for the perpendicular—sometimes overhanging—walls of rock rose up to a height of from one to two thousand feet, almost bridging over the desolate chasm below. We had made slow time thus far, on account of the storm, but we now began to make up for our loss. For four miles we shot down the chasm, rocking fearfully from side to side according to the curve of the walls, and passing over bridges several hundred feet above the roaring falls and cataracts below.

At length, beyond the north end of the gorge, we caught glimpses of beautiful valleys, and green hills upon which the setting sun sinking in the west was throwing his last lingering rays. A few miles further on we put up for the night at the village of Choir.

Going by rail to Zurich, we were surprised to find that the cars were built after the American style. We saw none similar to them elsewhere in Europe. We were not obliged to

OUR FUNNY FELLOW-PASSENGER.

enter small apartments from the sides, in which two seats facing each other ran crosswise the whole breadth of the coach; and we were not obliged to freeze because there was no fire.

As we passed along, we were amused to hear such a clatter of different languages all in one country. In Switzerland there are about 1,750,000 Germans; 550,000 French; 130,000 Italians; and 45,000 who speak a dialect very similar to the old Roman or Latin language. In our coach the three former were about equally represented. It is strange to me, why these languages do not become more mixed in Switzerland than they do. Suppose a German marries an Italian lady, and the children of this couple marry into French families, what language would the grandchildren speak?

At one of the stopping-places, the funniest-looking man I had ever seen took a seat opposite to us in the car. It was a great relief when the train started, giving us a chance to vent our mirth by roaring at something we fancied we saw out of the window. The passengers, including our funny neighbor, stretched their necks to see what it was that we were laughing at, but were unable to discover the cause of our mirth.

The country along the road was most beautiful, with lovely valleys, hills and lakelets. In the villages, and frequently in the country, we saw handsome little gardens, green with grass, shaded with trees, and divided into beautiful figures by curving paths; while in the centre of grassy plots might frequently be seen sparkling fountains.

In the course of a few hours we reached Zurich, beautifully located at the head of a lake of the same name, and surrounded by mountains—the Alps being visible in the distance. We stopped here a day or two, but as it was only a scene of beauty, we soon tired. There were no ruins gray with time, no magnificent cathedrals, no astounding architectural structures of any kind, nor was it the capital of a great nation. So we went on to Basle in the north-western part of Switzerland.

From Basle we made a tour of observation into Germany, —that is to say, we walked across a bridge over the Rhine and visited a small town on the German side of the river. We only remained an hour or so, but have the satisfaction of knowing that henceforth, when recounting our travels, we can say truthfully that we have been in Germany.

CHAPTER XLVIII.

PARIS AND LONDON.

ALTHOUGH our passports were all right, we felt but little at ease as we approached Paris. The high walls surrounding the late imperial city appeared to us like relics of barbarism, and seemed to say," Beware how you intrude." But when we entered, and were driven along the broad streets, shaded avenues, and unrivaled boulevards, lined with palatial windows, all aglow with diamond-set jewelry which had been left undisturbed during the siege, I then realized that modern war meant mercy, when compared with the wars of earlier and less civilized times. I could hardly persuade myself, as we wandered through the gaily-lighted streets, that this was poor down-trodden Paris, whose most affluent children had starved or been fed on scanty rations of mule-meat during the siege.

The west end of the Tuileries, nearly a quarter of a mile in length, had been considerably damaged during the troublesome times, and workmen were repairing it when we were there. The imperial family who so lately occupied the palace were refugees in other lands; and we happened in at an auction sale of the private property they had left behind them. An American lady present bought a quantity of under-clothing once belonging to the dethroned Empress; and when we saw her examining critically a pair of pantaloons shuffled off by the skedaddled Emperor, we concluded that there was little chance for speculation; so we left the auction, and soon afterward the country.

But of course, like all good Americans, we visited Versailles, a few miles from the metropolis. This was once only a small village in a forest, where Louis XIII. had a hunting-seat; but his successor, Louis XIV., at an enormous expense, converted it into a royal residence, large enough and grand enough to lodge all the kings and queens of Europe. Here the voluptuous monarch began his intimacy with the famous, or infamous, Madame de Marntenon, who, while acting as governess to a lady of the court, charmed and captivated him by her winning ways.

As a specimen of his devotion to the lady, it is related that when on one occasion she expressed a wish for a sleigh-ride, he caused the avenues for a long distance to be covered, during the night, with salt and sugar; and when she arose in the morning a sleigh stood at the gate to gratify her whim.

A SUMMER SLEIGH-RIDE.

It is said that the couple were privately married in 1865, soon after the death of the queen, Maria Theresa; but she was never publicly acknowledged by him.

We wandered at evening through the parks and pleasure grounds of the palace. Everything seemed laid out on a gigantic scale. The trees were trained into fantastic shapes;

PARK AND FOUNTAIN AT VERSAILLES.

ruined columns were standing here and there; and statue-lined avenues stretched away as far as the eye could reach. All seemed a gorgeous dream; and as we halted on the brink of a lake, the moon, emerging from behind the clouds, revealed to us what appeared to be a mythological being in a chariot drawn by floundering steeds rising from the water.

Versailles was devastated by the revolutionists in 1792; but Louis Philippe restored its splendors, and concentrated there many illustrations of the history of his country. Paintings, sculptures, and other works of art now fill the splendid halls of the noble palace.

As we rode through the country on our way to the English Channel, we saw many traces of the late war; and the greater number of women than men working in the fields, told of absent husbands and sons. But if success in raising beets was an indication of prosperity, they were a prosperous people. Immense piles of these vegetables, hundreds of feet long and twenty or more high, were frequently to be seen along the road. They were to be used in the manufacture of sugar.

We saw the artificial embankments which had reclaimed many homesteads from the dominion of the sea. Down the net-work of narrow canals the peasants paddled boats, gathering their farm produce. Some were homeward bound with loads, while others were going to the nearest village to exchange their vegetables for family supplies. These Holland canoes, though less fanciful, seemed as useful and indispensable as the gondolas which I had seen shooting like arrows along the watery streets of Venice, or silently floating amid her anchored palaces.

*　　*　　*　　*　　*　　*

We didn't sleep much the first night we were in London, as every two or three minutes a train of cars whizzed beneath the foundation of our hotel. When I did doze, it was to dream of St. Paul's; and as the next day was Sunday we thought it was a favorable time to visit this great cathedral, which is worthy of the first place among the edifices of Protestant Christendom.

On inquiring the way thither, we were advised to take the underground railroad. Victoria Station was close to our hotel, and we were soon shooting along beneath palaces and hovels, stopping at numerous stations and starting again with amazing rapidity. After going three or four miles we left the regions of darkness, and took our place among the worshipers of God in the cathedral; but we were more interested in the building and its monuments than we were in the officiating clergymen.

Among the renowned personages buried in this cathedral are Wellington, England's greatest soldier; and the naval hero Nelson, who, just before the battle at Trafalgar, said to an officer, "Now for a peerage or Westminster Abbey." There are monuments to Sir John Moore, Lord Cornwallis, Bishop Heber, and many others who have reflected glory on the British Empire by their virtues, heroism, and achievements at home and abroad.

Later in the day we visited that mausoleum of departed greatness, Westminster Abbey. To rest at last in this sacred spot has been the highest ambition of many a British worthy, and England can show no greater honor to the memory of any one than to bury him there. The place abounds in all kinds of monuments, many of which are beautiful works of art. The pavements, over which hundreds of people were passing, were carved with the names of the dead; marble slabs represented the reposing forms of the kings and queens of the Middle Ages, and along the walls, in the aisles and transepts and chapels, and everywhere around, were tombs, tablets, statues and inscriptions.

In the "Poet's Corner," the busts of Milton, Shakspeare, Pope, Dryden, and others, looked down upon us from niches in the wall bearing epitaphs written in Latin and old English, which we found very difficult to read. Beneath the seats were the resting places of others whose names are familiar to the world; and while standing on one stone, we read upon it the name of Charles Dickens. Time softens envy; and rivals in wit, in literature, in theology, in beauty, in power, and in royalty, sleep here peacefully, side by side.

In the evening we went to hear Spurgeon, the eminent Baptist divine, who justly ranks among the most eloquent preachers of the age; and that he is one of the most popular of them, no one can doubt who goes into the neighborhood of his church (called the Tabernacle), while his congregation are assembling. Everybody then in the streets seems attracted to the same common center, and everybody seems to be in a hurry.

GOING TO HEAR SPURGEON.

Although we arrived early, vast crowds of people were already waiting in the damp streets; and when the iron gates were thrown open, the front yard, wide steps, and capacious portico were speedily filled. We succeeded in getting a position at the front, where we were pressed against one of the doors by the throng behind us. In this uncomfortable place we were kept for what seemed an hour, but amused ourselves by listening to the noise made within by the pew-holders, as they entered by private doors and called out the numbers of their seats to the ushers.

At last the key turned, the door opened, and we were at once shot far up the main aisle by the advancing throng. We secured seats on a vast elevated platform, below another platform upon which the preacher stood, and where we had a good view of him during the service. Every seat in the building seemed full, but still people flocked in by hundreds.

The singing, in which Spurgeon joined, was truly wonderful, and the strains poured down from the lofty galleries like the voice of many thunders. Then followed a fervent prayer, in which the supplicant seemed to plead and argue as if face to face with his Maker. The sermon was listened to with profound attention, and could be heard distinctly in the remotest corners of the vast room. The vehement eloquence and serene faith of the speaker seemed to carry the audience along as willing captives; and his pathos and good humor provoked alternately smiles and tears.

London is well provided with public parks, gardens, and pleasure-grounds, into which the crowded streets pour out their throngs to enjoy a new life, and gather health and recreation. One of the largest in the city is Hyde Park; and we here saw a great many people skating on the river within it. At the Zoological Gardens, in Regent's Park, we saw specimens of every animal, bird and reptile which we were acquainted with, and a good many others.

Trafalgar Square is one of the finest squares to be found anywhere. On one side of it is the National Gallery of Art, where we saw the largest collection of paintings in England. This is a free gallery, and it is one of the most frequented places in London. In the square, opposite this edifice, is Nelson's Monument—an imposing and very handsome column, surmounted by a figure of Nelson.

The Crystal Palace is about ten miles away from the city, but so easily accessible by steam cars that it is very popular as a rural resort. The grounds are magnificent; and the edifice, made entirely of glass and iron, is perhaps the most wonderful structure in the world. Beneath its elongated dome, Nature finds at all seasons of the year a tropical home. Fountains play; broad leaves, between which dart golden fish, float upon the surface of lakes; birds of rich plumage perch upon branches; vines cling to trees and to rocks, among which barbarous natives of various climes, as natural as life, spear the springing tiger; while upon the sandy desert, Arabs spread their tents and rest their camels. Under the glassy wings of the Palace are ancient buildings adorned with statues as in the days of their glory; and thousands of gay and happy visitors wander through the courts and temples of Egypt, Greece, Rome, and other countries, as if treading the rich apartments of proud kings.

NELSON'S MONUMENT, TRAFALGAR SQUARE.

We were astonished at the number of beggars that we met with in London. They seemed to be of every age and in every condition of beggary—objects of pity that rent our hearts. Puny arms were held out to ask alms, or else to implore us to purchase some trifle or other, which was only offered as an excuse for begging. One poor thing, a little girl of thirteen, perhaps, followed us the whole length of the Houses of Parliament, beseeching us for God's sake to give her a trifle, for her mother was sick and had not tasted food for two days. Another girl, a young woman in fact, entreated us, with a cheerful face, to buy a little bunch of flowers. She told us how grateful she would be, and even promised to pray for us; but when she finally despaired of effecting a sale, she actually turned away and cried bitterly. We couldn't stand that; so we paid her the price of the flowers and then made her a present of them.

But Heaven only knows when tears are shed in earnest; for these beggars study their profession, like actors on the the stage, and know well every way to move the hearts of men. They strip off their shoes, and walk in the middle of the damp freezing streets, singing mournful songs. A blind couple will borrow a family of deformed children, and train themselves as a band of musicians. Such a party played near our window at dead of every night for two or three weeks before Christmas, and during the holidays.

"THERE SHE SAT AS USUAL."

Day after day and month after month, thousands of street-sweepers stand at their respective crossings, using their brooms dexterously when they see a stylish party approaching, and holding out their hands for a reward; and thousands of other persons have sittings where each one constantly exhibits a basket of fruit. Were I to return to London, I should expect to see a beautiful girl, with one leg and a few sticks of candy, still sitting on a little box before the Queen's gate; which gate, by the way, we once mistook in the fog for the entrance to St. James Park—finding out our mistake when halted, almost at the steps of the palace, by the bayonet of a guard gorgeously arrayed in red coat and bear-skin cap. By another mansion I should look for a woman with two children—one in her arms—sitting on the stone step. When I last passed the place, it was on a cold night just after the clock in the tower had struck ten; but there she sat as usual, with bare arm projecting from a thin shawl which partially covered her shivering children. I still seem to see the pallid hand holding out a penny match-box, and to hear her piteous words of appeal. No; if I returned I should not expect to find her where I last saw her, but in her grave.

But notwithstanding the appearance of penury and misery which are seen so often on the streets of London, far more touching scenes of woe and wretchedness could doubtless be found in the hovels which line both sides of many of the squalid lanes, courts and by-ways of the city, where poverty-stricken families who have not lost the sense of shame find a retreat from the sight of the world.

One day, with a heavy heart and a light pocketbook, (for the expected remittance had not arrived,) I left the post-office and wandered down towards the river to see the "Lord Mayor's Show," as the newsboys, running about with long pictorial programmes of the procession streaming in the air, called it. For two miles or more the magnificent stone embankment, fifty feet wide, with all the roads leading to it, was densely packed with people, waiting for the newly-elected mayor and his endless retinue to pass by, on their way from the Mansion House to the scene of inauguration at Westminster Abbey.

Before long I found myself among a jolly set of rough fellows who, devoid of care, were boxing, knocking off hats, and occasionally throwing a dethroned tile over the heads of the crowd into the river. In the midst of this sport, one of them suddenly cried out "Spurgeon;" and though I tried to seem unconscious of the fact, I became aware that the remark referred to me. Again a wide mouth bellowed out "Spurgeon;" another one, "Apostolic Spurgeon;" and I was somewhat frightened to find that wherever I turned, hundreds of eyes were staring upon me. I was reminded of a drove of Texan cattle, which, with wild curiosity, encircle a lonely footman, bellow, and toss their heads, until one makes a pass at him and the rest trample him down.

AMONG THE ROUGHS.

At length one of the fellows was shoved against me; then another, and another, until the pressure was greater than my temper could bear. Fear left me. Giving my fists full play square in their faces, I started hastily forward, and was soon met by policemen coming to my rescue, who saved the beggarly rascals from the disgrace of rifling my empty pockets.

We spent considerable time in the British Museum, which is one of the chief attractions of London. Here, for more than a century, have been accumulating a vast number of antiquities and curiosities, and the collection is probably unequaled in interest and value by any in the world. A library of nearly a million books, printed in various languages and treating of every imaginable subject, constitutes one department of the museum. There is also a reading-room which will accommodate three hundred readers at a time.

We saw at the museum, arrow-heads of flint and axes of stone which had been discovered in various parts of England; and could trace how the son improved upon the work of his father in the manufacture of spears, arrows, and other implements of war. We could see where bronze came into use, where iron, where steel. We could see when the Romans came into Britain, and could trace the new ideas which they suggested. We could follow the race up through its various improvements, from the time when London was but a collection of British wigwams, and painted savages paddled in the river where now floated the Great Eastern, just returned from laying a cable in Oriental waters.

We also saw the various pieces of broken stone covered with strange-looking letters, which, on being put together and deciphered, proved to be an Assyrian account of the deluge. These stones had been exhumed from the palace of one of the last potentates of the doomed city of Nineveh. In this palace the monarch could walk from hall to hall and from chamber to chamber, and read from inscriptions on the vast slabs of alabaster which lined the walls, the history of his country; while representations of battles, sieges, and pursuits of enemies, carved and painted on stone, with eagle-headed figures, winged lions and flying bulls, everywhere met his gaze. Subsequently the province of Babylon revolted and marched upon Nineveh; the waters of the Tigris were turned through the city; the king in despair killed himself after setting fire to his palace, the apartments of which were filled with the falling ruins. Excavators have recently brought again to light the long-hidden stones, slabs, and statues, and many of them have been placed in this museum.

In the Nimrod palace I took an interest in the manner in which one of the royal descendants of the mighty hunter was showering his arrows upon the head and breast of a roaring lion which was endeavoring to show that turn about was fair play. It would have been an easy matter, apparently, for the hunter's bearded attendants to have broken ranks and taken a hand; but they believed in keeping step in those days. It is a wonder that the lion did not upset the chariot and spill out the king; but he did not, for the next slab represents the hunter at home, with beardless eunuchs around him offering cups of beverage, and a dead lion at his feet.

CHAPTER XLIX.

HOMEWARD BOUND.

WE were now about to part. Caleb was resolved to remain in London a few weeks longer, while I was just as determined to return to America without delay. So without any pulling of hair, or similar demonstration, I bade him good-bye, and was soon on a railroad train bound for Liverpool, where I intended to take a steamer for New York. Although it was mid-winter the hills and valleys were still green, but the everlasting fog was hovering over all.

I took passage by a steamer of the Inman line, and with the other cabin passengers was conveyed to the vessel, which was anchored a short distance from the shore, in a small steamboat. The steerage passengers, with their bedding, tin ware, and other traps for housekeeping purposes during the voyage, had previously been taken on board. They were a motley-looking crowd, setting out to seek their fortunes in the western world. There was a little delay in starting, and I became impatient even to restlessness till finally the agitation of the water showed that the great screw at the stern, whose gigantic force was to propel us across the ocean, had begun to move.

When one day out from Liverpool we stopped at Queenstown, a port at the southern extremity of Ireland, to take on board some more steerage passengers—men, women, and children. They were a jolly and noisy set, and some of the men seemed intoxicated, or partially so. The women scolded, the children squalled, the men laughed and joked, tin dishes clattered, and all was confusion. This confusion was increased when it was found that some of them must go into the lower steerage—a dark apartment below the surface of the water—as the upper one already contained as many passengers as it could accommodate comfortably, or even uncomfortably. Some of the women remonstrated, till they found it was of

GOING BELOW.

no use doing so, and that there was no other place where they could be stowed away.

One couple—lately married, I judged—were particularly conspicuous among the new-comers—the man by his willingness to take up his abode below, and his wife by her obstinacy about doing so. Finally, however, she yielded to his solicitations, picked up her bedding, and tripped it lightly down the stairs. Her tipsy young husband, with his hands full of tin ware and frying pans, and with other articles of the same culinary nature tied together and strung over his shoulder, started to follow her, singing a lively refrain and keeping time thereto with dancing feet. At the top of the steps he stumbled, lost his balance, and went tumbling down, head first, while the din of his tin wares rose above the screams of his astonished better half. We all thought that he was killed or seriously damaged, but he jumped quickly up and began dancing again as if nothing unusual had happened.

I never ventured to go into the lower apartment occupied by these emigrants, but sometimes visited their more desirable quarters above. Here, at meal-time, the passengers ranged themselves in rows, and held out their tin cups to receive the soup or gruel which the stewards dipped out to each from an immense can dragged along the floor; or they held out their tin plates and hands for more solid rations in the shape of meat and biscuits, which were distributed from large pans and baskets. There was at times considerable of a strife for the places near the head of the table (figuratively speaking,) where the stewards would begin their dispensations of good things to the hungry crowd. Occasionally a boy, after having been served at the upper end of the line, would swallow his hot gruel, stick his biscuit in his pocket, and slip slyly down to the lower end, there to receive a second allowance. Sometimes however the stewards would detect the trick, and then the rogue would receive a biscuit aimed at his head.

On the whole these emigrants seemed, at the start, to enjoy their voyage much better than the cabin passengers did. On some evenings they sang hymns or love-ditties, and on others they danced merrily to the music of a fiddle. But afterwards, during a fearful and protracted storm, with all the port-holes and sky-lights closed to keep out the water which came sweeping over the vessel, these steerage passengers must have suffered terribly in their close quarters. Many, no doubt, wished sincerely that they had been better contented at home.

For a week the weather had been fine for the time of year, and we were anticipating a quick and smooth voyage. But on the seventh day the wind began to rise, and it increased during the night, causing the vessel to roll and toss considerably. Next morning it blew harder, and small waves were occasionally dashed over the deck. Only a few of the boldest passengers ventured out, and as the storm increased even they were glad to seek again the shelter below, but even there the water found its way. Although the sky-lights

A DANCE IN THE STEERAGE.

of the upper deck were closed, the water at times poured in torrents through them into the cabin below, and some of the passengers tried to escape from it by jumping upon the settees. During the night the vessel labored heavily, and every timber in her seemed to groan and creak.

I shall never forget the scene which I peeped out upon the next morning through the boxed-up door. The wind was blowing harder than ever, and almost took away my breath. The salt vapors, like a driving mist, blinded me. The waves were chasing each other in the wildest fury. The steamer would rise apparently mountain high and then dive headlong down the waves as if nothing could prevent her from going to the bottom. Not infrequently the prow struck under a great wave, the vessel trembled as if she had run on to a rock, and immediately the waters above came thundering over her entire length. All day long the situation was, to landsmen at least, truly alarming.

Night came on again and darkness spread her black wings over the chaos of waters, but brought no change for the better. Towards midnight a fearful wave crashed in the bulwarks, and the waters came pouring in, causing great consternation among the passengers. Almost immediately afterward the steamer's whistle was sounded, and this fresh cause for alarm brought out of their bunks all of the passengers who were not too sea-sick to care much whether we sunk or not. One man ran up and down the cabin, crying, "We are lost! we are lost!" Another one, who was a cripple, hopped about in a way that would have been most laughable at any other time. A third person, who I judged had rather a poor opinion of his fellow passengers, startled us all by ejaculating, "We are all going to h——". For my own part, I felt that I would give a small fortune to be put safely ashore.

We soon learned however that no serious damage had been received; and that the whistling was to guard against collision with other vessels, as we were in dense fogs off the coast of Newfoundland.

The long night passed slowly away, and morning came at last. During the day the storm slightly abated, and on the succeeding day its fury was over, though the waves were still running high.

Another morning dawned, and land was in sight at last. The passengers assembled on deck, and as they gazed

"On old Long Island's sea girt shore,"

many a face which had been pallid through the voyage, brightened up with joy—many a terror-stricken heart warmed to life again.

As we steamed up the noble harbor of New York, Castle Garden, the spire of Trinity Church, the North and East Rivers with the ferry boats shooting across them—everything in fact looked wonderfully familiar, though I had visited New York City but once before. I was greatly elated, and felt at home again in my native land, although still separated by many hundred miles from the friends who awaited me far beyond the Mississippi.

I remained in New York only a short time, but saw enough of her stately buildings, fine parks, thronged streets, shipping and commercial bustle, to convince me that Americans have no reason to be ashamed of their metropolis—that even France and England might be proud of such a city. Though she has not as many fine streets as Paris, her commercial importance is proportionally greater; and though her population is small compared with that of London, her natural location is better and her surroundings more attractive.

From New York I went to Washington, that city of jobbery and corruption, and arrived just in time to attend the President's levee. Early in the evening people by the thousands—aristocrats in coaches and plebians on foot, honest men and rogues—had begun to assemble at the White House. I had been told that there was considerable crowding on these occasions, but had not the slightest idea of the extent it was indulged in till I experienced it myself. I would not be knocked about again as I was that evening for the privilege of shaking hands with all the presidents in the world.

Policemen were stationed at the outside and inside doors to check the surging crowds, and succeeded to some extent in doing so. Occasionally some one of the ladies ahead of me would scream out, and though I at first supposed they were merely taking advantage of a good opportunity to fall into friendly arms, I thought differently afterward when I reached the thickest of the throng and was myself more than half suffocated.

At last I emerged into the charmed circle where stood the President and his wife, who looked at me so pleasantly that I thought they mistook me for some old friend. I was then introduced, and shook hands with each. As I was leaving them, with the idea that they felt honored by my presence, I discovered that a benevolent-looking but very home-

A PRESIDENT AND PRESIDENT-MAKER.

ly negro was the next visitor to be presented; and from his hesitating steps it was evident that he was much embarrassed. But the President smilingly reached out his hand to him, and, as far as I could judge, received him as cordially as he had me.

Passing on through elegant apartments and halls I at length reached the open air. Visitors were still flocking in by hundreds; and I could but feel pity for the occupants of the White House who were thus undergoing one of the penalties of their exalted condition. I went away thankful that I was but a private citizen, and formed a resolution never to attend another president's levee, if I could avoid it.

456 HOME AGAIN!

From Washington, I proceeded leisurely westward, visiting the Mammoth Cave in Kentucky, and other places of interest. I tarried for a few days at Cincinnati, Chicago, and St. Louis, and reached my home about the middle of May. Caleb joined me in due time, coming by the way of Canada; and under the same spreading apple-tree where we had originally planned our travels, we recounted to interested and sympathizing friends many stories of the people we had met in OUR WESTWARD FLIGHT AROUND THE WORLD.

SOME OF THE PEOPLE WE HAD MET.

The Columbian Book Company,

OF

HARTFORD, CONN.,

Are Publishers of First-Class, Standard, Illustrated Works, which are sold By Subscription Only.

They will bring out only works of high moral tone, rare literary merit, and positive and permanent value—works, which from their intrinsic and sterling worth, will be welcomed to every Home and Fireside in the Country, and be a credit to the Canvassers who introduce them.

As their plan of conducting business enables them to make very large sales of every work, they supply Agents at a very small advance from actual cost, (giving them nearly all the profits,) thus ensuring to energetic men and women large pay for their services. The established retail prices are always lower than books of equal cost and character are sold for at bookstores.

In mechanical execution their publications will always be first-class—well printed on good paper, and tastefully and substantially bound. Publishing but a limited number of books, yearly, they are enabled to give particular attention to their manufacture, and to expend money freely in illustrating them. Subscribers for their works can always depend on receiving what they contract for.

AGENTS ARE WANTED

to sell these Books in every town in the United States.

Agents for GOOD BOOKS are a lasting benefit in any community, and their calling is a noble one. To men and women wishing honorable, pleasant and lucrative employment we offer great inducements. Young men who engage in this business will gain a knowledge of the country, and of men and things which will be of great benefit to them.

Agents who canvass for our Works in the Western and Southern sections of the country, will be supplied with books from our offices at the West and South.

Circulars with full information are sent promptly to any one wishing an agency. Address,

COLUMBIAN BOOK COMPANY,
HARTFORD, CONN., AND CHICAGO, ILL.

JOHN PAUL'S OPINION OF HIS BOOK.

From the New York Daily Tribune.

To the Editor of The Tribune.

SIR: To you, who know my modest nature well, it is not necessary that I demonstrate how it pains me to find myself forced into a personal mention which, to the prejudiced eye, may look very much like an intention to advertise the work of my hands. But you, who have so often remarked upon my unwillingness to exalt my own horn (or blow it), unless the public good were to be subserved thereby (and it could be done in a way which passed all human ingenuity to find out), can give indignant denial to any such suspicion. To the many requests that I would state, with the weight which a responsible name ever carries with it, what sort of a book mine is to be, when it is to be published, and several other particulars in regard to which I am erroneously supposed to be well informed, I long turned a deaf ear. But when His Illustrious Majesty of Prussia, King William, politely requests that I will ease his Imperial mind on those points, can I longer refuse?

Briefly, then, I will not positively say that my book is the best which the century has produced. But when I say that no book of early or late date has so forcibly attracted my attention, that in none has my interest been enlisted to such a degree, I trust that it will be believed that I speak only the truth! Looking over it now, after several very careful readings previously, I do not find one line which even a dyer "could wish to blot;" and certainly one could not take away a page without spoiling the Table of Contents—already in press; nor could you add a page without making the book too big to be carried round by hand!

For there are already 684 pages of it, to say nothing about the portrait-page at the beginning—about which the less said the better, perhaps. And all the illustrations are full-page—though as all the pages are not full of illustrations, this is not quite so bad as it might be.

As to when the book will be out, I don't know. The compositors who should have set it up, stopped and sat themselves down instead to read, and many of them took the copy home to read to their families. The consequence was an interesting "revival" in Hartford, but a delay to the book. However, along toward the middle of this month, if householders wish to get out of its way and avoid agents, they had better leave the country.

Notwithstanding what has been said, it must not be rashly concluded that it is, strictly speaking, a theological book. The truth it contains is the result of accident mostly rather than of design. And this perhaps is one reason why it works on the wicked human system so powerfully; I flatter myself that to me belongs the credit of moving upon sinners strategically, and taking them by surprise. Before they know that any one is gunning for them, you see I've got 'em where the capillary growth is of minimum length, and the best thing they can do is lie still and say nothing about it. And I may add that though orders for my book may not come in from Sunday schools at once, I am confident the demand from that source will never be less than it is at the beginning.

Ladies will like the book unquestionably. With the hair-drawn pencil of poetic prophecy, Mr. Tennyson foretells this when he paints the Lady of Shalott:

"But in her Webb she still delights."

And I see no reason why ladies should not delight in my book, whether they are given merely to the mild shallott or confess to an insane preference for a more virulent form of onion.

As I was saying, when interrupted, I cannot say exactly when the book will be out. However, I can state positively that the publishers are out already, and will probably be out more when the work gets further along. But being a wealthy and powerful concern—the Columbian Book Company of Hartford—I guess they'll manage to worry through.

I was obliged to go to Hartford to avoid existing jealousy and contentions among our local publishers. Now that none of them at all has it, they sit on their ragged anxieties with much more of calm and comfort. And as I was saying, as the present month wears along it will daily become more and more hazardous for any householder to express a wish to buy the John Paul book in the hearing of a man that looks like a minister, for he may be entertaining by that remark an agent unawares.

And now I trust that King William of Prussia is satisfied, and that he will instruct the chambermaids about the palace to economize in the use of Prussian blue, so that the Royal family may be able to buy a copy of my book.

Respectfully yours,

JOHN PAUL.

www.ingramcontent.com/pod-product-compliance
Lightning Source LLC
Chambersburg PA
CBHW031956300426
44117CB00008B/780